Practical Manag

# Practical Management Development

*Strategies for Management Resourcing and Development in the 1990s*

GORDON McBEATH

Basil Blackwell

First published 1990

First published in paperback 1994

Blackwell Publishers
108 Cowley Road
Oxford OX4 1JF
UK

238 Main Street
Cambridge, Massachusetts 02142
USA



*British Library Cataloguing-in-Publication Data*
A CIP catalogue record for this book is available from the British Library.

*Library of Congress Cataloging-in-Publication Data*
A CIP catalog record for this book is available from the Library of Congress.

ISBN 0–631–19346–4 (paper)

Typeset in 11 on 13 pt Photina
by Butler and Tanner Ltd., Frome, Somerset
Printed in Great Britain by T.J. Press, Padstow, Cornwall

This book is printed on acid-free paper

# *Contents*

# *Preface*

There is gradual recognition by top management that a sustainable competitive advantage will only be achieved through people. Human resources are the most important assets which any organisation has. The effective management and development of these resources is the key to gaining competitive advantage. Success is most likely to be achieved if all activity is linked to a clear vision of the corporate future, and to the achievement of clear and attainable corporate objectives as an integral part of strategic management.

This book was written to meet a particular need. It is the sort of book I always wanted to pass to involved line managers and less experienced human resource practitioners, but could not find elsewhere!

An enormous amount is written about human resourcing and development; from disjointed collections of essays in 'handbooks', through the great range of largely academic books and papers on specialised aspects, to the 'Excellence' books full of what someone described as 'warm feelings and no practical solutions'.

What I sought was not a 'how to' book, but a book which showed how management resourcing and development fitted together, within and as an essential part of managing the business; to show its contribution to the business – and its lack of purpose if approached in isolation. As a practising manager, that was what I needed.

So there you have the purpose – to provide a comprehensive framework of management resourcing and development, integrated with business operation and development, and anticipating further changes in the rapidly evolving business environment and in cultural attitudes – around which any organisation can structure its own management development processes, knowing that all the influences and factors have been taken into account, and that the language and operation have been adapted to corporate style. Management development planning must be given the same priority as the planning and preparation for achieving overall company goals. Every organisation needs its vision of where it intends to be in the year 2000, and knows that it will need to prepare its management for that achievement.

I make no apology for using a systems approach. The whole area is too complex to handle in any other way without the risk of significant omissions – no matter how open and participative the corporate culture. System is there as a discipline, to make sure all relevant issues are identified. It does not stop a manager rejecting the relevance of any facet and moving on, but he will have made a decision to do so and not have simply overlooked what might be important. Indeed, there should be sufficient flexibility in any system to accommodate selective non-conformity and to give free rein for flair to override other considerations!

We hear a lot about developing chaos; that the extent of change is getting too complex to handle. We must be able to deal with the many aspects of change by the assembly of data and logical analysis, building up scenarios of probabilities to provide a basis for managing. We shall still require great flexibility, and readiness to adapt our forward view, but if we reject this approach, then, by default, there is no forward vision, so that managing will be like driving at full speed at night with no headlights. Managing is increasingly about envisioning, but using intelligence rather than a crystal ball.

Nothing can be achieved except through our human resources, of which the most crucial group is management. In an increasingly hostile and competitive world, it is only through people that we can achieve any competitive advantage, and what these people believe and how they behave goes right to the heart of the organisation. It is people who have vision, who develop the strategies, innovate, and design the products, who achieve the sales, who manage and utilise the resources. It is our managers who lead and motivate, who encourage personal contribution, learning and growth; who encourage the vitality and co-ordinated drive in an organisation which achieves competitive advantage.

Gordon McBeath
*London, January 1990*

# *Note*

Throughout the book, the word 'manager' is used for convenience as a universal term to cover any individual with a supervisory, managerial or directing role, plus senior specialists, without regard to position title.

Similarly, the male pronoun used throughout is for convenience only, and all such references should be taken to apply equally to the female.

The examples in this book are fictional creations designed to illustrate principles and practices. In general, they are based on a number of events in more than one company, and, in all cases, names and characters have been invented.

# PART I

# Introduction

# 1.1

## *The competitive edge*

### LOOKING TO THE FUTURE

The ways in which business is organised and managed will continue to evolve through the 1990s, influenced by the continued rapid change in the business environment and attitudes to the way we live. Technology, and particularly information technology, will continue to progress, as will the market place. We shall increase efforts to anticipate and better the strategies and actions of our competitors. 'Green' issues will continue to grow in importance. The scale of change will not constitute 'chaos', but will demand skilled analysis and comprehension of influences. Towards the envisioned corporate future, our assessments of the future business environment and what we can realistically expect to achieve will lead us to update our short-term business objectives and strategies more frequently, and to steadily adapt the organisation and the culture which we use to achieve them. We shall need a clear assessment of the skills which our future managers will require to be effective, to enable us to help them prepare for that future, and to take the initiatives which will give competitive advantage.

It is one of the essential tasks of a manager to envision the uncertain future. Competent analysis of obtainable data can minimise uncertainty and enable options to be identified and evaluated. Planning systems make substantial demands on management time, but planning provides a pay-off by helping managers with vision to take giant strides; by clarifying what is possible, identifying obstacles, defining intentions, objectives and environment, and by setting out a clear scenario as a basis for positive decision-making. Subsequently, differences between the actual and anticipated scenarios become clearly evident so that thinking and actions can be adjusted. There is a degree of security in always having a firm view of the future, even though we suspect it will be found to be inaccurate, as it provides the ability to adjust that projection in a controlled fashion while providing a base for all forward thinking decisions. This is nowhere more critical than in our projections of individual career development and in the planned utilisation of our managers.

## MANAGEMENT DEVELOPMENT

Management development cannot operate in isolation. Without purpose it becomes meaningless: it must be integrated into the total business strategy to provide the managers needed by the business, and be adapted in line with evolving needs. Much traditional management development and succession planning has been based on current organisation with no recognition that the business environment and objectives, organisation and required competencies are all changing. Much past failure is attributable to a lack of awareness that goalposts were moving. "We got our people ready, but the organisation/jobs/needs had changed."

Yet management continuity is essential to the company's future and requires the cultivating of existing people to provide the further generations of management required to meet identified future needs. Those future needs must be properly identified, and specifications should be evident from, and be derived from, business plans, strategies, and changing environmental scenarios. These requirement specifications provide the guidelines for all management resourcing and development policies and action strategies.

Future business targets, objectives, plans and strategies tend to be complex if they are realistic and meaningful. Typically they concentrate primarily on financial measures, but incorporate a range of functional detail such as investment and product plans and strategies, marketing strategies, etc. In the past many tended not to cover human resource requirements or strategies in the same detail, although examination of the achievability of plans would show that the availability of appropriate managerial resources was the primary limiting factor, and that positive human resource strategies and actions were essential to minimising or overcoming that limitation.

*All management resourcing and development strategies and policies must stem from this source* – they must be designed to provide what the business needs. Business situations frequently come down to people situations, and there is increasing recognition by top management that *a sustainable competitive advantage will only be achieved through people.*

## Competitive advantage

It is an objective of many organisations to gain 'the edge' over competitors in order 'to win'. A competitive edge might be defined as 'some form of advantageous lead in the market place leading to enhanced market share and profitability'. The strategies and tactics of achievement may not be well defined, but gaining a competitive edge is very much associated with people. If a sustainable competitive advantage can only be achieved through people, then human resources are the most important assets of any organisation. At the core of this resource is the critically important *management* resource. The effective management and development of these human resources is the key to achieving competitive advantage. Success is most likely to be achieved if all management resourcing and development activity is linked to achieving challenging yet attainable corporate objectives and is an integral part of strategic management.

Many companies claim that 'the one advantage which they have over competition resides in their people'; that they have the 'best people'. Of course not everyone can have the best, so what is claimed is that they have the best people for their business, organisation, culture, etc. But however good the people, they still need direction. Leadership, whether by an individual or a management group, with clear vision and realistic purpose, with properly designed organisation, carefully selected people and a thought through culture, can provide a cerebral and inspirational management environment which encourages innovation, challenges the 'now', and creates a competitive advantage.

## Limiting resource?

The limiting resource for most corporate ambition is human resource. In the growth and development of businesses, the absence of an individual or a team to 'make it all happen' may be the sole reason for not proceeding with a new product, with a major development, or with an acquisition. The overall concept may be clear, as may the product idea, the availability of technical and manufacturing facilities, the identified niche in the market and viable costs; but if you have all that and cannot resource the opportunity with appropriate people, you have nothing. Even more disastrous is having the resources but so restricting their deployment and initiatives by management systems or cultural inhibitions ('the way we do things around here') that opportunities are lost because no one believes success is possible.

In contrast, some managements believe that anything is achievable. Obstacles are things you only become aware of when you take your eye off the objective! Relatively small Japanese companies with ambitious corporate vision quite out of keeping with their resources have surged through to be world players. The achievement potential of small dedicated groups of high ability people in supportive environments can be extraordinary, and has been the secret behind many critical advances.

## 'Excellence'

Much excitement has been generated by books on 'excellence' which, as one commentator observed, "leave the reader with a warm feeling but do not, unfortunately, leave any prescription for action". While many pointers appear in the text, there is a need to identify and assemble a full set of relevant factors and influences in order to determine a course of action, or the result could resemble a jigsaw with key pieces missing. 'Excellence' implies all around excellence. As one company put it, "We simply want to be the 'Best Company' ". But best at what? Profitability, technology, best products, service, as an employer, at communication, or all of these things? Any such ambition is extremely demanding and must be thought through in terms of relevance to the business. Once objectives are clear, positive actions and open communication will ensure that all employees understand and are striving in the same direction.

One constant in 'excellence' seems to be a corporate culture which is focussed on corporate quality, and particularly on the quality of service to the customer; on meeting customer needs; putting the customer first, meeting his requirements and leaving him feeling satisfied; on high quality in all thought and action. Corporate beliefs, attitudes and behaviours must be considered essential to the achievement of excellence in business performance, rather than incidental.

## Culture

Culture is about what the management group believes and how it behaves. Ultimately, its attitude will have a massive influence on how well people are used; whether they are encouraged to use their initiatives, to grow, to *participate* in the business – or simply to behave as moderately intelligent but unthinking robots. Cultural style has an effect on business which can range from 'turbocharging' to crippling, influencing the effectiveness of all activities and the full achievement of corporate potential; but enthusiasm and drive are not enough.

Culture must be matched to business objectives and be supportive, but as culture stems from the individuals who make up the group *the appropriateness of the people to the situation* is the overriding key. It is individuals who have vision, intellect, ambition, drive, competencies, and experience – the abilities to generate great achievements. It is for management resourcing and development strategies to assemble the appropriate individuals in the right place and at the right time. These strategies will be implemented through a range of purpose-shaped activities which combine to produce the required results.

## System and flexibility

Whatever the culture, any large scale and complex activity requires a *disciplined and systematic approach* to clarify what needs to be done and to establish an ordered sequence for the process. The uncertainties of the timing and form of the evolving business environment, and of the timing of business developments, and of the readiness for advancement of individual managers are notoriously difficult to balance. Planning must allow a degree of flexibility, both in the anticipated business development and in managing the deployment of an inventory of managers to staff the opportunities.

If this suggests that the desired cutting edge may be achieved by 'putting into place' a series of procedures and strategies which, together, will produce results, it grossly understates what is required.

Achievement requires wide-ranging analysis to ensure the best use of people to provide the optimum opportunity to contribute to business development and to grow personally, and flexibility on *how* the company can reach its longer term vision.

A systems approach is necessary because we are dealing with substantial complexity, which requires a disciplined approach to ensure that all considerations and influences are identified and taken into account (where any more informal approach would risk oversight of key elements). A systems approach will also ensure rapid response to unexpected changes, as prior consideration of most options and the outlining of anticipated scenarios will enable the unexpected to be assessed quickly and the implications integrated into scenarios and plans swiftly.

It is essential to avoid overburdening any system with administrative rigidity, for the system must serve managers rather than the opposite. This is particularly so when the system is concerned with the managing of individuals. Part of the flexibility required should take account of managerial 'flair', where there may be a limited logical basis for decisions which a manager takes instinctively. Some managers believe that at least 10 per cent of all actions should be 'outside the system' in any dynamic and successful situation. I do not quarrel with this view on people decisions, since the data we have on people can never be total and objective: and, as noted above, virtually all business decisions have a strong people component.

Use of a Review process designed to involve managers at every level in the integration of business needs with the development and deployment of all management resources, from their perspective, is the most important recommendation in this book. Involvement and 'ownership' go hand in hand, and the Reviews ensure that all the elements contributing to management resourcing and development are focussed on real corporate needs.

This activity is targetted on the provision of current and future managers; on improving their effectiveness now and preparing them for future assignments. That preparation involves infinitely more than 'providing some training', although training is likely to contribute. The real aim will be to create commitment to personal development as part of an open and participative style of managing, so that everyone contributes naturally to the development of the business; and learning, in the fullest sense, is part of the way of life.

## SUMMARY

It is worth noting that managers who are good at encouraging the growth of their subordinates get considerable satisfaction from their achievements. Also, that they gain one enormous advantage in that all the best people want to join them – which in turn leads to excellent personal performance.

This book is about planning the development and deployment of managers within the business, and about making things happen through people to achieve that elusive competitive advantage.

# PART II

# A Planning Approach to Business

# *Introduction*

The corporate vision of where the organisation is heading in the long term provides both broad direction and a backcloth for planning business development in the shorter term. Anticipating and preparing for the future, in parallel with addressing the immediate and shorter term direction and objectives, appears to be an essential element of every managers' job.

The business environment is changing very rapidly in many respects. Talk of 'chaos' is negative, for there are many pointers to the form and extent of future change. While that change may be massive and complex, systematic planning involves managers in anticipating and preparing for change. Success in avoiding being wrong-footed by competitors and in identifying and exploiting opportunities can provide new competitive advantages.

Most change has human resource implications, and it is in the development of appropriate human resource strategies where much competitive advantage is obtained. These strategies determine the management resourcing and development requirements and actions within the business, determined in exactly the same way as, for example, product development and marketing strategies. All are fundamental elements which are inseparable from the total business.

# II.I

## *Planning: a vision of the future*

As managers, you are in the business of foretelling the future for, apart from managing the 'now', you have to be preparing for next year and beyond. You have to have a vision of what you expect to face and what you expect to do, and, most of all, what you want to do in the longer term.

Whether formal and systematised or not, planning becomes part of the way of life – part of the way of managing for most managers. It comes with recognition of the range and scale of change and its impact, and of the 'comfort' provided by anticipation of events. The time taken is acknowledged as valuably spent, with a worthwhile pay-back.

### VISION AND CAPABILITY

#### Planning ahead

As an early part of the planning process, it is necessary to look at your vision of the company's place in the envisioned future, and to ensure that the scale of your thinking is adequate. As an example, consider the general view of Japanese industries in the 1960s and early 1970s. Few western business planners paid serious attention to them as competitive threats, as it seemed that many Japanese companies at that time had what might have been regarded as grandiose and unrealistic plans to achieve certain goals over a 20-year time frame. Those plans were defined in brief statements of aggressive intent, which became their *long-term and unchanging missions*, with short-term strategies continually revised and restated as means of progression towards the achievement of the all important long-term goals. The pace of advance of various of these companies from nowhere to global household names, however, shows the results.

Where much business planning very properly sets out to optimise the use of available resources, matching them with opportunities, it is evident that some long-term missions can appear completely out of step with the available resources and organisation capability of your company now. But 20 years is a long time, and in that time frame resources can be built up systematically towards the ultimate vision. It is indeed visionary, and demands enormous commitment from managers to move a company from complete 'misfit' in its resourcing and capability to close the gap and build competitive advantage.

As one British managing director said, "I think that a business mission has got to be stretching; it has got to take your breath away".

Once that vision is there, it has to become an obsession 'to win'. It must focus all the actions possible to develop small but cumulative competitive advantages, and progress the company to a stage where the questions are about the steps which may be taken to change the business environment to advantage and to take the initiative from competitors. One way may be to develop an alternative concept of the market and what the customer wants, such as when Canon sold copiers to users who wanted decentralised copying facilities while Xerox was still concentrating on managers of central duplicating services.

Is this at all relevant for a *small company*? It is said that a young Japanese man stood on a box in the middle of the garage where he built small motorcycles and told his 20 employees, "We are going global!". His name was Honda. The story may not be true, but the message holds good – a vision of your future objectives is possible at any size. Of course, small companies have small resources, but they are less visible to the big groups and have much greater freedom of action if they identify their opportunities carefully. Time spent determining the future course is relevant regardless of size.

## The scope of planning

Achieving a competitive edge involves not only vision and even obsession, but also a great deal of detailed preparation so that there are few or no surprises, events are anticipated correctly, there is preparation for likely change, and initiatives are ahead of the competition. This sort of anticipation involves open-minded and critical analysis of self, of all elements of the business environment, and particularly of competitors, which enables strategies to develop which continually place the company at advantage.

The biggest uncertainty in planning may arise from a focus on existing resources and competitiveness, and a failure to identify the potential resourcefulness and future capability of one's own organisation, or of competitors. The ability to achieve a major change in capability is probably linked to cultural factors; to the belief in self and to a willingness to challenge the way things are.

Some of the most dramatic advances have been achieved by tiny teams rather than by the concerted efforts of a heavily resourced organisation. The capability of an organisation to unleash many small teams of dynamic innovators to seek out and exploit competitive advantage may enable achievements to outrun apparent resource limitations. It is very easy to underestimate resource potential, and when competitiveness is still out of reach, strategic alliances may provide a route into new areas.

The suggestion that 'playing by the rules of the industry leader is suicide' encourages the search for unconventional thought and alternative tactical approaches to market structure and technical applications. Real commercial advantage can follow from wrong-footing competitors.

Waterman wrote that "Nothing creates momentum for change like crisis", but crisis is not essential to getting the adrenalin running and creative thinking becoming productive. The excitement of seizing opportunity can do the same if the culture is right, and it can enhance the capability of an organisation enormously.

## Planning: a way of managing

If planning is to work well, it must first shake free of today's problems and move on to tomorrow. It will require a level of dedication and determination from all the participants – a high degree of natural commitment. Planning cannot be effective if the activity is limited to a tiny elite at the top or to a specialist department, or if it is approached inflexibly with the system all powerful. There must always be an opportunity for 'flair' to override system. It is most effective where group culture encourages openness and can draw out all information, ideas and contributions from every level; where people have the self confidence to be open minded and analyse critically; where there are no sacred cows or any need for political caution. Where arrogant and able people with 'an almost divine discontent with the adequacy of now' and a need to do better find themselves in such a culture, the continual challenge to 'how we do things around here' and the search for perfection becomes a great driving force for business development.

A further contributing element in this culture is the attitude of facilitating the growth of people within the limits of their abilities and preferences. This too generates an upward thrust of ambition and ideas which identifies and exploits opportunities, and drives the business towards its long-term goals.

The development of subordinate managers is one of the most stimulating and rewarding aspects of management. As management is essentially about getting things done through people, this initiative is likely to have a business pay-off. Even so, encouraging development can be time consuming, and therefore expensive, so that a clear, business related justification should be expected. Every business needs people, now and into the future, in order to operate. Those people need to have relevant competences to be effective; to be motivated to achieve; to fit corporate needs and style better than competitors' staff; and be capable of initiatives to take the competitive edge. The manager who can inspire his following to these heights will not only be a high achiever through them, but will also attract the cream to come and join him.

Few companies achieve optimum use of their human resources and capability. Not every company even thinks in these terms, but those which do strive to develop a culture which encourages the growth of business through the growth of people may attain a combination which can prove formidable.

The least constructive 'forward objectives' are those which are simply a projection from past achievements, providing little direction from top management and being modified only marginally when business analysis indicates necessary or preferable alternatives. For example, an imposed target of achieving profit growth of 15 per cent may look suspect against anticipated competitor actions to bring out new ranges of low cost products; or a requirement to improve market share may seem illogical if the accessability of product niches will offer excellent profit growth with little change in market share.

Similarly, 'challenging' objectives about staying at the 'leading edge of technology' may be modified by the daunting cost implications and by marketing staff showing that the customer wants proven technology and would be unwilling to pay any premium for unproven, leading edge products. Corporate ambition may be enhanced by potential excitement, but may need to be curbed by commercial realism. Every time, it is necessary to come back to the need for a clear vision of the longer term mission.

If objectives require the company to maximise short-term cash extraction from a declining, 'cash cow' product range, some short-term penalty may well be acceptable if the product life can be extended with the potential to double the residual profitability. Analyses open up those options which are practicable and place large warning signs on dangerous avenues and non-achievable ambitions. The planning process must identify the options so that they can be weighed, one against another, and so that an achievable plan can be developed consisting of achievable tasks and making balanced use of resources and capability; but always placing some resource on more speculative projects to enhance competitiveness and progress long-term strategy.

The degree of *commitment* to using the total planning process as a way of managing is critical. As a part of the culture of an organisation, planning can be approached in an almost evangelical manner of total belief and commitment, or in some more casual way. Limited commitment can be dangerous – as in the company which assembled an attractive looking plan without looking seriously enough at some developing competitive threats, the impact of which produced an unforeseen down turn in business which unseated the chief executive.

## A SYSTEMS APPROACH

In addition to corporate vision, there is also a need for system and the discipline that essential systems bring. Enthusiasm and drive, even combined with considerable intelligence, will not necessarily produce the best result. An efficient system should ensure that nothing gets overlooked, that everything necessary is taken into consideration and covered properly. Through system, we can ensure the effective use of resources and direction of effort, to optimise the capability of the organisation and direct its development.

A systematic approach allows for the activity concerned to be subdivided into a number of parts, which will be addressed sequentially to achieve an end result. It implies *acceptance of thoughtful analysis and forward planning as the logical basis for managing a business* towards its goals. Of course, this is complicated by the need to continuously re-appraise assumptions, projections and intentions, so that much of the plan will be 'under review' at any point in time and any recorded version will inevitably be a passing snapshot already partially out of date. System and planning does not imply slowness of action or excessive caution: rather the availability of an information base enabling fast, informed and considered decisions.

A systems cycle starts with review of the organisation's *capability now*: an in-depth analysis of the business as it is; its immediate objectives, people, organisation and culture; the environment in which it exists; and what its resources are potentially able to achieve. All planning will involve progression from that starting point.

Much of the business environment is changing at a tremendous pace and many elements of that change have human resource implications – some relatively minor, but some radical and complex. Planning must amplify the weak signals warning of future change. The form and degree of potential implications must be assessed, for there may be substantial advantages to be exploited or obstacles to be overcome in human resource terms in order to optimise the potential of the organisation. And there will be a vital time dimension as the plan unfolds. Time *is not* a resource in the sense of finance and people, but it is finite and is used to set key 'milestones' towards achievement of human resource and other strategies. For example, time, in the early or delayed readiness of a team to exploit a market opportunity, can make the difference between achieving a dominant market leadership position or an unprofitable also-ran situation.

## THE ACHIEVABLE PLAN

The product of this approach should be a clearly stated plan in which the long-term corporate vision is followed by shorter term detailed business objectives, supported in turn by statements of the anticipated business environment and the strategies (including particularly human resource strategies) which must be implemented to ensure successful achievement.

The emerging plan needs to be comprehensive. For example, it needs to be clear on forward organisation requirements and how these are to evolve from what exists now; on forward culture and style, and how these will evolve; on future management needs, detailing the evolution of changing skill requirements or profiles; and on the expected evolution and impact of management information systems. Against these human resource needs can be set the current inventory of management and the latest forecasts of individual development.

As demand and supply (needs and inventory) are matched, there may be some supply limitations which force reconsideration of aspects of the business plan. The degree of *adaptability* of people, organisation and culture may be key influences on what will be achievable.

## The time dimension

The time dimension is critical, as already stated, but it is also a variable. Many of the environmental changes built into the plan will have been assigned degrees of probability which will be acceptably accurate, but the anticipated timing of technical and competitor movement is frequently the greatest uncertainty. The overall plan, and particularly the human resource elements, is under continuous reassessment as both the timing of requirements and the readiness of people are reappraised.

No matter what the size of the company, management will have a vision of the business sectors and markets they favour, the market shares and margins they would like to achieve, with levels of profitability and cash flow, in various time scales. Objectives or targets can be proposed and evaluated, but these start as ideal targets, stated in rather general language. These will be modified for the short term as they get translated into hard requirements for business resources and actions, and 'achievability' considerations are added based on the assessed real capabilities of the organisation in the anticipated environment. The potential capability of small dedicated teams with limited resources to tackle tough new initiatives should not be discounted in planning.

The ultimate 'achievable' plan for the shorter term may incorporate targets which are substantially different from the 'corporate vision'. This does not imply that the vision is worthless, but an understanding of the 'deviation' and its longer term contribution to the ultimate objectives should be sought. It is useful to have a preferred course when there are many options, some offering favourable and profitable short-term opportunities; but these must not be allowed to distract from the unchanging long-term goal.

## What is 'achievable'

'Achievable' means that everything required to lead to successful outcome is available or possible. Not only is the product range expected to have completed the design stage and to have progressed into production, but the market place is believed to be receptive – competition can be matched or beaten on design, quality, delivery, price, etc. All that will not be enough, however, if there is a problem in human resource terms which might limit the ability to exploit the opportunity. So corporate ambition must be tempered, but hopefully not seriously inhibited, by the capability of the organisation as the achievable plan is assembled.

The corporate vision or mission should provide a backcloth for defining specific long- and short-term objectives in greater detail; probably financially orientated with capital, required profit and sales topping the list. From 'target numbers', the detailed business plan grows to state exactly *how* the objectives are to be achieved, including the resources to be used and the strategies to be employed to overcome obstacles. As the skeletal form of the plan is fleshed out, the need to assess the present capability of the people and the organisation and how it may be increased, and to see how the competitive environment is likely to change become paramount; after which an *achievable plan* and the strategies required to support it can be determined.

# II.2

## *Corporate capability now*

### RECOGNISING POTENTIAL

Organisation capability means the full potential which the organisation is capable of achieving, *if* it can maximise the use of all its resources, including particularly its human resources.

Most organisations fail to achieve their full potential by a combination of factors, including in particular failing to mobilise and motivate small innovative teams; but also by pursuing objectives for which they are not ideally resourced; by unbalanced resources; by organisation structures and cultures not designed to achieve the objectives, and so on.

The only sound base from which to improve capability and to plan the future is a very clear statement of *where you are now plus an evaluation of how well you are doing.* The enterprise may not be strong enough to tackle future tasks until you have made sure that your current business operation is more efficient, or until you have taken action to bring aspects of the business performance up to acceptable standards. This requires a complete 'check-up' – a comprehensive analysis to clarify the 'now', and to assess how effective the enterprise has been in using its resources and strengths to achieve its recent objectives, including how effective each function and department has been in handling relevant parts of the overall programmes.

In parallel, an assessment of the overall *capability* of the organisation is needed. What would the organisation be capable of achieving beyond present objectives if resources were so directed, fully utilised and motivated? This should be considered against the background of long-term corporate strategy, and how the deployment of limited resources might enable potentially major programmes to be initiated needs to be examined. This assessment should not concentrate simply on improving overall productivity or efficiency, but on the business strategies required, and then on the compatibility between objectives and the utilisation of resources. *The organisation exists, with people, purpose and culture.* You should be able to measure and make judgements on how effectively it is operating now, and on its potential capability.

### ANALYSIS OF 'NOW' AGAINST COMPETITORS

#### Sources of information

The range of analyses to be used is likely to begin with an examination of every meaningful financial ratio in the business concerned and extend ultimately to just about everything which is quantifiable. In most cases it will be possible to set current figures against those for the past several years to identify any deteriorating trends. Perhaps more important, how do these compare with any equivalent data gleaned from competitors? Their main financial ratios are generally available from the annual reports of public companies (not always easy to get for overseas competitors), but breakdown into product line detail tends to be concealed in these documents so that other sources must be found.

Curiously, much may be gathered at industry conventions and professional gatherings where individuals compete to demonstrate status and achievements and sometimes provide detailed information. Collection of this material for evaluation against other data can prove valuable. Of course, a range of data is collected and published by national and industry bodies.

Salesmen are an excellent source of competitive data as they pick up news from customers about competitors' claimed achievements, problems and future plans. Drawing out this information and encouraging sales people to seek it, may require specific reference and even reward within the commission plan, but systematic data gathering needs to be established on a permanent basis.

Recruitment interviews provide a further potential source of intelligence as the job hunter tends to be expansive about what he is working on, about achievements, or perhaps about some business development which results in him being in the job market. Candidates who are cautious during pre-employment interviews may be debriefed once they are recruited if they have come from a competitor and have 'changed sides'.

## Methods of analysis

Much of the analysis is likely to focus on comparisons with competitors, and there are probably two particular analyses you will use to help – a SWOT analysis and the Boston matrix. These will give assessments of where you believe you fit in relation to competitors and their products (or product ranges), related to the growth rate of the market and relative market shares.

*The Boston matrix*

The matrix, which examines relative market share against the rate of market growth, was developed by the Boston Consulting Group. It is designed to give some indications of the present market position and future prospects of current product ranges. Products are categorised as follows: A relatively new product with a high market share in a growth market is a *Star*, likely to be adequately self-financing in terms of cash flow. Yesterday's Stars, which have retained high market share and profitability in a market with little or no further growth, become *Cash Cows* with strong positive cash flows. The *Problem Child* did not achieve a dominant market position in a still growing market, or may have slipped back, and is a cash user. The *Dogs* have no future and are also a drain on cash.

At any one time, a range of products is likely to contain a mix of these categories at different stages in their product life cycles, and the matrix gives a quick initial review of the 'health' of the overall product offering.

A number of organisations have developed more detailed forms of this basic matrix, and more precise measures along the axes, relevant to their own situations. Such analyses can provide a more accurate assessment of the 'health' of a product portfolio and can be used to highlight movement in the positions for each product, year on year.

*SWOT analysis*

A SWOT analysis (Strengths, Weaknesses, Opportunities, Threats) is probably the most valuable analysis which can be made as part of this study – provided it is made with proper thoroughness. I recall one company which made such an analysis but missed key indicators to imminent changes in competitor strategy, and was quite unprepared for developments which halved its market share within two years and wiped out its profit. Yet the directors had been confident of their future, having predicted a clear way ahead following their SWOT analysis.

There is a great temptation to be complaisant when looking at strengths, and a tendency to turn a blind eye to weaknesses which have not been too critical in the past or which are 'unchangeable'. It is dangerous to start this analysis unless the participants can be open-minded and self-critical; able to look at the company against competitors and admit to being worse. For it is only when realism is injected and a problem is identified that any corrective action can begin.

In the second half of the analysis, there is usually some excitement over opportunities, although the logic and capability to address them may be more sobering so that real capability is under-rated. I find the analysis of potential threats to be critically important, and more difficult to analyse comprehensively. It requires substantial knowledge and understanding of the activities of each significant competitor and potential competitor; a knowledge of product technology and likely developments; and a host of other data. Even then, the greatest threat comes from competitor initiatives which do not conform to your analysis pattern and lead to unexpected threats. Sensibly, the threats category should be overdone so that there can be consideration of responses to quite low order probabilities, and the probabilities themselves can be properly assessed.

The SWOT analysis may be carried out by functional specialists and then reviewed by the top management team. The analysis can be used to give an overall picture, but may also need to be carried out in greater depth for segments of the business such as product lines or geographic areas. These analyses will identify areas where the company appears to be outperformed by some competitors – or potentially so. How specific is the evidence and what are the differences? Are hard data available, or an assembly of non-quantified indicators? What does cold logic suggest in the situation? All conceivable influences should be listed, and notes made against each one of the known or suspected situation. Such a list might include:

- sales figures, by product
- product design
- price comparisons
- delivery performance
- product performance (quality and reliability)
- customer relations
- after sales service
- profitability (overall and indications by product)
- capital investment programmes
- manning levels (including adequacy of skills, etc.)
- pay levels
- staff turnover
- culture differences
- location advantages and
- any other factors which seem relevant.

## Assessing the analysis

Also using the SWOT approach, an assessment of each main competitor against your present standards will produce a rank order and a view of the form the competitor's edge takes. Establish his pattern of thinking! The greater the detail which can be provided, the greater the opportunity to identify both an effective response and a means of gaining the edge.

There is generally an assumption that a competitor will continue to follow established patterns of competition, but Xerox were wrong-footed when Canon targetted secretaries and their managers who wanted distributed photocopying, rather than the 'traditional' central duplicating departments.

Increasing capability appears to involve identifying series of relatively small opportunities and 'running a marathon in 400 metre sprints'. Challenges and opportunities have to be addressed in relation to long-term strategic objectives and actions selected to progress towards achieving and retaining the desired competitive edge.

There may be a danger, as conclusions begin to be reached, of reacting too quickly or over-reacting: "It is clear that we are overmanned so we must cut our headcount by 10 per cent across the board immediately." If there *are* indications of overmanning, then the areas of concern need to be identified and the basis for the conclusion evaluated. There can be very sound reasons for differences in manning between two apparently identical companies, and indeed for many other differences once superficial conclusions have been probed.

For example, comparisons between two large companies in the hand-held computer business showed that one was concentrating on very high volume, low cost models, while the other aimed at state of the art models for technology application. The organisation structure and the management and staffing mix were substantially different between the two, although initial assumptions were based on their apparent similarity. However, if the conclusion *had* been that there were close similarities of operation but variations in manning standards, the task would have been to find a means of using people better, to 'work smarter'. If work is analysed to determine what is essential – to identify and discontinue the non-essential and duplicated activities, then to sort out the best system – productivity improvements are invariably achievable. However, some allowance for 'discretionary' (non-essential) work should be made on a considered basis.

The initial purpose of the SWOT and other analyses has been to answer the question, "How well are we doing?". It is most unlikely to have produced a resounding, "Outstandingly well!". Even if the conclusion is 'pretty good', there will be a range of points where it is sensible to be less than satisfied, while if the conclusions were much more disturbing, the dissatisfaction with current performance may be deep. But the purpose here is not just to assess how well the company is doing in relation to its competitors and how operations may be made more efficient. You should be examining how capability may be improved by realigning the deployment of resources to achieve longer term objectives; altering the way you behave to achieve more positive actions and gain more initiative.

The problems identified may be associated with a particular function or be across the board, but the reason behind the problem is almost certain to have some roots in the human resource area:

- Is the *organisation* best structured to give the right focus and dedication to the problem issue?
- Is the *corporate culture* supportive of the behaviour necessary for most effective actions or does it find them alien?

- Is the *inventory of management* (their individual skills and strengths) adequate and appropriate to carry through the tasks required to achieve objectives at the performance standards necessary?

## Improving the 'now'

Many of the conclusions from these analyses will take some time to initiate fresh actions and implement, and suitable strategies will need to be embodied in the corporate action priorities, but there should be instances where actions can be immediate and where an early response may be anticipated.

The analyses are likely to result in a list of tasks to support the required strategies, which may be weighted to short-term efficiency improvements. These may take the form of 'headings' with supporting detail covering present and target standards. The means of achieving the improvements may require a numer of interrelated actions by various departments or functions. A fully detailed strategy for each main task should be prepared so that the actions, the expected results, the timing and resources required are all evident and recorded for subsequent monitoring of progress.

At this stage the human resource actions can be extracted and an overall human resource programme determined, highlighting timed targets as 'milestones'. If this should indicate some unmanagable peaks of activity, then the phasing of some programmes may need resheduling. (There should be similar extracts covering each of the main functions or elements of the business, particularly if the scale of fast improvement scheduled is substantial.)

The form which the *human resource action plans* take (and typical headings) is much the same as that covered in some detail on pages 57 to 69 with regard to the human resources implications for business objectives (chapter II.4). Indeed, the elements may be virtually identical, with only the time horizon being shorter. Typical issues would include a lack of key competencies (see chapter III.3), changing skill mix, shortages of categories of specialists, manning standards, or recruiting difficulties; organisation issues including general ineffectiveness, an excess of levels, or a mismatch of organisation structure and objectives. There may be a cultural mismatch. Pay policy may be inappropriate and not encourage people to focus on the key business issues. And there can be many other issues.

Human resource problems will frequently be associated with problems in another function. Possibly a radical review of both marketing strategy and marketing staff is required; or manufacturing management may not be keeping up with the flow of orders in spite of being well resourced. In these programmes, the human resources constituent may be the critical one.

There needs to be an *assessment of the realism of the total improvement programme*, the targets and the timetable, to ensure that these are achievable and that the company is not simply fooling itself that, having identified problems, they will inevitably be overcome. It may be judged that the total programme involves more upheaval than can be managed within the preferred time scale. By selecting priorities and deferring some less critical elements, a large programme to upgrade capability can be progressed.

However, there may be cultural factors which will be difficult to address within a short time scale, thus reducing the probability of achievement on other parts of the programme; or there may be other restrictions, such as sales volumes, which make the desired level of automated manufacture uneconomic. If there is no way of achieving the targetted standards or change of attitudes, etc. which will enable the enterprise to compete successfully, it may become appropriate to question, 'Are you in the right business?'. A review of business objectives against clearly identified limitations may help to identify new and achievable objectives and a way forward.

All planning should loop back to its opening position in this way. As the enterprise begins to plan its future, the starting base must be firm and clearly understood as a live situation, with the first stage of improving capability already built in.

## RADICAL CHANGE

### Assessing the need for change

The degree to which an established management team can achieve a radical change in the capability of an organisation is probably rather limited. It is reasonable to assume that the team has been endeavouring to do well, and that past achievements represent its best efforts. It may have learned by experience how it might perform better, or from its analyses the reasons why some aspects of performance are less than acceptable. Unless it has shown some real flexibility of mind, and the drive and willingness to take a radical rethink, it may not be possible for the team to respond dramatically under its present leadership.

The elements which need to change may have been pin-pointed, and may even focus on one area or function which is limiting the overall capacity. Team attention to this limited area may achieve some breakthrough, or a more major change may be triggered by one committed individual who sees and grasps an opportunity.

> An electronics company found that it was suddenly losing market share in an important product area which it had previously dominated to a young, relatively small company with an excellent new product. Redesigning its own products traditionally took three years, followed by extended adapting in manufacturing before the result was tried out on marketing. The time scale was long enough for the market to be lost, but the management team had no answer.
>
> A younger manager proposed a multi-disciplinary team and crash programme. He asked for resources which were felt to be totally inadequate; for example, seven design engineers instead of the usual team of 70. He was told to go ahead and allowed to pick his team because no one had a better idea and it would not waste too much money. No one in the management team believed it would achieve anything.
>
> The team also included tiny numbers of selected marketing people, production engineers and buyers, as well as the design engineers. In nine months they were delivering volumes of their new product, which had a real edge over their competitor, and were reclaiming their market. The tiny team had been unencumbered by previous behaviour and administrative systems and had shown the way the market had to be tackled.
>
> There ought to be a happy ending, but the management team was unable to adapt to the challenge and moved to impose their traditional approach, swamping and destroying the new high achieving team, most of whom left.

There is generally awareness of need for change within an organisation, but the minds of the senior management may be closed to *accepting* that need. An aging team may be unwilling or unable to face the upheaval. Only if the organisation is dying and becomes vulnerable to takeover can a new team take control and implement the necessary change. Alternatively, the threat to survival may trigger actions which result in a new leader and a revitalisation of the enterprise.

## Maximising capability

Maximising capability has a number of elements, but the most critical is optimising the opportunity to contribute by the human resources, where corporate culture will be the main influence. For example, an authoritarian style will place blocks on the ability of a large proportion of people to contribute initiatives or non-directed actions, thus severely diminishing potential capability. In contrast, an open culture, with transforming leadership which encourages and motivates business related initiatives and behaviour, is likely to generate a much higher level of success. In such a culture, high personal objectives are likely to be set and exceeded, the only concern being not to over-extend the capacities of individuals.

At a different level, maximising capability involves matching achievable objectives with resources and modifying one or both to a 'best fit'. There must also be a matching of objectives with the organisation's strengths so that opportunities are exploited through a willingness to use the small committed group to work miracles. It makes more sense to utilise strengths to expand capability than to dwell on limitations, but critical weaknesses must be addressed to minimise their impact.

The objective will be to reach the full potential which can be developed by diminishing restrictions on creative initiatives and by encouraging the most effective use of all the resources of the organisation – by seeking to bring into balance achievement of 'impossible' business objectives through the expansion of human capacity.

# II.3

## *Environmental change*

### INTRODUCTION

The conditions which surround our organisations, within which we exist and function, make up our environment – and it is changing continuously. This chapter is about that change and the ways which change will influence business objectives and their achievability; the strategies you need to develop to achieve them, and the way you manage. Business environment has a very real impact on business strategies and on human resource requirements.

### Forecasting change

Nothing is 'for sure' beyond a three-month time horizon, let alone one of 10 to 20 years, but managers are in the business of forecasting change over extended periods. Understanding the changes taking place or developing around us has to be one of the most important preoccupations of managers in the 1990s. In this process, there is an overriding need for objectivity, with no room for complaisance. Only an open-minded and critical analysis of what you think may be possible will open your eyes to all aspects of potential environmental change and the impact it is likely to have on your businesses.

### Managing change

The best way to *manage* change is to anticipate the forms of change which may occur and to plan how to respond to them; and perhaps to develop contingency plans for the possible but less likely considerations.

This does not require a visionary, but envisioning helps. Anticipating future opportunities and difficulties is what business planning is all about, yet many planners fail to make sufficiently comprehensive studies of potential change, or to follow through to examine the implications. In this book, I am concerned particularly with environmental changes which will affect the business and may have human resource implications; with changes which may affect your requirements for and uses of human resources, both now and into the future. In a high proportion of business situations the critical element in determining the achievability of a plan will be human resource factors in some form or other. *It should therefore be of the greatest concern that many business objectives are at risk due to lack of awareness of impending change, compounded by lack of preparation by managers to cope with that change.*

## Types of environmental change

The range of aspects where environment may change and affect human resource issues is obviously very large and any grouping will result in some overlap. However, the following checklist may provide reasonably comprehensive cover:

- New technology: its impact on possible products, product design, manufacturing methods, materials and costs; its impact on information technology and office automation.
- Competitor activity: changes in the behaviour or strategies of competitors which alter the market situation; impact of increasing internationalism of markets.
- Legislation: controls and regulations which alter freedom of action; tax changes which affect costs and profitability.
- Economic trends: changing levels of inflation and wage indices, geographically; other national economic statistics, interest rates; health care costs, etc.
- Demographics: changing age mix of population and work force; supply of graduates and of various skills; male/female mix of work force; minority groups.
- Social values: changes in society and attitudes to work and authority; participation; quality of life.
- Pollution of the environment ('green' issues): changes in the

acceptability of pollution; high cost implications of pollution/pollution controls.

- Energy: energy management; safeguarding natural resource reserves.

## Making change acceptable

The human resource aspects of these issues are many and various, and the strategies needed to deal with those implications will be similarly varied. Strategies need to be essentially practical and effective rather than idealistic, to support business objectives which are also realistic and achievable. Further, the human resource strategies must be potentially acceptable to the people who will be affected, for unless their support is forthcoming, strategies may not be allowed to work.

The culture of an organisation, and the degree to which it is participative and supportive, will have major influence on the communication and acceptability of any radical strategy proposals, which require careful presentation and understanding if acceptance is to be gained. Time is a further ingredient in this process, i.e. time for people to comprehend and come to terms with a problem, with the solution proposed and with its implications for them personally. Time must be adequate within the culture.

### TECHNOLOGY

## The pace and scale of technological change

The pace and scale of technological change appear to be increasing and will have enormous effects on many aspects of business operations as well as life in general. Some features of this change are the opening up of fundamental new areas such as genetic engineering, which has enormous potential; the development of new materials and advances in electronics, which have domino effects on a variety of other technologies; and the advances in computer information and communication technologies which will fundamentally alter our lives. Virtually all advances in technology will have some impact on the uses and management of human resources.

Technology itself is not a competitive advantage; it is only a tool.

The purposes to which that tool is directed will determine whether there is competitive advantage.

The advances in electronics are making cheaper computing power readily available and leading to the installation of computer chips in a wide variety of equipment. Various domestic equipments are controlled in this way, offering a wide range of programmes (such as in washing machines, dishwashers, microwave ovens and so on). In the same way, computers are beginning to feature more in cars, progressing from 'toys', to control petrol feed, avoid wheel lock, sense for black ice, and provide an increasing range of useful functions. Utilisation of computing power will continue to escalate in line with increasing capacity and reducing costs of chips which enable new low cost options to be offered. The power of hand-held and personal computers is extraordinary by the standards of ten years ago: a further decade is likely to show comparable growth.

For most products, the product life cycle is getting shorter, and each new generation or variant must be designed and delivered to the customer more quickly. Failure to match the development pace of competitors can leave a company stranded with obsolete and unsaleable products. This pace has forced the use of integrated teams in which marketing influences product design and manufacturing engineers ensure the emerging design is easily and cheaply made and maintained. This breaking down of traditional barriers is not universally popular but has proved essential in the more competitive situations, and this type of project team will become the norm in organisations in the 1990s.

Judgements of the acceptability of new technology and its cost to the customer may quickly or universally determine how much new technology is utilised. Some companies strive for 'state of the art' products for customers prepared to pay. Good examples exist in aeronautics, defence, computers, and medical products. But many customers in other fields are happier with proven technology, which may be somewhat slower but is lower priced and felt to be more reliable. Apart from the design of the product, the ease with which it can be made and serviced also has price implications. Organisations with state of the art technologies may need other divisions which can utilise their experience with these technologies as they become 'proven' and more widely accepted.

Knowledge of what is possible (or becoming so) in technological terms is vital to the marketing people who are determining future product strategies on which the business plan will be based. Innovation may be vital at the leading edge, but judgement of when the 'possible' will be acceptable and economic is difficult, and it is easy to run ahead of the market place. The design and production costs of the Concorde provide an example; and the continual updating of the Nimrod specification, another.

Manufacturing automation has provided the basis of substantial reductions in the cost of large volume items (and parallel reductions in manpower) and further advance can be anticipated (if not yet fully identifiable). The potential for further manufacturing technology change remains considerable in many industries and has been notable for the resulting extreme changes in numbers and skills of people.

The growth areas of bio-technology and genetic engineering have wide potential applications to farming and agriculture, as well as to pharmaceuticals and medicine, and may well provide the greatest fundamental changes in technology during the 1990s. So far, the applications to the design of new plants and animals, new drugs and treatments are largely experimental, but over a further five to ten year period many of these applications will come into everyday use and begin to revolutionise the industries concerned, particularly pharmaceuticals. The human resource implications within industry are difficult to assess as yet, beyond the shortage of suitably qualified researchers, but must concentrate minds in these industries.

Last and by no means least is the impact of advances in information technology and telecommunications, which will continue the revolution begun in administration. This has the same potential for taking out very large numbers of the lower skilled, routine office jobs which automation has removed from manufacturing during the past decade. In turn, this will alter the content of many managerial posts, and the numbers required. The implications of much of this initial summary can be seen to be substantial for the human resource function. Change will come partly from the changing numbers of people involved, but also from the considerable changes in skills required to do the work.

## Product technology

*The marketing approach*

New technology does not necessarily mean new products, only the opportunity of choice for customers, who may prefer lower cost, proven technology and products. Determined sales staff may manage to sell what the company has decided to produce, but what is needed is a marketing approach.

Product life cycles are shortening. New materials are becoming available. Computer power is providing a new dimension for many products. The need to have products which the customer wants, with the designs he likes, with the technology he prefers with guaranteed quality, at the right price, available at the right time: all these are essential to holding a competitive edge.

The force which is driving product development is *increased competition, to which product innovation is the major response.* Companies have sought to achieve a competitive edge by increasing the added value of products, by increasing complexity, by more specialised focus on products to target more precise groups. And the focus has moved from European orientation to address global markets. The major shift of emphasis is away from production orientation to marketing, with attention to identifying and meeting customer needs which may require product innovation or may need attention to other aspects of customer services.

Marketing staff must have a comprehensive understanding of technological advances relevant to the business they are in, and how these advances may be utilised in product development. From discussion of this application potential, they must build up a view of the product specifications which will sell, some months (and years) later. It is only when the customer begins to ask for particular concepts that a potential new product begins to become marketable. Until that point, the excitement of the technical staff and product designers must be controlled and the anticipated requirements of the customer met.

*Business planning*

From time to time, a technological breakthrough may have a devastating effect on an industry. There was a substantial valve industry before the advent of the transistor. In a few years it had been swept away, with the exception of tiny niche producers of extremely specialised products, while a whole new transistor industry had grown up. When such a development is recognised, determining the most cost saving route out of a capital intensive business may be the only option, although the full implications of the transistor revolution were not recognised immediately.

The starting base for a business plan includes an evaluation of the range of existing products and of the market place, knowledge of existing applied technology, plus what has been achieved in laboratories or should be technically possible within the time frame. Advances in manufacturing technology are equally important. Development of market orientated future product specifications can then be incorporated into the plan, with judgements of the human resource implications.

A high technology company is likely to want to push to incorporate new knowledge into products at maximum rate, to give itself competitive advantage. This can be highly advantageous if the customer is supportive. A small computer company with a marketing stance of always offering state of the art technology will satisfy its usual customers by this tactic; but a similar organisation which stresses proven technology would not need to be at the technology frontier. However, there can be dangers. For example, the Ministry of Defence has, on some contracts, continually updated a specification to keep pace with research, but made it impossible for the supplier to complete a design and bring it to production, in spite of increasingly horrendous costs (Nimrod was such an example). There has to be a cut off point, after which there is a crash programme to complete a design, to get it into manufacture and into the customers' hands.

The human resource requires a multi-functional team to design, make and sell, with high ability management and a supportive culture which is at ease with such teams. Functional boundaries can not exist and inter-functional conflict should be alien. The creation and re-absorbing of project teams will be a major feature of 1990s' organisation.

Product development in 'lower technology' companies, or where technology is evolving at a slower pace, involves much the same task. Planning future products starts with what exists, current technology and anticipated developments, and marketing knowledge of customer requirements. The slower pace of change places more emphasis on product redesign to reduce product costs and manufacturing complexity, to increase automation, and to adapt designs to fashion changes or customer preferences.

Some vulnerability may stem from the possibility of rapid advance which renders an existing product obsolete. Within electronics, this may be a step forward in the capacity or cost of a chip which radically changes the capability or price of units and requires a reassessment of marketing objectives. This may affect the whole organisation – management requirements and skills, numbers and skills of employees, and even geographic locations. If such events are considered possible (they may be identified as 'probable' in the business analysis, but with time as an extreme uncertainty), some contingency plan should exist, including initiatives to gain advantage (or at worst, to ensure survival).

## New technologies

The emergence of bio-technology and genetic engineering fits easily into some existing businesses, but there are large opportunities to create totally new businesses. These may develop as spin-offs from large companies, but it is evident that many will be smaller, capital intensive, research orientated companies which may grow very rapidly after the fashion of some 1960s'/70s computer or software houses.

In these 'exploding' units, the organisation and culture will be critical, needing open communication and strong encouragement of individual growth to attract and utilise the specialised human resources required. In the upper part of the organisation structure, the rapid change in job content and development in the scale of managerial responsibility will stretch occupants to the limit. Exceptional rates of growth are extremely difficult to manage, and any compromise on standards near the top is destined ultimately to fail. Individual merit is the only justification for holding such a position, with recognition that even fast developing managers may not be able to grow at the pace demanded by evolving jobs.

In these new industries many of the required skills will be coming from universities, with the use of academics as part-time consultants an essential factor in staying ahead. A cellular structure around projects, rather than functional organisation, is likely, although in larger companies the future success of the 'new area' division may be put at risk by being staffed more traditionally.

## Information technology

The major developments in information technology are the increasing availability of computing power at reducing cost and with increasing 'user friendliness', and the advances in telecommunications which enable information to be transmitted or accessed from remote points.

*Computers*

The effects of this can be seen most easily in the enormous growth of personal computers and computer terminals; in the ready and increasing availability of distributed computing power. All the indications are that there is potential for considerable further development of this technology and associated application, and the extravagant projections of further expenditure on information technology during the first half of the 1990s may even prove to be understated.

One immediate impact has been on large scale administration processes, where vast numbers of similar transactions have in the past occupied armies of clerical help. Computers have been used for some years, with the ability to process all routine paperwork at great speed and to present comprehensive summaries and analyses in parallel, to wipe out large volumes of relatively low skilled work, and to alter the tasks of associated managers. Availability of 'end result' data enables the manager to deal with the implications straight away rather than have to focus on getting analyses done. He can take decisions and move on to his next task. In this process, it is not only clerical and analytical jobs which disappear: management jobs reduce in number and change in content.

Computers have moved up from clerical and management desks to the top level, as databases have become more comprehensive and the computers themselves more friendly. Software can shape a mass of data into analyses or colourful graphs, drawing on company-wide sources through a network, and directed through friendly touch screens. This has radically altered the ways managers can manage, the ways they plan, report or run meetings. One executive has commented that meetings which took 80 per cent of the time sharing information and agreeing what was correct can now spend 80 per cent taking decisions.

Further developments in systems technology, to assist the

assembly and analysis of data to aid management decision-making, may be assisted by voice activated instruction, and by highly developed scanning processes. The complexities of monthly/quarterly/yearly cycles will be replaced by total daily updates of all financial numbers. The task of the manager over the next decade or two will change as dramatically as that of the farmer over the last century.

*Interfacing with telecommunications*

When combined with telecommunications developments, it is possible to utilise computer power from anywhere, provided that there is a telephone line and a modem. The remote small computer can download batches of data from its giant and distant cousin to work on locally, or can feed new data straight into the main frame. Geographic flexibility is straightforward.

The reducing need to concentrate great numbers of administrative staff in large offices will have a fundamental impact on human resource requirements and management. One option is to decentralise the administrative process to numbers of satellite locations with significantly lower office costs and probably lower staff costs. As an extreme example, one American insurance company has all its claims from clients in the Eastern States processed through an office in a country town in Ireland, which is on-line to the New York office. It achieves substantially lower accommodation and staff costs, with virtually no delay in printing out approved statements in New York. General routine administration is covered easily this way, but non-standard problems may need re-routing to specialists. More and more large scale administration and service activities will be handled this way. Your account in a bank or building society is on-line for withdrawals or information. The state of your account with the gas and electricity authorities, with your credit card company, and so on, is accessible via an operator on a terminal.

The telephone number you want is accessed quickly through the directory enquiries operator using a terminal. Your holiday and air bookings are confirmed over a terminal. Car registration and television licence administration is computerised. All this is a normal process, though not yet universal, with some concerns expressed about national databases which contain personal data.

As it becomes easier to do work away from an administrative centre, home will be the logical work place. Much experimentation is taking place already, particularly with 'home workers' doing commercial programming and some processing work, sometimes loaded and unloaded at night. Some key workers are able to continue in full-time roles, 400 miles from base. By 1989 there were already in excess of 5,000 employees of large concerns permanently based at home, and the numbers are growing rapidly. Work volumes and accuracy are self monitored by the home worker so that achievement or performance is evident to both manager and managed, and the *control and discipline elements in the manager's role largely disappear.*

Using the same telecommunications technology, teleconferencing with television pictures of participants is technically possible, providing 'face to face' conversation at a distance with facsimile transfer of documents in parallel. Even a board meeting will not require the directors to assemble, as teleconferencing facilities will enable the business and discussion to proceed, with the speaker visible on screen. Only the business lunch which used to follow, and the off-record side meetings, will be lost, or be covered separately.

At a more sophisticated level, medical diagnosis by computer will evolve from current experimentation. Where integrated databases presently concentrate on only one segment of medical practice, the emergence of even larger scale data evaluation should permit integration of the segments.

In the field of education and training, there are rapid advances in the development and use of packaged courses for use on a distant learning basis. Schools broadcasting on television and Open University material are flourishing. The possibility of developing high quality video presentations of all basic 'teaching' on a national basis would enable learning to be more individually paced and encourage individual tutorial back up on a larger scale. The real application of information technology has yet to take form in the field of education.

### *The human resources implications*

Information technology developments have enormous potential implications for human resources at every level, influencing organisation, skill requirements and management style, as well as the numbers of people required; and there is a sense that this 'revolution' still has a very long way to run. Such is its significance that achieving and maintaining a competitive edge will almost certainly involve achieving a high degree of effectiveness in information management as one of the most essential factors. A long-term vision of information technology strategy, embracing the expected technological advances and the planned in-house applications, is to be recommended.

### ENVIRONMENTAL POLLUTION

Political pressures from the 'green' movement, the ecology pressure groups which have built into a political force, have brought many aspects of environmental pollution into media headlines and public interest. Managers generally will need to be well informed on pollution relevant to their organisations, and companies will need to spend time and money to meet ecological standards which will become more stringent.

The overriding concern is with the overall 'health' of the planet as the 'greenhouse effect' arising from polluted atmosphere and the changing balance of vegetation begins to alter the world-wide climate with some potentially disastrous implications. But there are many specific and more local elements where public concern is going to ensure greater management attention, either where historical perspectives are being challenged or where new conditions are emerging. It takes only one small report or incident to attract media attention for a major national storm of protest to follow.

The cleanliness or otherwise of rivers, beaches and the sea is given a high profile, particularly when accidents occur, but also concerning long-term steady pollution which has an adverse affect on wild life. Cleaning up rivers to encourage fish breeding or the return of salmon can have major implications for large industrial users of water, requiring expensive equipment to ensure that returned water is acceptably clean, or even the right temperature. Once a river is 'clean' any irregularity is likely to have immediate visible impact, causing public outcry.

Clean air is equally important, with concern about toxic fumes and acid rain. Lead emission from cars will result in steady pressure for lead-free petrol to become the norm. The concern about the effect of CFCs on the ozone layer must eventually result in world-wide controls, but meanwhile there is substantial investment in chemical plants producing CFCs. People cannot see most of this pollution, but public awareness is substantial and increasing, so that the countries, industries and companies most responsible are under growing pressure.

Protection of wild life and the country will continue to be popular concerns, but there will be conflicting pressure for allocation of green belt land for housing. On a world scale, population growth is a key factor in the continuing destruction of rain forests which is contributing to the 'greenhouse effect'. This seems unlikely to be halted, so that the change in weather patterns already evident will go some way further – even over the next decade – and generate other changes in the global environment, both business and ecological.

At a different level, industrial health and safety is likely to continue to generate further legislation, which managements will need to understand and respond to fully. On the fringe of this will be pressures such as the anti-smoking lobby in some developed countries, which is achieving non-smoking areas in many public places and at work, but where there is an opposite pressure for individual freedom of action. A similar lobby is that concerning nuclear energy, which has many ill-informed opponents; while food additives are showing the potential to become a third.

The potential costs involved in many aspects of pollution can be enormous, both in terms of equipment to overcome pollution and with regard to damages which may be awarded against the polluting organisation. For these reasons, pollution is likely to feature more prominently on the list of concerns for managers in relevant companies, as a highly political issue sometimes involving governments.

## ENERGY

Energy factors tie in closely with pollution factors as hydrocarbons and nuclear energy feature significantly in both. The pressure to reduce the production of carbon dioxide by the burning of oil, coal and gas will lead to some reduction in use, with reduction of other pollution from hydrocarbons involving some cost increase. The logical progression to nuclear fuels will be opposed by 'green' groups and may not increase rapidly. A great deal more effort will go into new industries concerned with the generation of other forms of energy – solar energy, hydro-electric, heat from the earth's core, wind power, tidal power – most of which will have limited impact on human resource management.

Energy conservation will become more important, particularly if energy costs rise. This will place new demands on management time and is already resulting in a new specialisation in businesses which are heavy energy users.

### THE MARKET PLACE: COMPETITORS

The customer is king! Meeting his needs is fundamental. Only attention to product specification and design, quality, service (including delivery) and price will enable that competitive edge to be attained.

## Assessing competitors

The behaviour of competitors is one of the most important aspects of the operating environment, and one which can be expected to change to your disadvantage. Intelligence on the strengths and limitations of competitors, the threats each presents, and the opportunities which may occur are all of great importance, together with all information on their operating strategies and tactics, present and future. If a competitor succeeds in launching a significant initiative or innovation without warning, his advantage can be substantial.

> The essence of marketing strategy lies in creating tomorrow's competitive advantages faster than competitors mimic the ones you possess today. But if you have competitive advantage, you must be wary of competitive surprise, arising from unseen strategic intent, unconventional entry tactics, or simply underestimating resource factors. Then advantage can be lost quickly if you do not respond effectively. (Hamel and Prahaled)

Some large international companies have appointed backroom analysts to be their 'Mr IBM', or whatever the names of their major competitors may be. The role of these individuals is to absorb every bit of detail they can on the competitor organisation from all possible sources, to get to think like them, and then to brief senior management on any development or possible action which may be significant. Such intelligence work is expensive, but a good researcher with a range of contacts can put together an astonishing amount of detail; can identify anomolies in a pattern which hint at impending actions; or anticipate opportunities to gain advantage. This competitor focus should be sought at every level of the organisation, to emphasise the 'enemy challenge' and motivate employees to respond.

The single most critical factor here is the internationalising or globalising of markets so that the major players are competing across the world and have developed strategies covering each territory. Organisations which operate more locally must always be aware of the financial strength of global-scale competitors, and may need to accept that they can compete successfully only in niche markets. As there are probably too many competitors in many markets there can be no prospect of any let up in competitive pressure and the need for innovative and effective new strategies.

Initially, these developments affected the manpower intensive manufacturing companies most severely, but the progression has extended universally. For example, in financial services deregulation not only opened more international doors, but encouraged banks, building societies and insurance companies to look at each others' fields as areas for expansion, triggering many new developments, mergers and associations. The additional factor of widening use of information technology in financial services is progressively altering their business strategies, their cultures, and their human resource requirements, and doubling the impact of the revolution.

All this change provides challenge and stimulation for flexible, change orientated managers, but also great stresses and career casualties.

## The single European market

The emergence of Europe as a single market of some 320 million people is leading to substantial rationalisation, both within international groups and through mergers and alliances between smaller companies. Reappraisal of commercial objectives and favoured markets will trigger other changes as companies endeavour to position themselves to use their strengths to best exploit opportunities. The implications for human resource management will be severe in many cases as differing corporate cultures and organisations are brought together. Inevitably, some mergers will break down over cultural incompatibility, and others will lead to substantial changes of people which will adversely affect company performance.

## Identifying competitors

If the potential effect of a competitor gaining market share at your expense can be fairly disastrous, there is high incentive to obtain and feed back to a central 'processing' point all data that can be obtained. The first stage is to ask 'who are the competitors?'. A full list is desirable, but if the market is very fragmented there may be little advantage in trying to list all of the small fry. Yet 20 years ago some Japanese companies which have become international players would have been ignored as 'small fry'. So include 'small fry' which show dynamism and innovative strategies!

A competitor list is needed for every territory where you compete or are thinking of entering on a world scale. A detailed assessment is required of all the major 'players'. That starts with all the factual data obtainable: organisation structure, names of management, pay standards, numbers of people and where they are located; details of products, prices, delivery times, quality, customer reaction; information on technology and how it is being developed, product developments, response time from a new concept; something of their management culture; and any specifics on the strengths or weaknesses of the company (e.g. a rich parent company, or an independent rather short of funds, etc.). If they show any signs of maverick activity, such as unconventional but effective tactics, and tend to come up with surprises, treat them as dangerous.

What is your overall view of them? Where do you have an edge – or where do they beat you? Ranking all competitors against your own performance covers this in an enlightening way. Probe for signs of change – in anything. Changes of organisation or personnel may be significant, for example. Determine what you judge might trigger changes in behaviour by a competitor. How do you anticipate that they will develop, and what are the probabilities on some alternatives? Particularly, is there anything that might suggest impending changes which might hurt you?

## New competitors and the changing market place

Apart from the identified competitors, what is the scope for new 'players'? If some interntional groups do not operate in all overseas territories, there must be a risk that they will widen their field of operations. Also, if technology is changing, the cost to new competitors of entering a market may be reducing; or technologies may be converging, encouraging offensive/defensive strategies. It is worth examining how well positions can be defended in the market places where you operate, although the best defence is attack to gain further advantage.

The SWOT analysis of competitors mentioned earlier in the previous chapter (of strengths, weaknesses, opportunities and threats) may link competitor strengths to threats, and weaknesses to opportunities. However, a two to five year projection of own and competitor strengths and weaknesses may show a rapidly changing picture, with the possibility of a change in balance. The assumptions and projections will need to be coldly objective and comprehensive or they have the potential to be dangerously misleading if wrong. I recall a company which was complaisant about its market share, believing that it was well protected by patents, yet within two years it was scrambling desperately to retain half its previous volumes, not having foreseen how it could be attacked.

Perhaps the most serious threat comes from 'comfortable' thinking. In this last case, there were ways in which the patent protection could be overcome using a parallel technology which gave a lower quality product, but which was nevertheless more than adequate for more than 90 per cent of the customers.

Similar fresh thinking helped Canon to identify that secretaries and their bosses wanted decentralised reprographic services to replace central duplicating departments, and that the target customers generally had more 'clout' than the duplicating department managers who were the prime customers of Xerox. And Canon approached their identified market through agents who were already selling to their target customers rather than by building a fresh sales force.

Strategic marketing requires the identification or creation of such market opportunities, and the analysis of markets and competitors must be unlimited.

## Human resource implications

The human resource implications of the marketing strategies which follow possible competitor scenarios will vary widely. Recognition of a need for more market intelligence and higher level marketing skills to develop necessary strategies is more or less universal in the present environment and likely to be a feature of the 1990s. Other human resource implications are interlocked with technology, where changing product ranges may alter skill requirements, or result in radical change in the market place and market shares. Loss of market share, of course, may have repercussions well beyond the marketing function.

Competitive pressures on market shares can be assessed up to a point. As noted above, planning tends to be influenced primarily by the resources competitors are known to have, and by their recent behaviour, but judgements may not be realistic about the developing capability of competitiors or their ability to 'change the rules' – the ways the market is analysed and attacked. Unforeseen competitor initiatives can change the game overnight.

If technology is changing and opening the way for new players and changed margins, or if there is a sense of oversupply and moves to 'reduce the field', strategies will have to be thought through very carefully. However, new opportunities are continually being identified and exploited, even in very competitive sectors. The growth of Tie Rack and Sock Shop in retail niches are good examples.

Competitor action which raises pressure on productivity and profitability and cost levels can change affordable staffing levels and lead to the trimming out of discretionary activity. It may also affect the shape of many managerial posts as the changing skills required gradually alter the skills backgrounds of managers, and may even alter the required style of managing. Profitability may affect the demand for some specialist activities; for example, recognition of an increase in competitor activity and a need for improved competitor intelligence can lead to an increased requirement for, or higher standards of, marketing management.

The human resource requirements of moving into a new market or territory will include the nucleus of a management team, prepared for or adaptable to the territory's language and cultural factors, backed by local recruitment of the supporting resources.

The *service industry* is far more local and less affected by global considerations, although this may change. One of the largest service industries is that covering health care, where there is already a strong trend away from in-patient hospital care in the most advanced nations, simply because it has become too expensive.

Hospital organisation has got into deep trouble, frequently overburdened by non-value-adding administrations and overmanned services, and under resourced on medical staff. It may take until beyond the 1990s to sort out the future in Britain, but gradually we should expect to progress to a smaller number of centres of excellence – high technology centres (related to our ability to afford these services) and a much more decentralised general medical service which maximises preventative medicine and minimises in-patient care.

## DEMOGRAPHICS

### Impact on human resource management

There are three aspects of demographic change which are going to have an impact on human resource management over the next decade.

First, declining birthrates in much of the developed world during the late 1960s and 1970s are followed by reductions in numbers completing school, from a mid-1980s high, through a reduction of one-third by the mid-1990s. Regional reductions vary between 10 per cent and over 40 per cent. Reductions are much greater in the lower social groups than in professional groups.

Decline in graduate output in the UK is expected to be less severe, probably less than 10 per cent, partly because undergraduates come more from parents in the professional groups (where the reduction in birthrates has been lower), and partly because more older candidates, particularly women returning to work, will fill some places. Output of technical graduates, for whom demand will continue to increase, is expected to decline slightly within this pattern.

Secondly, longer life spans will offset birthrate reductions to provide a fairly static total population over the period to 2025, but the average age will rise.

Thirdly, the tendency towards earlier retirement, plus the reductions in numbers of school leavers available for work, is expected to be offset by further increases in the numbers of married women at work and the substantial use of pensioners and others on a part-time basis, so that the overall work force will grow slowly but steadily. The numbers of jobs in professional/technical areas will grow significantly, while 'office automation' will reduce the numbers of clerical jobs.

Against these aspects, a number of subsidiary points are relevant. The UK pattern is being followed in France, Germany, and the USA.

The birthrate decline is most severe in Germany where projections suggest a progressive decline in population, reaching 20 per cent by the year 2025. Birthrate reductions have been marginal in Catholic southern Europe and Ireland, and the rate is apparently unchanged in many ethnic minority groups.

For all the slowing down of birthrates in developed countries, world population is increasing by one billion every 14 years at present, with implications for the world economy.

## Implications for the supply of human resources

The most critical area of concern appears to be the adequacy of the supply of graduates. The UK supply, particularly of technical graduates, is likely to be insufficient to meet local demand, yet the probability of additional demand from European employers is real and will worsen the situation. This may be offset partly if UK employers increase their recruitment from the rest of Europe, but there are severe problems in terms of relative pay levels so that the net flow may be towards mainland Europe. The impact of these pressures may reduce graduate intake in some companies and, more significantly, change the utilisation of some graduates. Also, graduate entry schemes will need to be modified to enable more mature graduates to be recruited.

As many organisations see graduate entrants as their primary source of future management and senior specialists, projections of future organisations which assume reductions in management requirements will find increased favour. These are projected to reflect the impact of information technology on the future form of management, but other researchers are forecasting *increases* of up to 20 per cent in the number of managers over the next decade! This picture is developed by including the increasing numbers of senior functional and other specialists, comparable in 'rank' to the manager of today, most of whom will be drawn from the higher intellect sector of the population. I anticipate that the rising specialist population will be balanced by the declining requirement for 'managers'.

Shortages of school leavers will vary substantially by region, depending on work availability and the local supply of both school leavers and married women and pensioners. The employability of youngsters from poorly managed schools, where lack of discipline has been accepted and teaching has been ineffective, may present local problems. Further automation of lower skilled work, particularly in the office, may reduce demand; and a continuing movement of ethnic minority groups plus people from southern Europe into service occupations may offset opportunities locally. However, where supply shortages do occur, the pressure on youngsters with university potential to move immediately into employment may cause some losses from the potential graduate output. One particular use of intelligent youngsters may be as narrow specialist technicians, underpinning shortages of graduates following intensive training.

In summary, employers will need to evaluate their *local* supply position, and determine the strategies they will need to ensure adequate manning if competition for some categories of employee is expected to become intense. Inevitably, the most critical categories will be management and specialists, and retention of key people will be vital.

## SOCIAL VALUES

### The changing ethos

Society commitment to the 'work ethic' appears to be declining, with much higher acceptance of non-employment. Other values are changing, with 'freedom' of choice strongly emphasised by some. The higher crime rate, with violence and use of drugs, plus the decline in marriage, a high divorce rate and a rising proportion of 'illegitimate' births, all point to a breakdown of previously accepted standards of social behaviour. Many younger people (including many potential managers) have much greater concern for their 'quality of life', and their preferences and ambitions need to be taken more positively into account. The development of 'whole people' needs to be supported.

The following excellent quotation (unfortunately unattributable) summarises the situation: "Todays workers and customers seem increasingly to expect the company and its leaders to stand for something; they expect a compassionate, fair, civic-minded, understanding and humane corporation. They expect to see these values reflected in the way the company conducts itself."

In employment terms, enormous numbers of the jobs which were done by the lower ability or less educated proportion of the population have disappeared – and will continue to do so. The availability of lower valued 'service' work could increase significantly, but this is not seen as 'socially acceptable' by many. Jobs demanding higher levels of skill and intellect do not appear to be on the decline. If this picture is correct, there may be less opportunity (that is, acceptable opportunity) for the less able on a permanent basis, giving rise to a major social problem by the end of the century.

Given that many youngsters in this category have little education and are disinclined to accept earlier norms of self discipline and social conduct, there is the probability of significant numbers of 'lifetime unemployables'. The emerging, more open style of managing will not be able to cope with individuals who are inherently incapable of the self discipline which goes with greater freedom in the workplace.

## Meeting the changing needs

Education will need to adjust, and many in the teaching profession will have to come to terms with working more closely with parents; with the children themselves to acknowledge their perceived needs; and with community representatives who 'own' the employment opportunities. As education must also come to terms with the potential offered by information technology, and with the increasing acceptance that education is a life-long activity, the scale of the education industry's readjustment is immense.

As the twenty-first century begins, life-styles will have evolved to substantially increased leisure time for most people. It is not easy to see how that time and energy will be used, but education offers substantial scope for many, as evidenced by the use of the Open University by many older or 'leisured' folk; but the heavy demand for video entertainment in areas of high unemployment offers a different scenario where the culture discounts learning.

### LEGISLATION

Legislative change is something we all live with. Much of it is initiated by national governments or by local government, but there is an increasing output from authorities with responsibilities for activities such as health and safety, and also from the European parliament and even the United Nations.

Management's concern must be to ensure that it heeds and

conforms to this legislation. It must allocate time to watch for changes and may lobby for or against proposals for change. Its concern will be particularly with any legislation which is particularly restrictive or likely to involve unreasonable increases in administration or costs which may influence business viability. This is part of the increased political sensitivity and involvement required of managers through the 1990s.

The starting point is always the pattern of controls and regulations which currently exists, which constitute part of the business environment. The planning process needs to identify the most likely changes and the probable form and rate of change. Subsequently an assessment is needed of the probable impact of changes on human resource issues.

Within the lifetime of an established parliament, the accuracy of the projections should be reasonably high, but where an election is pending with some doubt about the likely outcome, a range of possible scenarios may be more appropriate. In less democratic situations, forecasting the likelihood of a coup, and by which faction, may provide some of the scenarios.

The impact of changes in taxation and the movement of government resource allocation to new priorities may provide the largest exposure, both in financial terms and in impact on human resource management. Either may influence overall manning levels. For example, tax changes, or a reduction in development area concessions, may alter the cost projections of major investment projects and, therefore, competitiveness and the scale or location of business. Current social policies are likely to have had an influence on tax levels: for example, increases in expenditure on social services will need to be paid for, and higher income tax will generate demand for higher remuneration or benefits.

Legislation on employee representation in management, as favoured by a majority of the European parliament, can generate requirements which many continental organisations are finding restrictive; which reduce competitiveness and the speed of reaction sometimes required to retain a competitive edge. (Of course, the management culture in some companies can have a similar effect!) High standards of communication and employee participation exist in highly efficient companies, so the concern is with the form these may be required to take within the management decision-making process.

Legislation on health and safety at the workplace is gaining in complexity and requires specialist help and interpretation to ensure adequate coverage of all requirements, including emergencies, relevant staff training, and the auditing of safety procedures, all of which add to costs and to demands on managerial time.

Grant support for new activity in depressed areas and city centres provides a cost influence on decisions to locate a new plant or administrative centre; perhaps offset by non-availability of suitable skills, or militant employee representation.

At an international level, legislation may favour locally manufactured products and encourage foreign companies to establish local manufacture to overcome trade business or import tariffs, although all research, development and design may be retained at the foreign base. This process may be encouraged by availability of grants for certain areas, and by the availability of raw materials and skilled labour. Variations between national labour costs and attitudes to work are further contributing factors.

## ECONOMIC TRENDS

Variations between national labour costs, availability of skills and attitudes to work can be key contributors to decisions on where to locate an overseas subsidiary – or where an American or Japanese organisation may choose to locate manufacturing in Europe.

Changing levels of inflation, interest rates, pay rates between geographic areas or between countries will tend to influence the location of business activities, particularly those with high people costs such as manufacture. Where low labour costs go with adequate skills and a positive attitude to work and quality, it is hard to justify operating in a higher cost area – particularly if inflationary factors are strong. Part of the price of being able to trade in a country may be the setting up of an organisation to provide some local employment.

Development of the open frontiers European market will enable groups which previously have needed small national manufacturing units to consider evolution towards larger, more economic units, plus an efficient distribution system. Current and projected labour costs and achievable standards of efficiency will be major factors in selecting the best centres.

Another worrying dimension visible in the developed world is the rapidly escalating costs of health care or medical insurance, giving rise to the question, 'Can we afford to be located here?'. Two contributing factors are the increasing costs on a national scale of providing services to an aging population and dealing with the increase in AIDS patients. While these are not directly costs to an employer in respect of his own employees, they will have an impact on medical insurance costs, while the national problem may come through in the form of increased taxes.

## SUMMARY

This chapter has covered many (but not all) aspects of change in the environment in which we operate. Change can be large scale and fast moving, as well as more evolutionary. It is an essential part of the job of every manager to envision the future; to anticipate change; to get ahead of the crowd and into a lead position. His views are critical to all management development actions, for these may be the *most* critical of all, in preparing and positioning managers to optimise future opportunities.

# II.4

## *Human resource strategies in the achievable business plan*

### INTRODUCTION

We need to draw out the key actions required on human resource issues so that appropriately designed human resource strategies are developed and implemented to enable business objectives to be achieved.

The business planning process assembles a considerable volume of information, primarily on the direct influences of corporate ambitions, the present situation, the changing environment and corporate culture; and also on the many spin off analyses triggered by what/if type questions. Planning, as we have seen, goes through a stage of evaluating probabilities and options, the potential scale of which may be enormous, and in each of which resource allocation may be crucial.

Corporate ambitions are likely to indicate the broad path the company would like to follow, but against the ideal, what are the internal and external influences and pressures which will either enable the track to be followed, or will obstruct and limit progress? Availability of key people and organisation capability or cultural factors may register heavily; or the growing strength of competitors may cast doubt on what is achievable. Or there may be a straightforward shortage of appropriate skills, which could be overcome by positive action.

Alternatively, there may be opportunities outside the central area of corporate preference which provide new avenues for profitable development. If the enterprise has the management skills and the human resources to exploit such a situation, then the planning system should ascertain whether corporate ambitions are flexible enough to take in the opportunity.

PLANNING THE UTILISATION OF RESOURCES

Planning includes a large element of planning the utilisation of resources, particularly any critical and limited resources required to achieve specific business objectives and to enhance overall capability. Management resources tend to be crucial and frequently represent the single critical factor which limits what the enterprise can or is unable to do. Financial resources are essential, but substantial additional finance is generally available to a well run business and is not generally the limiting factor. Equipment, space, etc., can be covered under the general heading of finance – the ability to pay for them – although there are time considerations on availability of specialised space, equipment and materials to be taken into account. The other resource which does impose limitations on achievements is time, which must be managed but cannot be supplemented!

## Availability of management

In assessing the optimum mix of options in assembling a plan, availability of resources will be the key determinant, with availability of management the most critical factor. Planning the use of managers or specialists is particularly difficult where the timing of possible scenarios is uncertain and the same set of people may be required for several different purposes at the same time. For key human resources (say on product development teams or management teams) availability must be matched to demand, and the management planning task is to flex the scenarios to smooth the workload; to reschedule the peaks and troughs and handle sudden surges. The ultimate response to events will depend on the effectiveness with which resources are managed.

Matching demands to availability for the favoured options is one key element of planning activity. The ability to acquire planned additional rescources is an important factor. Additional finance may be readily available, but additional management may take months or years to recruit or develop, and a first class management group may take several years to assemble and settle into an effective team, imposing very real limitations on business development.

### Human resource limitations

At lower levels, the human resource limitations may arise from a lack of skilled manpower for a wide variety of possible skills, which may be overcome by recruitment or by training. Some programmes have required deskilling of work and restructuring of jobs to concentrate the available short-supply skills and get work done in new ways. Automation is another way out of short supply, but is capital intensive, requires an adequate volume of activity to be viable, and is rarely as quick to implement as is needed. The use of information technology enables some administrative work to be done at a point remote from the area where skills are short.

The need to tie down key human resources for a long period may reduce the favour with which some projects are seen. Return on investment on key corporate assets (management and specialist resources) has got to be as sound as in any other financial evaluation. It is appropriate to compare options, but accept that the quantitive financial answer may not be the final consideration. Any project or opportunity with potentially high visibility will come into a special category. A project which fits the direction the company wishes to pursue may be selected as an important element in the overall plan, even if it involves a higher than normally acceptable risk and will be a heavy user of resources. Such options place a heavy strain on any plan. Record the logic for selection and the assessed risk, to ensure that it is possible to review progress and keep options open if the probability of success drops too far.

## ACHIEVABLE BUSINESS OBJECTIVES

The ultimate business plan and set of objectives consists of the assembly of selected options covering the immediate years, progressing towards the envisioned future. These objectives should use the available and acquirable resources fully, and result in financial and commercial results which are acceptable. Use of critical path analyses may be relevant where key resources are to be used on several programmes with some uncertainty of timing, so that use and progress can be optimised and potential damage from programme delays minimised. This emphasises the need for detail in a plan. The interrelationships between the parts of a plan need to be clear in each resource and functional area with time scales for progress; 'mile stones' are usually defined for monitoring purposes, and contingency plans determined.

*A plan is not complete unless the means of implementation are clear.* There will be a range of critical events where achievement is essential to the success of the overall plan. How each of these is to be covered needs to be known. These strategies should be supported by a series of tactics which, if properly implemented, should ensure business success.

## Human resource strategies

Many action plans will tend to be multi-functional, but it is the human resource elements which are of concern here.

> A new marketing venture will need to be resourced. The manpower requirements are defined, but cannot be met wholly from inside, so some recruitment is required. The skills needed to analyse the market more closely and establish tactics must be supplemented by recruitment, and some specialised training will also be necessary, designed and run in-house. Action programmes to cover these needs may assume the use of external recruiting and training support, plus marketing consultants until new staff are appointed. For success, it must be assumed that staff retention will be high, as the jobs should be interesting and challenging, but remuneration will need to be appropriate and management style positive. Actions cannot be taken on this area in isolation, and complete human resource policies may require revision.

At a more general level, the range of requirements across an enterprise may involve a wide range of actions. One might require a significant increase in graduate recruitment, starting from a base of limited university contacts, rising national demand for the relevant graduates, and a decline in numbers of new graduates qualifying. In such a situation a clear and determined programme will be essential to achieve the desired result, and a contingency plan will be advisable to cover partial non-achievement.

In a company with its top management close to retirement and facing rapid environmental change, the strategy to bring through the next generation of managers, properly prepared to deal with the changes, may need to be brought forward if there is any slowing of pace at the top or concern at the scale of impending change.

As each business grows and becomes more complex, it is an important responsibility for every manager to plan his human resource requirements systematically and carefully. The repercussions of missing the significance of some key element of environmental change have been noted. Failing to plan for and acquire adequate talent can constrain achievement of objectives and future growth; and over enthusiasm for maintaining tight controls over human resource levels and costs can be similarly damaging. A proper balance must be maintained.

The line manager does not have the time to work from first principles every time he puts together a plan, so there follows a *checklist of human resource strategic issues* – changes in the business which may have human resource implications:

- Expansion of existing business activities.
- Addition of new capacity (new plants, equipment, facilities, etc.).
- New ventures, acquisitions or divestitures.
- New products or services.
- New technologies or applications.
- New systems or changed information technology.
- Changes in operating methods or productivity improvements.
- Impact of projected inflation rates.
- New, pending or strengthened national or local government legislation or regulations.
- Adequacy of organisation structure.
- Adequacy of management.

These human resource implications may affect the achievability of the business plan through such factors as:

- shortage of any skill category in labour market
- areas of technical incompetency
- competitive recruiting activities
- imbalances in age distribution in any category
- inadequate or excessive turnover
- individual or group performance problems
- career advance of able people blocked
- employee mix does not match needs
- equal employment opportunities being achieved
- adequate supply of potential general managers
- adequate supply of appropriate managerial skills

- sufficient breadth and depth of experience among existing managers.

Examples 1 and 2 show forms used by large organisations to pin down the *actions to be taken* against key human resource objectives, while Example 3 provides an illustration of one action plan using a similar layout. These are likely to fall into 'areas for action' such as:

- modifying culture to improve response to objectives
- development and training initiatives
- improving communications
- recruiting programmes
- modifying recruiting/selection
- organisation/position changes and implementation
- improving appraisals and counselling
- remuneration policy changes
- job evaluation
- new specialisations to be resourced
- career counselling
- retraining of people with obsolete skills
- terminations
- accelerating career advancement (general or on a selected basis)
- reassignments/lateral moves
- accelerating management development
- establishing 'mentoring'
- cross function/division moves
- changing staffing levels
- implementing new systems or procedures
- modifying job requirements
- reassignment of work in restructuring.

Where action in any of these areas is identified as being essential to the successful business development, the objectives and the strategy for achieving the objectives need to be clearly stated and implementation monitored. In particular, *it is likely that all aspects of management development will form part of and be driven by essential strategies arising from business objectives.*

| List your key human resource *objectives* for the planning period. | List the specific *actions* to be undertaken to achieve the objectives. Assign responsibility and state time. |
| --- | --- |
| | |

**Example 1** Key human resource action plan format

## Management development objectives

Within most businesses, there will be a top down philosophy on management development which may read something like, 'Ensure the provision of effective management level staffing, in purpose designed organisations, to provide the management and leadership which will enable the enterprise to meet its business objectives'. This will have originated in the corporate objectives and/or the culture. In the business plan itself it is the management development specifics which require actions which give management development programmes their legitimacy. There is likely to be a range of requirements, perhaps on the lines of some of the following paragraphs, the first of which is written as within a plan; the others noting a range of situations with a need for strong human resource action.

> "Successors will be required to fill the listed management positions over the next 2–5 years; and for the estimated additional number of positions each year to cover unplanned promotions and transfers, terminations, and unplanned additional posts. Short-lists of adequate quality will be required in advance, so that any decisions to look outside can be taken sufficiently in advance to ensure vacancies are filled when required. A detailed action plan will be required, but the development actions to prepare internal candidates for all these opportunities should be shown to be deeply rooted, flexible and effective. Adequate early warning must be provided for all requirements which must be met by external resourcing."

> Strengthening the marketing function may be essential to some business strategies. Timing will influence how far this can concentrate on the development of existing personnel but the programme is likely to include a requirement to recruit externally to a number of identified management and specialist positions within a time scale, as well as to develop existing people. This might involve using consultants to help create and implement specialised training programmes to take the levels of knowledge of specified people up to new defined standards and even to provide operational support as these new skills begin to be exercised. Precise objectives will determine the needs.

> Where substantial MIS developments are planned, there may be

<table>
<tr><td colspan="4">Human resource action plan (prepared at ............................)</td></tr>
<tr><td colspan="4">Issue:</td></tr>
<tr><td colspan="4">Objective:</td></tr>
<tr><td colspan="2">Action plan:</td><td>Complete by (date)</td><td>Responsible manager</td></tr>
<tr><td>Position reports:</td><td colspan="3">Prepared by:</td></tr>
<tr><td colspan="4">1<br>date:</td></tr>
<tr><td colspan="4">2<br>date:</td></tr>
<tr><td colspan="4">3<br>date:</td></tr>
</table>

**Example 2** Key human resource action plan format

requirements for a range of specialist and management recruitment, and for a range of specialised training, ranging from 'management briefings' through to 'how to operate a desk top terminal' (and utilise the available data and analysis facilities), to highly technical systems and language training.

The anticipated environment change may need to be defined more tightly: a project team may be assembled to carry out a comprehensive analysis and make recommendations for action. Such a project could require secondment of some key people at short notice and provide opportunities for temporary assignments for future successors. This type of project may be specific to one aspect of business environment and, for example, require a number of marketing people to become expert on individual competitors and highlight their likely strategies and actions which may need to be countered.

Proper communication of new technology applications will require articulate non-technical briefings for other managers to ensure widespread appreciation of potential change – threats and opportunities. Locating and training individuals to do this effectively is always difficult. Or there may be developments in legislation which can have a critical effect on the business where a plain speaking legal person is required to communicate the requirements and implications.

'Green' issues have become a major issue which the line manager of every facility potentially able to pollute must understand and heed. The costs of avoiding chemical pollution can be extremely high, though not as high as dealing with a catastrophe, so that the level of expertise required by managers to safeguard the natural environment at minimum cost may represent a critical new skill and an important additional training need.

Graduate recruitment is a permanent task, but the demographic effect on the availability of relevant graduates and the form of competition are constantly changing. As most companies require fairly steady but increasing intakes to cover current or future manning requirements, strategies for attracting and retaining sufficient individuals of appropriate calibre and with the right skills requires a continual update of those strategies and action programmes. The flows of people up through the organisation

*Objective:* To prepare for the next phase of Management Information System development.

*Task:* To explore and develop further the means of advancing the use of office automation by managers including:

- increasing the availability of data required by managers
- analysing individual performance to identify scope for increasing the efficiency of use of office automation by all employees
- developing experimental organisation concepts which depend on more substantial use of MIS and closely monitor individual response and performance

The ultimate task is to improve utilisation of both management and other human resources, and expensive MIS equipment.

*Action plans:*

1 Assemble state of the art information on decentralised use of information management equipment and systems, and explore how these might be utilised.

2 Update current management information system strategies to improve the accessiblity of digested data for managers, to meet all their information requirements. Ensure that this meets their requirements for analysed/summarised information and analysis of work flow.

3 As necessary, develop the skills of our MIS specialists.

4 Determine the costs and actions required to implement the necessary changes, identifying areas for optimum benefit.

5 Develop alternative organisation concepts which are made practical by the MIS changes; and evaluate the actions required to introduce them.

6 Conduct divisional analyses of attitudes to the introduction of systems and potential organisation changes to identify preferred introduction areas for experimental approaches. Initiate consultation in selected areas to identify training requirements and any potential resistance.

7 Develop detailed implementation plans for selected applications, develop timetable, gain approval, and implement.

One year costs of studies as budgeted: costs of proposals to be reviewed as budget exceptions.

**Example 3** Human resource action plan

and the ability to resource future management requirements, may be directly affected by inadequate supply at the bottom end.

The ways in which the company responds to performance, individual achievements and failures, is most visible to managers in the form of remuneration – changes in salary and award of bonus. If business priorities are changing, there may be a need to overhaul the remuneration system to direct reward to achievements related to business imperatives and to encourage management focus on current key issues. Company response is also visible through promotion policy as other managers note who is promoted, and the achievements and behaviour which appear to be rewarded.

Management training is not going to influence business effectiveness unless it is focussed on the priority business strategies and is seen to be contributing directly to business results. The projects to be used in training can be 'live', from the pressing issues now.

The business justification for management development is far more than that it safeguards the organisation by ensuring that the management resource requirements are available with the appropriate skills in the numbers and quality required, necessary to enable business objective to be achieved. The management development process is an integral part of the management process, and its many elements contribute separately and together to increasing organisation capability and gaining competitive advantage. Human resource strategies should be developed with that purpose in mind.

## SUMMARY

Development of a corporate vision, and then a comprehensive business plan, is an essential part of knowing where you want to go and how you are going to get there, embracing every aspect of business performance.

Almost all actions which contribute to achieving planned business development have a human resource element, which in many instances is the critical factor influencing success or failure. The development and statement of the combined human resource objectives and strategies required *within the plan* should lock the broad management development requirements and activities firmly into the business operation, so that achievement of management development objectives is integral with achievement of the overall objectives of the business. Then, and only then, management development has purpose and live commitment.

# PART III

# The Managers you Need

# *Introduction*

From your vision of the business future, and the objectives, plans and strategies for the shorter term, you can effect a translation into the required future organisation, culture, competencies, leadership, and teams, and the numbers and categories of managers you will require. Later, you will need to match these evolving needs against your inventory of developing people.

This Part of the book is about that translation; starting from the 'business development plan' (in whatever form it takes) plus the assembled judgements of your present capabilities, the ways the environment will change, the strategies you have adopted and the objectives set. In the process of developing these plans and scenarios, the implications and means of achievement will have been considered in various degrees of detail. The further task is to clarify the detailed management resource requirements so that you can ensure the proper preparation and development of individuals, on whose actions will depend the success or failure of the totality. It is unlikely that the complete requirements will be defined accurately, but sufficient detail should be possible, plus an understanding of available flexibility to cope with contingencies, for the results to be matched against the inventory of managers.

# III.I

## *Organisation planning and development*

### ORGANISATION PLANNING

When Peter Drucker writes that "The typical large business 20 years hence will have fewer than half the levels of management of its counterpart today, and no more than a third of the managers", you can be sure that the organisation revolution you see beginning around you has much further to go.

Organisation provides a means of getting work done in a co-ordinated way by a group of individuals. It defines the way in which work necessary to achieve business objectives is divided into 'packages' of similar activities and ultimately into 'job sized' units grouped under a manager. It enables a series of work groups engaged on separate parts of the whole task to work independently towards a common objective.

*The organisation plan can be considered as a translation of the business plan into managerial requirements.* Business planning sets out the future objectives of the entire enterprise against anticipated scenarios of environmental and cultural change, and incorporates statements of the major strategies, including those required for human resource issues. Within the grand design, there must be a clear vision of how the plan is to be implemented; how resources are to be utilised and managed – the organisation required. For example, each strategy will need to be converted into 'what needs to be done in order for the strategy to be implemented', how it is to be made to happen, and how it can be managed. The total volume of activities necessary to achieve the plan will need to be determined and then allocated to logical groupings which can be managed within an overall structure.

ORGANISATION DEVELOPMENT

## What is organisation development?

This chapter might have been called 'Organisation development' because that is what it is all about. However, the term organisation development tends to get shortened to OD, which has specific meanings for individuals which are curiously varied, so I will address OD specifically.

Thomas H. Patten wrote that "OD has never been known to be easily pinpointed and summarily defined". It is notable that OD specialists appear to have widely differing views of what OD is all about, and that some writers shy away from attempting definitions.

Bennis described OD in 1969 as a response to change, a complex educational strategy intended to change the beliefs, attitudes, volumes and structure of organisations so that they can better adapt to new techniques, markets and challenges, and the dizzying role of change itself; but some years later he suggested that this was abstract and perhaps not useful.

More recently, Margulies and Raia wrote that

> Organisation development is essentially a systems approach to the total set of functional and inter-personnel role relationships in organisations. An organisation can be viewed as a system of co-ordinated human activities, a complex whole consisting of a number of inter-acting and inter-related elements or subsystems. A change in any one part will have an impact on one or more of the other parts. Organisation development itself can be viewed as a system of these related elements – values, process and technology.

In later publications, Margulies and Raia stress the importance of core values which appear fundamental in all *management* development work and provide a "target which represents an 'ideal' state towards which the design, structure and processes of the organisation is directed". These core values include providing opportunity for people to function as human beings and to develop to full potential; seeking to increase organisation effectiveness to achieve goals; environment for work to be exciting; opportunities to influence; and recognising that human beings have a complex set of needs. They conclude that OD core values have endured over several decades.

It does seem that organisation development and management

development are inseparable. Much OD activity focusses on behavioural rather than structural aspects of organisation, and looks for progress away from hierarchical structures to participative management styles and freer forms of organisation, in which the significance of level of authority gives way to level of knowledge as the key influence on decision-making.

A further reference (unfortunately unattributable) describes OD as "an intervention theory which contributes better solutions to organisation problems and to the development of effective cultural and structural conditions in organisations". The aim is to develop organisation change strategies, with OD practitioners concerned with their own intervention tactic and strategies.

Discussion at a recent seminar suggested that the best OD practitioners have long since broadened the term to encompass all aspects of managing an organisation. However, many OD practitioners have concentrated on facilitating the achievement of business goals, and cultural values have been put aside. For example, necessary organisational 'down sizing' has resulted in a company needing to dispense with large numbers of 'its most important assets', which may appear to be in conflict with claimed corporate values.

## The need for organisation development

Organisation development probably developed as a response to two trends. First, there is gradual obsolescence of 'traditional' organisation depending on the command-obedience management style (although obsolescent, this is by no means finally dead!). Secondly, there is the, perhaps related, change in cultural values, which is involving the individual far more in work design and management structures.

Organisation development is ultimately concerned with the planning of future organisation and the implementation of organisation change. Patten and Vaill suggest there are seven issues to be addressed:

- The organisation now.
- Why change?
- Who is initiating change?
- Is there resistance to change?

- How is change to be achieved?
- How is change to be assessed?
- What values apply?

For organisation to develop, there must be a clear vision of forward business goals which the organisation is designed to achieve. These overall business objectives will be supported by an array of short- and long-term supporting strategies, which can be 'translated' into theoretical organisation requirements designed to ensure that all necessary activity is managed and carried out, with due consideration of information systems, management style, leadership issues, motivation, and teams. This theoretical structure should be developed for a series of points in time, linked to business projections, to determine the evolution of organisation requirements.

The detail of future organisation, together with evolution from the present structure, may be established through the process suggested by Patten and Vaill. The seven questions they pose can be used to determine the structure best able to achieve those goals and how it can be introduced. Part of that introductory process may well challenge and change some part of the company's cultural values. Achievement will also need to heed existing personal power and be politically sensitive, and to exploit opportunities such as those which occur when a post is vacated to introduce elements of change.

Organisation development interventions are unlikely to be effective if they do not have the support of top management. For example, the degree of time-consuming analysis and discussion required is unlikely to be comprehensively done unless that support is available. I particularly like the quote attributed to Professor Reddin about OD change agents who believe that they can initiate change from the bottom up, that "the penalty for mutiny is death".

One of the most valuable involvements of some OD people may be in their contribution to the rapid development of teams. It does take a long time for an *ad hoc* assembly of managers to coalesce into a team, and few established teams exist for long periods without some changes of individuals. Yet new appointments may be selected wholly on the basis of competence to do a job, and their fit with other members of a management group may be considered as of secondary importance, subsequently reducing team effectiveness.

ORGANISATION STRUCTURES

## The changing pattern

There are historical or 'traditional' patterns of organisation, some of which can be traced back at least two thousand years, but organisation patterns are being influenced by changed attitudes to work and 'quality of life', and further influenced by the information technology revolution which is removing some of the activities which take up much of the 'traditional' middle manager's time.

It will still be necessary to get work done through people and to co-ordinate their efforts towards common objectives, but it will become less necessary to manage information as computers will do that automatically, providing end results which managers will use to determine further and non-standard actions. Subordinates will be able to see their work load status as clearly as their manager, and will be able to manage themselves; to determine priorities or seek guidance at their own discretion. Spans of subordinates will be much wider, with reductions in the numbers of managers and the number of levels. In parallel, there will be continuing progress away from the traditional command/obedience mode (I command/you obey) as structures become more flexible and participative.

## The form of change

The starting point for much organisational change will still commonly be from the traditional organisation structures which have developed great complexity in the biggest companies to form accepted norms which have only recently begun to be changed. The logic of these structures is based on the grouping of like activities, initially into main blocks and subsequently into 'job-sized' work units. This process keeps associated activities together under managers who provide co-ordination, control, and a communications link. In this way, the pieces are linked into a whole through a series of co-ordinator/controller levels with broader and broader spans of responsibility, until the chief executive is reached. It is designed to enable the efforts of many individuals to be directed and co-ordinated to achieve the corporately desired end result. The result is a structure capable of achieving the required overall aim, yet consisting of a multitude of defined jobs with identified tasks and responsibilities. It is a constant management task to achieve optimum organisational groupings. If related activities or responsibilities become separated organisationally, it is more difficult to promote harmonious operation.

The simplest form of organisation structure is one in which there is a manager of a small team, to whom all employees report. The next step occurs when the number of people is more than can be managed effectively by one individual, and the first intermediate management levels appear. Growth will require a further increase in the number of levels and clarification of groupings of related activities. Around six to eight prime groupings are likely to emerge – technical and design, production, marketing (including sales), finance, personnel, legal and secretarial – subject to inevitable variation and the possible inclusion of distribution, research, quality, and planning, etc, dependent on the overall size and complexity of operation.

As a company grows, further groups of 'thinkers' and 'planners' or specialist advisers may be created alongside the mainstream of line operational positions. These staff people support the 'directing group' of the company, collecting and feeding up ideas and plans on all functions, auditing and analysing the line operations, and encouraging improvements in their functional areas. This separation produces an organisation form known as 'staff and line', which occurs most frequently in large decentralised companies where complex ranges of activities are divided into separate business entities to simplify management. The company divides naturally into units covering distinct product groups or geographical areas, each run by a subsidiary team of top executives and having substantial autonomy. Such decentralisation is co-ordinated by a central board, with a high-level staff advisory group whose role is to develop broad principles and policies. Another variant is the financial holding company with a very small central board to co-ordinate only what is critical to the central team, which may allow great diversity of systems and management in group companies.

Decentralisation and delegation of authority go together, ideally with a matrix of strong line management balanced by competent staff professionals; where central staff are accepted as the chief executive's major means of evaluating performance in operating divisions.

## Informal organisation

In parallel with the formal structure based on the logical division of activities and work requirements runs a second structure, based on all the personal relationships which grow up when a substantial number of people are in regular contact working towards common goals. This networking, the informal organisation of the company, plays an important role in distributing ideas and information which help to integrate the whole structure, and in cutting red tape by means of informal discussion to 'clear the lines'. The place of informal relationships must be understood as part of corporate culture and its growth encouraged. Formal and informal structures are complementary.

### FUTURE ORGANISATION

## Responding to change

Organisation patterns and shapes are changing. Over the next ten years it will not only be necessary to adjust organisation to address changing business objectives and environments, but also to respond to changes in attitudes to work and accepted organisation concepts. Radical changes in environment demand radically different approaches to organisation and expectations from the managers within. There has been much research into future organisation and many of the concepts have already been adopted in young, high tech companies, so that we can consider realities which are providing advantages rather than speculate about what might be.

The key elements of change are:

- Substantial reductions in the number of middle management posts.
- Deletion of 'co-ordinating' managers, as information systems make these roles unnecessary and all managers become 'computer literate'.
- Much flatter organisations with much wider spans of control, conceived as teams rather than hierarchies.
- More emphasis on specialists and higher levels of specialist knowledge. Fewer generalists (although managing specialists will continue to need a generalist outlook).

*The emergence of knowledge-based organisations*

Peter Drucker, writing on organisations in the future, suggests that we can expect fewer levels of management and fewer managers in what will be knowledge-based organisations, composed largely of specialists who direct and discipline their own performance through organised feedback, such as in structures like hospitals or symphony orchestras. Corporate objectives will be clearer and more widely communicated. These knowledge workers resist the present day 'command and control' organisation model. An information-based organisation provides for self discipline as requirements and completed actions are visible through the systems.

The nature of tasks will change; for example, capital investment analysis will be transformed from opinion to diagnosis by rational weighting of alternative assumptions. Management jobs which only co-ordinate collection of data and convey requirements will become obsolete as information is processed more effectively.

There will be many more specialists in operating units, but fewer centrally, and the way work is done will be different, and largely self-directed (enabling large control spans).

Task focussed teams will be normal, assembling and disbursing as required to bring groups of specialists together to resolve issues. These can be seen already; for example, integrating research, development, manufacturing, and marketing to speed the pace of new product development. Other commentators also emphasise the importance of teams which will replace hierarchial structures, suggesting a cluster of teams around a central co-ordination (and non-hierarchial remuneration structures also).

I believe that this concept is already a reality which can be found in the structures and management styles of many medium-sized organisations which are young and have grown in areas of high technology. The management teams are predominantly young and home grown, unspoiled by exposure to older management concepts. Use of information technology is advanced and universally accessed. Typically, the organisation is flat, with a near total absence of hierarchy in the working relationships across levels. Jobs do not need 'frontiers'. Project teams continually form and disperse to hit any problem. And the management cannot comprehend why many other companies do not adopt a similar flexibility to act.

Drucker uses the modern hospital to illustrate the new organisation. The many different medical and paramedical teams work in self-contained specialist areas with their own knowledge, training and even language; each with a relevant head person who effectively reports to the top. Many *ad hoc* teams form to deal with single patients. There is little direct supervision of medical operations from the top (except supervision of administrative services), as the objectives of the organisation are understood universally.

Similarly, a large orchestra has a conductor (the CEO), and then a large number of specialists/instrumentalists. Effectively, the whole orchestra reports to one individual, but the degree of management control is negligible for they are all working to common objectives – a single score. 'Information responsibility' is taken individually by each musician working from that score. 'Information responsibility' to others will be understood and acted upon. 'Who depends on me for information? and on whom do I depend?'

*Career development*

Career development for specialists will change form rather than become more limited. They will be able to move up within their own specialism, but movement between specialisms will be difficult or impossible. They will have awareness of other specialisms from task force exposures, but few will become true generalists. Generalists are likely to evolve from task force leaders, although leadership will be informal as specialists work together in task forces on equal terms. Compensation potential will be as great for specialists as for generalists. Large consulting and law practices provide parallels already.

The conclusions reached by a research team at Ashridge Management College were along similar lines. The Ashridge team concluded that management development which concentrates on the 'doing' aspects of management, and the 'pumping in' of specific skills and knowledge, will be addressing only one part of future management challenges and needs. They suggest that the 'being' elements of a person – the inherent personal qualities and persepective of an individual – will be at least as important. These will *not* respond to training, but only to organisational environment and culture.

They take a ten-year horizon (to Drucker's 20), and therefore see less radical organisation change, but conclude that future organisations will form a 'different setting for the practice of management'.

The organisation itself will be flatter, faster moving, market driven, more cost conscious, fluid and complex. It will be decentralised, even fragmented, but the parts will be integrated by overall strategy and culture. (This is closely in line with the evolving Drucker model, except that it anticipates a lesser impact of information technology.) Horizontal relationships (across organisations) will become more important than vertical (directing) ones.

The Ashbridge team conclude that there will be "unprecedented emphasis on people and talent as the organisation's most precious resources; on the need to utilize human resources fully and on the need to draw out people's commitments."

The form of leadership will change from directing to a 'mobilising and energising role'. Increasing 'elitism' of specialists is identified, plus the problem of identifying which individual specialists should be given generalist skills. There is concern that individuals should not be developed as generalists until they have established very sound specialist knowledge and achievement.

Flexibility is evidently going to be important, and the personal qualities which go with this are listed. The ongoing ability to acquire new skills continuously (in a changing environment) will be more important than skills acquired in the past. Finally, the personal qualities to be sought in a 'balanced whole person' are contained in a list of 20 factors which can be summarised by the first two: bright and intellectually robust, and mentally agile.

Flexibility also comes through strongly from other writers, linked to the need to respond quickly to rapid change in the business environment, where a shift in short-term strategy may require organisation modification to achieve a completely dedicated focus. This need to flex with changing priorities and opportunities should be straightforward in the future organisation styles with continually reforming project teams.

*The importance of individuals and small teams*

Supporting this pattern is the recognition that business growth may depend more on the inventive capacity of individuals and small teams than on the actions of top managers. It is from the resourcefulness and originality of small dedicated teams that fresh tactics develop which may lead to building new competitive advantage. There are many examples of extraordinary achievements by such teams, where most larger organisations with heavy resources have been unable to adopt the mental adjustment necessary to gain a breakthrough.

Given the inability of the 'heavy' organisation to alter course rapidly, any business which requires fast response or innovative actions to seize initiative will need to be designed with the ability to assemble small high powered teams for dedicated tasks, and must be resourced accordingly.

## The organisation plan

In the short-term, say up to 12 months, it can generally be assumed that the organisation is in place or that changes will be in the pipeline, adequately defined and scheduled. If the business environment changes very rapidly, the existing structure will have to cope for a while. Organisation change should not be implemented rapidly and without careful preparation and briefings. A sudden change may take some months to settle into effective operation.

For the longer term, you may have a view of organisation ten or more years ahead, but most of the detailed planning will have a three- to five-year horizon. Within this time frame, most of the major developments likely to impact on the business and organisation *should already be visible* if the environment has been analysed carefully, although the precise timing of various developments may be far from certain. A forward organisation plan may take shape, while the timing of implementation may remain flexible. The degree of uncertainty naturally increases in longer term plans, their value being in the identification of likely future changes.

Much of the detailed organisation planning will focus on the one- to three-year period, covering evolution from the now to reasonably accurate business and environmental projections. For this period, it is likely to be practical to put together the fine detail of organisation development, down to unit (or even individual) objectives, job descriptions and person specifications, on which management development plans and provisional appointments decisions can be based. Longer term organisational outlines should provide guidance on the competencies and numbers of managers required within the progressively flatter organisational shapes.

## Theoretical requirements

The forward organisational plan is likely to start with a theoretical model based on the business plan and some agreed organisation parameters, which then gets exposed to a great deal of 'what if' type discussion around possible options and how things are to get done or be managed.

The theoretical model should ignore the present structure and systems, and set out ideal structures with logical future groupings of activities, functions and divisions of responsibilities, and optimum shapes for the co-ordination of effort, and achievement of objectives by appropriately skilled groups of people or individuals. It can be as detailed as is required, with fine detail being used for manpower projections (see examples 10 and 11 in Chapter III.6). The model should be scrutinised to ensure that it takes account of all critical influences including, amongst others, those discussed below.

*Information technology*

Information technology is having a considerable impact on how much managerial and administrative work is done. It will dramatically change the content of many managerial jobs and is the largest factor contributing to the development of flatter organisations: fewer managers – fewer levels – much wider spans of control – teams.

Evaluation of the pace of this change in the organisation is essential and may benefit from external consultants' contribution, as the scale of potential change induced by information technology seems rarely to be appreciated until it begins to bite.

The telecommunications revolution, which will enable an increasing number of people to work from home or at distributed centres, will have an influence on organisation, in that self-monitoring of progress and achievement will be built into systems, removing that role from line supervision.

*The changing work ethic*

The changing work ethic and increased interest in 'the quality of life' may be similar factors impacting on the content of managerial jobs. A popular view is that the length of the working week is going to decline for everyone except senior managers, who will remain workaholics. Many of the young graduates currently moving into industry and commerce are expressing opposition to this concept – but perhaps they will not be the ones who rise to the very top.

*Quality*

Quality, in a total business sense, has become a more significant issue in recent years, and features more strongly in organisation. Originally, the focus of quality was on the quality of manufactured output, but with the advent of quality circles this began to widen to cover design quality, and subsequently become all embracing. Now it covers the quality of customer relations, the quality of service, the quality of information systems, and so on; but in the 'quality organisation' this shows through in quality orientation rather than something specific on the organisation chart.

*Mergers, acquisitions and divestments*

Mergers, acquisitions and divestments are a normal part of business with various organisational impacts. They can involve extremely complex organisation issues, particularly where two units are being brought together, but mergers frequently involve the linking of two very different cultures. Then it is not structure which should concern you, but the task of getting two groups of people with differing styles and beliefs to work together. Inevitably, significant change will be required of one or both parties, and this will take time to prepare and implement. Mergers or acquisitions can fail simply due to cultural differences where there is a necessity to integrate the units quickly. Only the virtual destruction and replacement of one of the management groups will create a situation where integration is practical, and even this may take two years or more, not to mention the devastating impact on the business. If cultures are different, there is likely to be greatest advantage in keeping the units separate, running in their established styles and even competing, and then gradually developing joint working and collaboration.

*Interfaces*

Interfaces are becoming more visible. New product development no longer involves independent initiatives by marketing, technical and manufacturing people, but is more likely to be handled by a flexible, multi-discipline team backed by all functions. The teams themselves will emerge from the form of strategies defined in the business plans, indicating the thrust required from the project teams. These teams will be major elements in the 'new organisation', forming and changing in membership as tasks are tackled and as the detailed work requires different skills. The project leadership role will be extremely important, not only for the operation of the business, but also for providing generalist development opportunities for high ability people.

*Specialist people*

The management and motivation of professional and specialist people will be one of the big challenges for managers. The combination of increased specialisation by function, increased self-monitoring of work and progress, and wider spans of control will generally encourage a higher degree of self reliance and independence. There may be a parallel in the management of commission-only sales people, which requires a very high degree of skill in personal relationships, close involvement in mutual objectives, and a supporting remuneration policy to keep the sales people focussed on the objectives of the business. While the future professional may get on with his activities extremely well without supervision, the broad direction of his efforts and priorities in a changing world will need influencing. Linking remuneration with objectives may become more significant.

Similarly, the entrepreneurial talent in the organisation will be unleashed by greater independence, but will need to accept occasional redirection towards changing business objectives rather than simply exploiting disconnected 'opportunities'. The task for the entrepreneur may be to seek out and exploit opportunities which fit into the broad objectives of the business, and the task of his manager will be to encourage and support conforming actions. Organisationally, the structure may appear traditional, though flatter, but the management behaviour patterns will be very different.

The extent to which detail is developed in an organisation plan depends on need, but it is likely that the main assumptions about the sorts of changes anticipated in management jobs and the timing will be recorded, so that individual development and continuity planning have something firm as a base. Also the form and effect of any changes in the plan will be clearly evident. Possibly, some additional human resource strategy requirements may have emerged from the review and need to be specified. Reduced requirements for managers may trigger one strategy, and the remuneration implications of changing management and professional staff roles may be another.

This note details organisation changes which were justified in the separate paper on business issues. The effect will be to merge five product merchandising and marketing subsidiaries which had considerable overlap in their customer bases into a single multi-product organisation which will be substantially more effective in costs and marketing.

The Group executive and top managements of the five subsidiaries will be integrated and virtually all jobs redefined. Inevitably, the total management requirement is reduced. A number of appointments outside the immediate organisation will be announced in parallel, and some managers will have been identifed for whom no placement will be possible.

Merchandising operations will be consolidated under a Senior VP supported by regional directors responsible for defined home and export territories. Initially, the entire field management and sales force in each territory will continue their present activities, but report into the revised top structure. This will allow time for combining coverage of all product ranges, evolutionary transfer of customer relationships, and gradually improving customer service.

In parallel, a Product Marketing VP will be appointed, heading a team of product directors for the five areas; co-ordinating the flow of new products and centralising competitor intelligence.

All other functions will be grouped under assigned functional VPs but will maintain existing organisations and activities initially. Working parties drawn from each subsidiary will plan and implement consolidation over a six-month period, with due consultation and counselling to optimise use of these resources.

All employees are scheduled to be seen within one week of the announcement to clarify initial roles and the process to follow. Those identified as likely to be redundant will be seen early.

**Example 4** Notes supporting organisation plan

Example 4 is taken from the supporting notes of an organisation plan. It is a relatively simple statement and covers the changing task of one organisation component and the plan to handle the people implications of the organisational change.

## CHANGING ORGANISATION

There can be a thousand reasons for change – increase or decrease in business size, change of mission, change of culture, new systems, and many others or a combination of several. Substantial change is increasingly becoming 'normal'. If the change is to be successful, the members of your management team must be committed to the change to the point of feeling that they 'own' it, due to their participation in its development; and preferably be motivated. This may be because all of the participants believe they have something to gain, but one exceptional motivator is corporate survival – with the probability of some casualties.

It is necessary to understand the form and scale of the change and the potential impact on each participant. If there are to be casualties, they need to be identified early, and the available options considered for each one and presented frankly. The urgency and timing of implementation of change must be planned.

## Evolution

Where a planned future organisation takes a radically different shape from the organisation now, implementation will require evolution, which must be planned meticulously. Implementing change always requires great care, beginning with clear communication of facts, handled with due consideration for individuals who will be affected in any way. There needs to be an explanation and justification of the changes if they are to be understood and accepted, followed by real help and training to prepare and assist individuals whose jobs or responsibilities are altered. Change cannot be considered to have been implemented until people are doing the different things required of them.

A frequent element is change of emphasis in the priorities within a job, such as a sales and marketing director being required to delegate more of his selling involvement and concentrate on marketing strategy. Where these changes do not play to the individual's strengths, it may be necessary to arrange some intensive training or other development, or to go back to the organisation design to see how modification of supporting roles can achieve optimum use of individual strengths and still address key issues. The objective must be to develop a fully effective structure, backed by a detailed and timed (and possibly phased) plan to introduce the changes with minimum disturbance. This may be achieved by moving through an interim or transitional organisation if this reduces the degree of upset and allows people to make a partial adjustment in readiness for a further step.

The Review process and management continuity planning play important roles here. Where there is major change, the application at quarterly intervals of the Review process described in chapter IV.1 will plan and monitor the implementation in detail, with full participation by the managers in the area. Even if some are adversely affected by the changes, the effect of participation is sympathetic and supportive, and will achieve progress to efficiency much faster than a less participative approach.

## Organisation charts

An organisation chart is a pictorial description or statement of an organisation structure. Standard organisation charts show the reporting relationships between all the posts in the structure which are covered, perhaps restricted to the top two or three reporting levels. Occasionally, there is an advantage in showing the *total* staffing of a department, giving the number and types of all employees reporting to each supervisor. In companies which operate strict manpower control, these posts may be listed in full.

More sophisticated, and in many ways more useful than the standard model, are *stratified organisation charts*. In addition to showing the straightforward reporting relationships, relative job value levels of all posts are also indicated, as shown in example 5. Very much greater appreciation of a structure can be obtained from a stratified chart. Its use for management development purposes is great, as it clarifies possible lines for career advancement which may be less clear on ordinary charts. This is also discussed in chapter V.13 with regard to management succession.

### SUMMARY

The planning of future organisations must be based on analysis of *how* achievement of future business objectives is to be managed throughout the period of the plan. It involves identifying what is to be done at each phase of the business plan, drawing on the environment scenarios and the defined business and functional strategies, particularly the human resource strategies. From these, the shapes of the operational and functional activity groupings and their tasks will emerge, plus important subgroupings, to provide a logical structure of management jobs.

In the process, to design an organisation relevant to the needs of the business and to excite the participating managers, and thereby be effective, it is necessary to make allowance for factors such as the impact of information technology on management jobs and the way work will be done or managed; the greatly increased use of

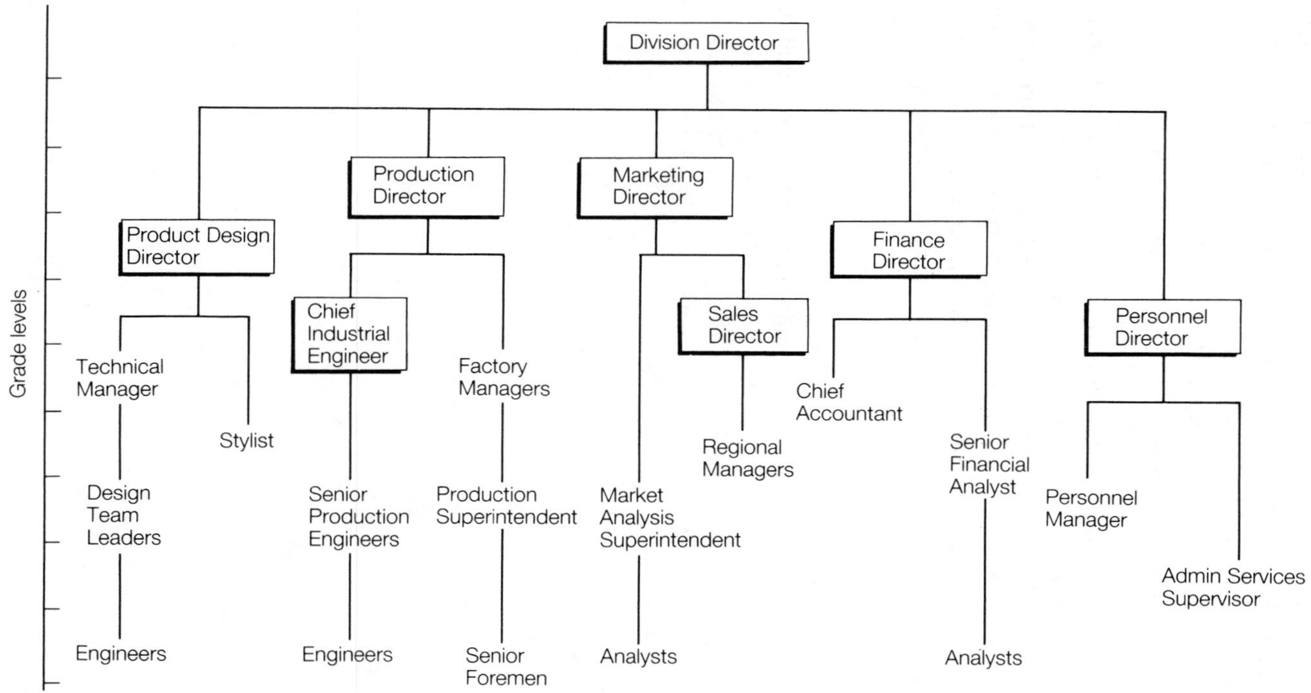


**Example 5** Stratified organisation chart showing job grade levels

multi-functional project teams to drive many programmes, changing perceptions of the importance of work; and so on.

These analyses can be seen as the beginning of an organisation development (OD) chain, with the detailed organisation change process as a highly complex activity, closely integrated with cultural change issues and the whole management development process. Certainly, organisation planning and change cannot be looked at in a narrow sense.

The end result of these deliberations should be a series of planned organisational forecasts which can be developed to show an evolution in the number, content and levels of management jobs, which identifies the requirements to be addressed for management continuity.

# III.2

## *Culture*

### CORPORATE CULTURE

### Introduction

Corporate culture is about company values; what the company believes and how it behaves. The company, for this purpose, has its identity in the body of directors, managers and other employees, whose collective individual viewpoints make up the total. The 'company view' should be provided by the top leadership, communicated through and supported by the management structure, so that a broad consensus exists. In a large company, product and geographic differences may lead to distinct variations of culture in different units, which are logical and sound. This broad consensus is evident in many organisations, but in others there is a fracture between the words of the leadership and their behaviour, so that an unspoken assumed culture is perceived.

Corporate culture is being credited with determining the potential success or failure of many an enterprise. If the business objectives and strategies of the company are strongly supported by the values and behaviour, or style, of the organisation, the will to achieve desired objectives will be strong; but where those values and behaviour are not supportive, the probability of success must be substantially reduced. For example, if sales objectives (and thereby profit objectives) are seen as being critically dependent on good customer service and product quality, and the company is developing strategies to improve these, then any historic attitudes that the customer is a nuisance, or of carelessness in manufacture, will require substantial and long-term effort in order to achieve significant behavioural change. Meanwhile, the sales objectives must be seriously at risk and the overall achievability of the plan uncertain, *solely* due to cultural factors.

The many pressures from the rapidly changing business environment can be met only by a highly motivated and integrated response at all levels of the organisation. Corporate culture is a critical element in determining achievability of business objectives and strategies.

In the last chapter, I examined organisation development (OD). While that chapter is primarily about the analytical preparation for, and implementation of, organisation change, a major and critical part in the process (which is stressed by leading researchers) is that corporate values form a key element in handling change effectively, and in developing organisations effectively.

- Providing opportunities for people to function as human beings.
- Providing opportunities for individuals to develop their full potential.
- Creating environments within which work could be satisfying.
- Providing opportunities for people to influence work.
- Accepting the complexity of human beings.
- Increasing organisation effectiveness.

These can be seen to be of primary importance, not only to organisation issues but to most of the activities within the management development process, and indeed are fundamental statements one looks for in corporate beliefs. If these values are incorporated into what the company leadership/management believes, and are reinforced by its behaviour, then the culture of that organisation is likely to be unambiguous and widely held.

## Culture and effectiveness

Corporate culture can be highly supportive in enabling an enterprise to carry through its objectives. Certainly there are organisations which seem to have things completely right and to be progressing with great energy as a result. In contrast, one finds companies in business environments which offer great opportunities, yet they appear to be unable to exploit those opportunities. On closer examination, such companies appear preoccupied with internal problems and may be unaware of events which have opened new doors for them. The performance effect of the cultural climate is critical.

The constraints which are culturally based are concerned with:

- interpretation of the environment
- interpretation of capability
- attitudes to performance standards and to opportunity
- willingness to respond to non-standard situations.

*Interpretation of the environment*

If the manager's view of the environment is complaisant, believing that change is not excessively threatening, then he may accept a declining sales and profit situation as of limited concern, up to the point where a threat to existence or to a sizeable proportion of the work force becomes real. Crisis will force a reappraisal and a radical change of attitudes. The outlook that 'we can do nothing about the things which are happening to us' and that it is all 'unfair', may seem ludicrous but is not uncommon. With this sort of attitude it is extremely difficult to accumulate the energy to change the stance of a whole group of managers to achieve agreement on new attitudes and a new line of action. Only when panic begins to rise can fresh and transforming leadership begin to have an impact.

*Interpretation of capability*

The view of capability is likely to be just as deep rooted in a mature organisation, so that the assumption built into strategic plans and into current scheduling may be very wide of what might be achieved, given an open mind, imagination and drive.

> In a company with a large design team with a tradition of taking 18 months to produce a new product design, followed by a year for production to sort it out and a further 18 months for marketing and sales to go through their ritual of declaring 'that the product is not marketable' through to the first sales, a determined middle manager created a tiny mixed discipline team and took a new product from design concept to highly successful launch in 15 per cent of the normal time cycle. Throughout the exercise, the surrounding culture muttered, 'Can't be done', until the point where it was publicly and evidently done, and done successfully.

'Can't be done' because it had never been done before in that company, was the cultural block on the real capability of the organisation, which *believed* that it could not be done.

*Attitude and willingness to recognise opportunity*

Similarly, an organisation may 'know' that it cannot respond quickly because it has a set of rules and procedures leading up to the making of a major decision which make it impossible to bid for a highly attractive order which it desperately wants. A rigid approach to 'the way we do things' would result in a strongly negative reaction to trying to by-pass the system, and deliberately block action which the organisation knows will lead to a favourable result. This sort of rigidity also leads to losses of key staff, where prompt retention action might be successful, and a variety of other 'shooting oneself in the foot' type situations.

Your concern should be to identify the elements of culture which support, or which may inhibit, your ability to achieve your objectives. At a straightforward level, are 'the ways we do things' effective? In much the same way as when you were looking at current organisation capability, look at how the business is run, ranging from how broad issues are being addressed through to the little things. For example, review the way new products are developed and brought to the customer; and at how information systems get changed.

There is a breed of individual who is naturally dissatisfied with 'the way we do things' and cannot help but continually strive for improvement. Such people cannot survive in a staid environment, but are the innovators who drive many successful organisations at every level within – who develop in others an acceptance that improvement pays off. And these are the opinion formers who look to set very high performance standards, and get them. So examine the managers who combine to provide the corporate consensus. How do you recruit, select, induct, train, communicate with, appraise and pay them – for these practices will influence who is attracted, and their communal attitudes and behaviour. How are actions approved, by delegation down the line, or reference upstairs? Are information systems and equipment up to date? Do competitors have advantages in how they do things, and if so, what is different?

It is necessary to examine what is meant by culture, how it develops and changes, and its relationship with organisation, systems, strategies, and leadership.

## What is corporate culture?

Most individuals who have had holidays abroad have been aware that the locals behave differently. They have different languages, dress differently, have houses which are different, eat different things cooked in unfamiliar ways, and so on. It is likely that their behaviour and attitudes will be discernibly different from our own, and perhaps that fundamental beliefs differ. We recognise that we come from different cultures. Within a country, there are many communities where we may recognise cultural differences which are just as marked, and most analyses of cultures within companies will show the same pattern.

As with many aspects of human resources management, discussion of what culture is, is likely to result in argument and a feeling that, for many, it is a rather woolly concept. Culture (without the 'corporate') has been defined by the anthropologist, Kluckhohn, as "The set of habitual and traditional ways of thinking, feeling and reacting that are characteristic of the ways a particular society meets its problems."

At a general level, it is easy to see differences between 'eastern' and 'western' cultures, and to see differences between, say, English and French behaviours. Within a country, there are evident differences between cultures of ethnic groups. Moving to corporate cultures, we can perceive differences between, say, Marks and Spencer and British Home Stores; between Allied Dunbar and a more traditional insurance company.

"The term Culture", argues Edgar Schein, "should be reserved for the basic assumptions and beliefs that are shared by members of an organisation, that operate unconsciously, and that define in a basic taken-for-granted fashion an organisation's view of itself and its environment."

Culture shows itself in a collection of rules, overt and covert; in principles and values, strongly noted in history, which influence behaviour within the organisation. It is the commitment which runs through an organisation to common objectives and values – once described as its soul, without which there is only a mob.

Corporate cultures are clearly visible from the way people behave, their interactions internally and with outsiders (particularly customers), and the systems or 'rituals' which they establish. There will be acceptable ways of getting things done, and resistance if the norms are challenged. There may be a declaration of values, associated, for example, with quality or equal opportunity, etc. And there will be a feeling about how the enterprise is managed, so that a company needs to be seen to be acting 'correctly', even if this occasionally causes some pain.

Culture may be said to be 'owned' by the group at large or by the opinion formers within. It is complex in a large organisation, in that any corporate culture is both an overlay and an amalgam of the cultures of many subgroups within the structure.

As culture is people-related, and people are continually developing and changing, culture too is in a constant state of evolution. Given also that the enterprise exists in a continually changing external environment, there are performance-related pressures on individual managers in the enterprise to adjust to environmental change, which may involve some modification of thinking, attitudes and behaviour.

The behavioural norms which develop in a corporate culture have been said to be those which solve the basic problems of those who shape them: providing solutions to survival and adaptation to the environment, and integrating the internal systems and processes which support those solutions. Within this, the development of a consensus between all those involved is a key element in the formation and evolution of corporate cultures. People will function easily together only where there is a high level of consensus which leaves them free to concentrate on their primary roles.

This consensus will cover a range of aspects, beginning with the need for a common language – a common interpretation of jargon or technical terms, without understanding of which an outsider would find difficulty in participating. Membership of a group and the means of gaining acceptance are crucial, as are all other 'relationship' rules related to direct and indirect authority and influence.

Expected standards for performance, which influence recognition as a high achiever or as a non-entity, are sometimes far from self-evident, so that learning the rules-of-play is essential for any newcomer, the consensus on these 'rules' having emanated from a small group of power figures. But even one committed manager can begin the process of modifying attitudes by his own actions and behaviour.

It is an important part of management's job to think through and establish not only business objectives, but also the values and behaviour applicable to achieving those objectives. An element in those values in most successful companies is the commitment to the development and growth of its human resources.

## Culture or climate?

There is a tendency for some writers to use the words 'culture' and 'climate' interchangeably, while others differentiate clearly. For example, references to a supportive climate or a supportive culture may be taken to mean much the same thing, unless the phrases are explained. A description of climate as 'work orientated culture' may indicate the relationship.

An article by Burke and Litwin emphasises the need to differentiate. They show climate as concerned with the "immediate, short term impact of the organisational environment on individual and group behaviour". Climate is very much a day-to-day matter, influenced by interactions and exchanges largely concerned with day-to-day management decisions, and readily responsive to change. These *transactional* issues focus on job requirements and motivation, and on practices and systems rather than fundamental beliefs.

Culture, in contrast, is shown to be concerned with the "underlying values and meaning systems that are difficult to manage, to alter, and even to be realised completely". It provides a framework which is "more or less permanent"; so that "instant change in culture is a contradiction in terms".

While culture has enormous inertia, it can be changed, even quickly, by the appointment of a *transforming* new leader. But he will be transforming factors which are deeply embedded in organisational life, supported by tradition, systems and power symbols which may need to be dismantled before a new culture can be consolidated.

How important, then, is climate? While clearly able to influence the effectiveness of departmental or company operation, climate should be seen as a 'sub-culture', strongly influenced in turn by the wider corporate culture, but more vulnerable to swings of 'mood' around incidents or the personal style of a particular manager.

## How culture develops

*The importance of leadership*

The founders of one enormously successful company set down on paper the basic set of beliefs and attitudes by which they wished their company to run. They were established businessmen and knew what worked well for them in their own field. They were successful in part because the open style of participative management they favoured is highly attractive to high ability people, and rare in their industry. The combination contributed significantly to the competitive edge which they have retained.

Edgar Schein writes that leadership is, beyond anything else, culture management; that "leadership is intertwined with cultural formation, evolution transformation and destination". Leaders' influence is exercised by how they behave, what they give priority to, how they deal with crises, how they communicate, and how they deal with all people matters, from choosing staff to rewards.

If corporate culture is created by 'leaders' who are sensitive to changing business demands, you can be assured that the resultant culture will adapt to fit the realities of the environment. However, this message raises the possibility that an enterprise may be headed by an extremely competent and professional management group which lacks the flair or sensitivity for 'leadership' and does not focus on the fine tuning of culture. Such a management group could have been moulded by the enterprise founder, but lack his visionary qualities as it carries on in the founding culture, until it fails to respond and the company gets into severe difficulty. A new *leader* will need not only insight to assess the limitations in the culture (and in the business), but also sensitivity to transform the thinking and actions of those around him.

*Combining ideas and behaviour*

An enterprise consists of a number of people, each of whom has an individual view of life with many variables – how they vote politically, their beliefs, involvement and attitudes towards religion, their response to violence and racism, and thousands of other factors. Within this population, some will be thoughtful and able to communicate their attitudes and ideas clearly. Of these, a few will also have the charisma to be strong opinion formers. Of the remainder most will be 'followers', who are influenced to varying degrees by the media or by leaders. Within an enterprise, the 'corporate culture' is an assembly of all the views and attitudes of the individuals who make up the work force, but the lead will come from the senior managers and any other dominant opinion influencers. For example, a manager who feels strongly about achieving high performance standards will endeavour to communicate his attitudes and to create conditions which facilitate superior performance.

Declared beliefs and behaviour dictate the pattern of behaviour required. If the pattern works and the enterprise flourishes, then the behaviour becomes the norm and becomes the culture. But if the perceived messages are ambiguous or conflicting, such as where stated beliefs are not reflected in actions, then perceived culture will be somewhat confused but generally reflect actions as more significant than words.

The ideas which develop to become part of culture may well grow from an unconscious consensus of views within a group which are tested gradually by events until they become 'lore'. Equally possible is that one founding figure, or a tiny group, has such a clear perception of the way to run the enterprise that he or it stamps his or its personality and beliefs onto it and the culture is set. There is no doubt that such personal sets of values and attitudes dominate some of the 'excellence' examples. If the formula is right for the business, the founder is suitably charismatic, and the business succeeds, the culture is well established.

*The established culture*

Once established, culture appears to be fairly static and inertia sets in. Individuals who join the organisation become indoctrinated, and may adapt some of their own thinking and standards to conform. To some degree, this may be essential if they are to get things done in their new environment, for there will be ways of getting things done – and also means of ensuring (quite indirectly) that they do not. There may be some scope for the charismatic maverick to operate, but he will be a tolerated rarity.

A long established culture 'matures' and the background to it may be rich in stories. If the norm is also of long service and a reasonably static business environment, then the patterns of thinking and behaviour may have become deeply entrenched. The style of leadership will be embodied in the culture, which in turn will influence management development and the growth of the next generation of leaders. In this way, culture can come to control the thinking of an enterprise, dictating how things are done, the form of systems, the form of organisation, and the type of managers, and influence the direction of the business objectives and operating standards. This dominance of thinking can inspire rigidity and dictate what the enterprise judges to be effective management, so that it becomes selective about what it hears of (or from) the outside world, thereby increasing its vulnerability.

The implication here is that culture cannot be allowed to mature into old age, for it is the enterprise that will die. Somehow, corporate culture needs to retain the flexibility found in young, emerging companies, ready to adapt to the changing environment; in fact, to have that quality of adaptability which is now required in organisation structures and in all the managers who fill them.

Inevitably, with the pace of change in the operating environment, the pressures on the ways the enterprise must operate will shift, and management behaviour needs to respond. However, it is also likely that, at any time, many aspects of the current culture have neither positive nor adverse influence on the efficiency of business operation. In the management of culture as the environment changes, concern needs to focus on identifying any elements in the culture which appear to inhibit the speed or effectiveness of the response required to anticipated new pressures. These are most likely to have developed from a lack of flexibility to think or act in a different mode.

It is frequently the case that the *cultural* change required is relatively minor, but it may need to be accompanied by significant organisation and strategy changes to improve effectiveness but which do not alter underlying beliefs.

## Analysis of culture

The concept of analysis suggests that a subject can be divided into a set of component parts which are clearly defined, each of which may be assessed to indicate quantitive judgements.

Corporate culture does not respond to straightforward analysis, first because there does not seem to be a tidy list of 'parts' and secondly because the aspects you may identify do not provide a basis for scales of measurement. Even the question of which end of a scale would be considered 'good' can evoke different responses.

For example, if 'management style' was selected as a component of corporate culture with a scale 'command/obedience – participative – communal', the end of the scale considered 'good' for an agricultural collective would not be the same as for an army brigade.

Analysis cannot come down to simple 'values', such as honesty, non-violence, or the need to develop personal potential. However, some companies have managed to assemble reasonable analyses of culture, in terms which make sense to themselves, by a series of self-assessments by managers and their subordinates on the ways they work, usually using a structured questionnaire. The language developed in each instance is usually only fully understood by participants.

> One large company attempts to analyse its culture periodically under a series of standard headings. The information source is primarily the people in each area and their perceptions of behaviour and practice. In addition to judgements of the actual position, they assemble a view of the 'should be' or ideal position from a wider audience to attempt some measure of 'cultural effectiveness'. These analyses have been useful in identifying excessive conformity in departments where a more adventurous entrepreneuralism is required; absence of team spirit in critical team working situations; and the fact that their recognition and reward systems are not perceived as rewarding factors in line with stated behavioural requirements.

The clearest analysis of corporate culture would appear to be that developed by Schein, and his approach to culture analysis is extremely thorough. He indicates that anything short of comprehensive, professional analysis is of concern. There is no doubt that there is a great deal still to be learned about corporate culture, how it develops and matures, and the effect it has on organisation efficiency. To attempt amateurish analysis is potentially misleading and must be approached with caution.

Having said that, there are several consultants working in this field who have evolved analytical approaches associated with reviews of organisation effectiveness. Claims of ability to change culture need to be treated with some caution and investigated thoroughly.

The real gurus accept that corporate cultures are difficult to define, even for them; that even a deep and time-consuming analysis may indicate great complexity in influences and beliefs, but no clear overall picture. Even where there seems to be a clearer picture, the language required to communicate that precisely to a non-specialist manager scarcely exists and may leave misconceptions. Cultures exist; describing them is possible, given sensitivity and patience, and the language to do this will develop further through the 1990s.

I must leave to the specialists the detail of how such an analysis may be carried out and the headings they would use to attempt their definitions of culture. It is sufficient here to note that the method should use single and group interviews and observations, to build up an awareness of actual behaviour and an understanding of the underlying assumptions and beliefs, and remain open-minded as patterns begin to form so that conclusions can be thoroughly tested. My concern here concentrates on the influence which culture has on strategies and actions.

## CULTURAL CHANGE

If culture is out of step with the achievement of future business objectives, it is likely that the inhibiting elements will need to be changed. While it is sometimes necessary to change aspects of culture, which involves altering the attitudes and behaviour of employees, many so called 'cultural changes' actually use the strength of existing culture to implement strategy and organisation realignment in response to changing environment.

Culture is difficult to change because it is made up of the deeply felt beliefs and values of the constituent individuals, which provide the individual contributions to agreed views on corporate beliefs and behaviour. For example, if community standards included high moral standards, corporate standards would not allow 'sharp practice', whatever the norms in the industry.

### Recognising the need for change

If changes in the business scene require different behaviour to enable the enterprise to continue to be successful (or perhaps to survive), managers must recognise the need and the form of change required before it can progress. But just as culture is not changed easily, so also it is not changed quickly. Any major change can take a number of years to consolidate, and during the early part of that time the tendency to revert to the original style will remain strong.

Within any sensitive working group there is likely to be continual striving at many levels to respond to the changing environment and to improve the internal workings of the company. Managers will seek to improve effectiveness. These activities continually modify behaviour – how things are done and how people relate to one another and to the situation. The culture of the group evolves unnoticed, with basic values remaining largely constant.

It is probable that every culture is as unique as a fingerprint, originating as it does out of the personal attitudes and strengths of initiators and evolving with pressures from the environment – continually adapting; hopefully improving. Interference in the process can come at many levels.

At its simplest, the manager who transfers a new person to a department, because it needs to think more in the style of the new individual, is setting out to influence and change the thinking and responses of that work group. The effectiveness of his action will depend on many aspects of the initial culture, as well as on the persuasiveness of the new individual.

Organisation development (OD) interventions can have as much to do with shifting attitudes, or culture generally, as they do with modifying organisation. Such interventions are rarely effective unless they are strongly backed at the top. In practice, any substantial change of culture must be understood and led from the top (but that can mean from the top of any organisational unit, not only the chief executive).

The reasons for setting out to change culture need to be clear. These invariably arise from business requirements. The aspects of culture which are limiting effectiveness and cultural development must be identified, possibly by an analysis of business effectiveness and cultural influences. In such analyses the realities of corporate culture begin to show up.

> A large organisation began to emphasise its requirements for young entrepreneurial managers to take existing and new business and expand them rapidly. Management training concentrated on the skills of the entrepreneurs, who were seen as bold risk takers who optimised opportunities in new markets, etc. However, the bright younger would-be entrepreneurs were looking at the experience of their older equivalents. It seemed that

there were no bold risk takers in middle to senior management, and the brighter younger managers observed the behaviour at the top. Managers who made any sort of mistake found this 'career limiting' or worse. Top management behaviour showed that the risk taking qualities of an enterpreneur were not acceptable in practice.

Another large organisation had settled into a mode where it concentrated on high level technical standards, ignored price factors and delivery dates, and expected customers to come to it with orders. For a long time this had worked, but the world changed, and the organisation had a tough time adjusting to the existence of a purposeful sales and marketing group (hurriedly recruited from outside), which had to demonstrate its value in order to gain acceptance before it could begin to alter critical attitudes of design and manufacturing staff – to accept that the customer knew what he wanted, when he wanted it, what the competitive price was, and so on.

Other organisations have faced similar problems of needing employees at large to come to terms with the importance of service to the customer when internal administration had previously been all important; or to improve quality which had been thought unimportant.

## What can trigger the process?

Change is frequently triggered by an event or realisation which leads to a significant change of business strategy, which leads to recognition of the need to alter culture and take transformational action. The event may be some business initiative by a competitor or a particularly bad set of annual figures, or simply the appointment of a new chief executive. A realisation may emerge from the latest business plan, a review of the environment or of organisation capability, that shows the company poorly equipped to face the future. Realisation that the company is in real danger is a strong stimulant. If panic results, the company may well go under, but fresh leadership at such a time will tend to reshape the company and restate a set of beliefs and required behaviour.

It does appear that many so-called changes of culture may be nothing of the kind. For example, there may be radical reshaping of the organisation to interface with a changing market place, and a crash programme of training to ensure the changes are communicated, understood and become effective. All these are more transactional and can happen without altering any of the fundamental beliefs and attitudes of the company – which indeed may help to push through the change in organisation.

Mergers, whether with an acquired business or between two previously separate divisions, may well bring together two strong but different cultures. Where this happens, rapid integration may destroy one culture and severely damage the business. If it is assumed that the established cultures are suitably matched to business objectives, the cultural differences may also indicate differences in addressing markets which are separately effective, so that integration will put at risk the retention of a market segment. As a preliminary to any action towards integration following a merger, an analysis is required of the separate business objectives and of the cultures, and of the extent to which aspects of either culture enhance or inhibit business potential. To this might be added any preliminary views of the objectives of the combined organisation and assessments of expected synergy. From this data, judgements must be made of the business logic of integration and of the cultural implications. If the ways of managing are to be changed, the effects will have been anticipated. It is relevant to note that there have been a number of quite substantial mergers and acquisitions which have subsequently been reversed for reasons of cultural incompatibility.

## Achieving cultural change

Change agents vary from the revolutionary, through the evolver, to the cautious adapter. There are as many opinions on how to achieve the desired change as there are options. There is rarely a 'right way', other than the near necessity that *cultural change should be planned.*

*The initial steps*

If cultural change is required, rather than changes in organisation, systems, etc., then it will be essential to define the starting position, the desired change and the required end position. It is said that if you really want to understand the culture in a company, you should try to change it. In attempting to achieve change, you may find that the initial diagnosis was wrong! Then the value of recording the perceived starting point and planned actions to achieve change is evident in providing a basis for reorientation and reappraisal.

Change commences then by defining the starting point. This need not involve a comprehensive statement of culture, but must cover in detail those elements of the culture which are of concern. The reasons for concern should also be noted. Woolly statements or generalisations at this stage must be taken as a danger signal, for inability to be specific will indicate insufficient understanding of the culture itself and of the justification for making any change.

Definition of the change required and the desired end result needs to be thought out with the same clarity, and that leads on to planning *how* the change is to be achieved. Who is to be influenced, by what means, and over what time scale? And how is progress to be monitored and appraised?

The first action should be designed to 'unfreeze' the existing set position: to destabilise the culture to the point where alternative thinking can be accepted for consideration. Having achieved a receptive state, the elements of the culture to be deleted or altered can be attacked and the substitutions brought in with heavy repetition and overt support. The change in behaviour must be widely visible and actively encouraged as people gain confidence. The more effective the demonstration of practical use, the more ready the general acceptance and development of a new consensus. As this is reached the change will gradually 'freeze back' into a stable culture which will respond to the new direction.

If the required time scale is short, as in a crisis, then strong and transformational leadership of the change will be essential. There will not be time for a consensus to develop; it will be necessary for a clear message to be stated and then accepted quickly. And it may be necessary for any opposing forces to be removed from influential positions to reinforce the intention to change, and to place articulate supporters in key posts.

### *Cultural change through changing people*

Of the various ways of initiating change, the most powerful is probably to change people. An incoming and transforming new chief executive can be a strong initiator, but corporate culture reflects the views of a wide range of people. If a number of key managers are removed and replaced by strong supporters of the new culture, it is likely that the message will be clearly understood and corporate opinion will be reshaped on the new course.

> In one example of dramatic change of this sort, the externally recruited chief executive decided that the only way a strong people orientated culture could be changed was by wiping out the existing top management completely. The combination of the 'alien' action of getting rid of top, thinking people and introducing a deliberately insensitive 'achieve or be fired' message 'unfroze' and destroyed much of the old culture quickly and enabled the company to respond more alertly to its rapidly changing environment. Surviving old employees insist that the company is no longer a good employer, but it is expanding and profitable after near bankruptcy.

If there is more time available for implementing change, the basic process is much the same as outlined above, but without the pressure for drastic actions. The leadership of change may still come from the top, but may equally develop as a consensus view across a management group, stimulated by the opinion formers within the group.

> One large company which realised that it faced a radically changed and internationalised market place increased its marketing management and staff by over a third, but, by a range of redeployment action and some redundancies, rebuilt a marketing organisation in which two-thirds of the managers and senior staff came from outside, in order to stamp new attitudes and practices on the function. They followed through with custom designed international marketing training for all their non-marketing management, within one year, so that all managers spoke a common marketing language.

Removing or transferring those managers who are unwilling to respond may be a radical step, but it is also a highly effective one if counselling has produced no change in style. In addition to providing openings for an influx of people who think and behave differently, one removes the blockages to progress as humanely as is practical. Supportive members of the previous teams adapt quickly to changed style and culture.

People change on a large scale is drastic but effective. The middle managers initially hang on to their positions, and gradually make their career decisions as the new style becomes evident. The message from the top and the style of the incoming group set out the behaviours and values required. The acceptance of these by the larger mass of people may be grudging to varying degrees, but over a period of months or years there is acknowledgement of 'the way things are now'.

Similar change may be achieved without redundancy, but by the deliberate transfer of individual managers who are not supportive of new attitudes. While older managers who are unable to cope with the change may be attracted by early retirement packages, younger but inflexible managers can be moved to less influential posts and may ultimately have no future. The key positions need to be filled by supporters of the new culture who are active opinion influencers.

A likely benefit of this movement is that it will tend to dislodge some of the older 'traditional' managers and open the way for young high fliers who will tend to be supportive of the change (or at least conformist because it opens the way for their advancement).

*Cultural change through 'indoctrination'*

Training and other communication can be used intensively to present 'new thinking' and emphasise the required behaviour. In the well known British Airways case, a very large scale programme of briefings and training, backed by strong internal communication, ensured that everyone was aware of the new thinking. The internal media were also used to publicise the 'heros' of the new culture – those demonstrating their understanding by acceptance and effective actions. At the same time, the non-conforming elements could be seen to lose out.

> The move by British Airways to recognise the importance of the customer, and to ensure that every member of staff not only got the message but believed it sufficiently for it to be reflected in behaviour, required a massive programme over an extended time frame. They found that top management had to allocate substantial time to the process, not only setting out a comprehensive strategy, but defining and getting accepted a unified, committed system of values, attitudes, and actions. Getting the right people into jobs was a further element. The change process itself depended heavily on a considerable flow of information and dis-

cussion at all levels, with top management staying closely in touch and steering the evolution. Inevitably, over a period of several years there were many people changes, monitored carefully; plus changes to match pay systems to the new standards and objectives.

This brief summary grossly understates the enormous amount of careful thought and planning needed to implement the change successfully. The approach and how it was achieved was distinctive to that organisation, that management team, that period in time. There is little doubt that other managers, facing the same objective could have moved differently.

Not all programmes go as well as the British Airways one.

Another chief executive, who adopted a slower pace and softer approach, working with and on his senior management and being unwilling to take harsh action against those unable or unwilling to follow, found that his middle and junior management lost heart. Stimulated and excited by the initial statements, they could see no evidence of follow through of the grand words, and settled into believing that the company management was making statements which it did not really believe; that the evident behaviour was unchanged; and that a two-faced attitude to many issues should be accepted as the norm. It will prove extremely hard to get this programme back on track with real commitment to change.

*Communication* of a new or modified set of beliefs, attitudes, values and expected behaviour is an essential part of change, but communication may not lead to accepting and absorbing beliefs. The use of *training* to explain the changes, to explore why they were necessary and to show how things will be different in practical terms, will go a long way towards establishing behaviour change – particularly if the coverage of employees is total.

Much of the most effective training is action centred and involves discussion between groups, so that people can ask questions, challenge and put their own points of view, and, with good leadership, come to a consensus favouring the change and to feeling a degree of ownership in what is created.

Playing out a variety of situations using the required behaviour provides a realistic understanding not obtainable from theoretical statements or lectures. Changing the manner in which employees respond to customers will not come easily, but salesmen (for example) will reinforce the actions and reactions within their group as they play out the new style, which will then feel familiar when they return to their jobs. Cascading programmes down through the organisation will further reinforce change by ensuring it is fully *understood at every level*. Of course, a steady pressure of communication and training is required to first establish the concepts in people's minds and then, systematically, to confirm and consolidate their thinking.

It has been said that often, where attitude or cultural changes have been achieved, the management at large will 'revert to style' as soon as the pressure to behave differently is relieved. It may take five years or even longer to consolidate a major cultural change, with many people changes and persistent communication and training to gain full commitment to the new values and behaviour.

## Reinforcing cultural change through personnel practices

If changed behaviour is required, the single strongest way to reinforce conformity is to reward it through remuneration policies, and to penalise continuance of previous behaviour patterns by the same means. If 'appropriate behaviour' is clearly rewarded while 'past habits' are penalised, the motivation to conform is strengthened and realisation that the new ways are here to stay is reinforced. Further, it must be evident that all advancements and appointments also reward supporters of the new way, and that managers too deeply committed to past practice are progressively moved aside from the main stream.

Achievement of these links between culture and various reward systems (in a wider sense than just remuneration) may require some modification of appraisal and counselling practices to ensure that there is hard data available for remuneration and other decisions and for the communication of the effects back to the individual. As remuneration is not usually the primary purpose of appraisal, some care must be taken, and emphasis on improving performance in the present job will need to draw out instances of achievement/non-achievement against required behaviour, etc. An objective will need to have been achieved in the appropriate way for it to be fully accepted as successfully completed.

## Monitoring progress

The purpose of the change and the details of the change required are defined at the beginning of the change process, and a detailed implementation plan developed which includes anticipated effects. Subsequently the progress of the implementation needs to be monitored carefully. There is always the possibility that the cultural elements identified as having an adverse impact on the business could be wrongly diagnosed, or that the changes being achieved do not have the expected result. The actions taken may lead to reactions which were not anticipated, and the programme may require a rapid re-evaluation. Close monitoring to identify any deviation from the plan and its expected result is necessary, with flexibility to reappraise the programme objectives at every stage.

### SUMMARY

Culture has developed as a highly topical subject, with recognition that corporate culture can have a strong positive influence on the ability of a company to achieve its commercial objectives. Equally, it may produce a serious negative impact. Although culture is immensely complex, it is necessary to identify the cultural factors which are inhibiting performance.

Our knowledge of our culture – the effects it may have, how it may be assessed and how it may be changed is at a fairly primitive level. Researchers such as Schein appear to have developed a high degree of understanding of its complexity and are able to carry out complex analyses. Many consultants have adopted far more simplistic approaches – more easily understood by busy managers, but perhaps also less precise.

Cultural change is almost invariably triggered by developments in the business environment or other strategic issues, or by a change of CEO (or both). Once the need for change has been accepted, the form of the change required and how it is to be achieved must be planned meticulously, and then progress monitored.

Influencing or changing corporate culture, which is basically a consensus of the beliefs and behaviours of the group of managers concerned, involves influencing those beliefs and behaviours. To achieve change it is necessary to jolt existing thinking into a receptive state, and then to gain acceptance of fresh results-producing attitudes which form new patterns of behaviour and modified beliefs.

There are only a small number of primary means of achieving such change. People may need to be changed or moved in order to place supportive opinion influencers in key roles and move aside those who oppose or cannot manage change. Communication and training have an essential and long-term role in indoctrinating, establishing and then reinforcing the cultural change. Remuneration policy is a powerful means of stressing the behaviour required and of demonstrating that success leads to reward.

Finally, monitoring progress is essential, to ensure that the expected changes are occurring as planned, so that the programme objectives are being achieved and the business performance is responding as anticipated. If anything unexpected occurs, the analysis of the cultural factors which may be causing the adverse effect requires swift reappraisal.

The volume of literature on culture is likely to grow enormously over the next few years, although the general level of understanding may remain somewhat limited, confused by jargon. It is an area which may justify calling in a very competent (but down to earth) specialist.

# III.3

## *Competencies*

### INTRODUCTION

Deployment of people to management positions is dependent on first having a clear picture of the individual who is likely to be effective in each position; not only currently, but with an eye to the future. Person specifications state the 'competencies' required, both in terms of skills and also in terms of the personal qualities necessary for effective performance. If your view of organisation incorporates significant change, the competencies you may require in your managers may alter to some degree, and you need to begin the development of 'future managers' to meet the new specifications as early as possible.

'Competencies' is relatively new jargon. The word did not feature in the indexes of most management development books published up to 1986. Yet the concept of identifying the skills and abilities required in a job is long established. Companies with well developed human resource practices have tended to produce detailed job and person specifications for very many years. So what is new?

It may be that increasing numbers of factors and complexity triggered the interest in analysing competencies, together with attempts to improve assessments by clarifying factors which could be used to determine the effectiveness of managers or their suitability for other appointments. Some other questions were 'What sort of people shall we need in the future?' and 'Who will be effective in that environment?'. Leading from those questions came 'What *sort* of graduates should we be recruiting to provide our future managers?'.

## DEFINING COMPETENCIES

Person specifications have always included a variety of factors, frequently beginning with preferred age and ideal educational background, so that most managers attempting to identify competencies had no disciplined tradition or framework to use, and so far there is no accepted definition of what competencies might encompass. Inevitably, there is considerable lack of precision about what is meant by the term and some variation in its use. For some organisations, competency means skills, capable of improvement by experience or training, which relate to the technical and professional ability to do a job. More commonly, the term is extended to cover the qualities, innate abilities or personality strengths which are found in effective managers.

In a recent survey for Ashridge into the use of competencies for various assessment purposes, Dr Jacobs asked "What is meant by competency?" – an extraordinary question in the circumstances, but a revealing one. He went on to ask "Is it an ability, is it a skill or a combination of the two?", and then to comment that the apparent lack of agreement about terminology and concepts reflects a continuing disagreement about the subject amongst both academics and practitioners.

The Institute of Manpower Studies has commented that "although most organisations use the same words, they more often than not mean very different things. Indeed, we found wide differences in interpretation both *between* organisations and *within* them".

In every organisation, the competencies identified in effective managers seem influenced by the culture, language and the jargon of the company concerned, particularly the language and the clarity with which competency factors are able to be understood. For example, one organisation may select 'leadership ability' as a key competency, while another may consider this too general and seek to use a range of qualities which it associates with good leadership. Another discussion might arise around the selection of 'analytical ability' as an alternative to the use of 'judgement', being a more significant measure concerned with *applied* analysis. Clearly they are different, but how many criteria do you want?

When we talk about competencies, we are asking questions about what people need to be able to do and about how they need to behave in order to be effective, normally in one job or a category or level of jobs, probably against defined acceptable standards or performance expectations. However, if it is a management job, any list of the 'qualities' which constitute being a good manager could be almost endless – and in that rests the real problem about competencies, made even more difficult by lack of consensus on what a competency is, or is not.

## THE RANGE OF COMPETENCIES

The purpose and intended use of selected competencies are very important. Once these are clear, establishing a common vocabulary among users will ensure that the results are intelligible. Even then, an excessively long list may develop, or there will be complaints of a narrowness of view of required behaviour!

If you take a look back some 30 years, the list of key management qualities was very much shorter. For example, a major oil company identified only five such qualities:

- 'helicopter' ability
- analytical skills
- imagination
- 'a sense of reality'
- leadership.

More recently, the list was changed to develop the last two and to introduce 'skills' to the more general personal qualities:

- 'helicopter' ability
- analytical skills
- imagination and creativity
- a sense of reality – worldliness
- decisiveness, which subdivides into –
    - influencing and motivating
    - effective delegation
    - ability to communicate
    - business sense.

The change of identity and subdivision of the old 'leadership' might lead to lively discussion in many companies regarding the adequacy of the selected competencies, even if you accept that they will vary between companies and situations. For example, in a world-wide organisation, where is 'global outlook' or an indication of the need for an ability with languages? Hidden behind other words perhaps, or of lesser importance than the selected short list.

## Determining the correct specifications

With the increased pace of environmental change, the sorts of people who will be effective in given situations has become more crucial. Person specifications (and the associated remuneration packages) may vary enormously between apparently equivalent jobs. For example, two general managers operating in the same industry, both requiring high standards of achievement, may have very different specifications because one post is in a straightforward operating situation and the other is in an extremely competitive situation and demands higher competencies. These differences are very important, so it is essential to get specifications right.

Lists of competencies have grown as both researchers and line managers have endeavoured to be more precise in defining appropriate 'profiles' for jobs. Increased use of psychometrics and assessments has added a further dimension to the language used. And, of course, there is the added complexity resulting from evolving organisation forms and cultural influences as we seek to define detailed profiles of future managers as an aid to management development. Sometimes, at least, we go into far more detail than has value!

Selection of competencies seems to generate much argument. For example, there have been a number of attempts to generate a 'universal set' of managerial competencies; but an IPM report states that "Significant research over many years has shown that there can be no agreement over such qualities and their relationship with managerial effectiveness when emphasised in the most general terms." For one thing, the relevance of individual competencies will vary with the task.

Would it be possible to determine sets of managerial competencies within functional areas? This has rather more merit, but I suspect that in any function, jobs and settings vary to a degree that would reduce the functional lists to guide-lines, with final selection determined for specific situations.

Some of this debate arose from a wish to establish a basis for national academic qualifications for management, and led to a variety of other considerations. Perhaps the most complex is the way in which very large lists of 'competencies' can be developed, from which various groupings may be assembled under 'general' headings. In practice, the selection of general headings and the grouping of individual competencies also seem to vary between analysts and for various situations. Even the precise meanings of words or phrases used appear to lose some clarity in this process!

Development of a specific set of competencies, for one group or level of jobs within one situation, which are clearly understood by the participants evolving the criteria and choosing the words, seems to be necessary for real understanding of the competencies themselves to emerge.

> A large food and drinks company used consultants to identify important areas of competence for its managers. They selected about 50 skills and qualities, in six main groupings. As the full list was somewhat indigestible, the company introduced only the main headings to line managers, and let subdivisions and terminology grow progressively and naturally within each of the subsidiary businesses. This is being used by the company's main board as part of a programme of progressive cultural change, and gives emphasis to newly acquired competencies as one element in encouraging change. I have some reservation about whether a fully codified and implemented set of competencies will remain clear at every level, and even more reservation that the same competencies could be relevant at every level in all functions and for all business situations.

> An exercise in a large insurance company to establish future competencies as a basis for assessments noted considerable *differences* in the competencies identified as relevant for different levels of management, and also noted variations between product divisions, related in part to differences in the competitive environment and business style.

Other difficulties which arise include the near impossibility of applying any logical measurement or weighting to selections of competencies, and also to their lack of permanence as business environment changes. Given that management is usually a team effort, should competency requirements be associated with individual positions, or as factors which must be relevant within the team as a whole?

Ultimately the relevance and value of competencies are determined by what we seek to do with them. There seem to be three primary objectives:

1 To provide maximum guidance on the specification required for any managerial position which is about to be filled.
2 To provide maximum guidance on the specifications you are likely to need for your managers on into the future, as this will influence the recruiting you do now and the development programmes which follow as you endeavour to prepare individuals for those future roles.
3 To help you to understand the differences between the 'now' and the future so that you can manage the change.

## Future skills

Some of the skills which future managers will need are directly related to changes in the business environment in their industries, but there are a number of other major influences which are more internal in nature. These internal influences include trends towards:

- flatter organisation structures and wider spans of control
- reduction in the command/obedience mode of managing
- increases in the use of project teams or temporary management groupings
- further advances in information management systems
- increased self-management.

These influences will alter the ways people manage and are managed. For example, as management information systems develop, masses of undigested data will be analysed automatically, so that everything from individual efficiency to priority issues will be readily discernible to each manager and to his subordinates. There will be little need to give instructions or allocate work when what needs to be done will be self evident, and any performance failure will be publicly visible.

From this list of likely influences, a number of traits seem likely to increase in significance:

- adaptability/flexibility
- breadth of view (functional specialists will need a general rather than functional outlook)

- self-reliance/self-discipline/self-starting
- support of team efforts and other people/departments
- computer literacy.

The middle three in this list are particularly related to changing organisation philosophy and ways of managing. The profile of competencies required by the future managers of some companies may change significantly in these respects.

Research in another organisation drew out three different headings considered to be especially relevant to the future (but does not deny the considerable importance of other criteria in different situations):

- flexibility
- social or interpersonal skills
- leadership.

Of *flexibility*, it is self evident that the degree and pace of environmental change will prove disastrous for managers who are not quick on their feet, adaptable to new situations, analytical and logical in their decision-making, strategic in outlook. And there you have a short list of associated competencies!

Of *social or interpersonal skills*, the influence of environmental change allied to changing management style will increase the importance of these skills. Consider some scales:

| | | |
|---|---|---|
| Listing skills | v | Poor listener |
| Effective relationships | v | Low profile |
| Powerful influence | v | No presence |
| Socially confident | v | Reserved |
| Effective team player | v | Insular |
| Communicates well | v | Poor communication |

The competencies you will require of a future manager seem clear cut, while the other ends of the scales may be acceptable (*or non-critical*) in some specialist, non-managing roles.

*Leadership* will also break down into a series of subsidiary competencies, but you do need to be specific about who is to be led and the situation in which the leader is to operate. A leader has to be accepted, not just appointed. Leadership has an intellectual requirement too. If the leader has an intellectual and visionary grasp of the business – where it is now, where it is going, and how it will get there, the *way* it will get there – plus the personality to gain acceptance, then his potential for leading effectively is enormous. If these qualities generate a certain arrogance, even this may be acceptable.

## SUMMARY

Appointments to management positions now, and development of managers towards future management positions, should be influenced by the competencies identified as relevant in the future. Analysis of the demands arising from changing business environments and internal factors such as changed organisation design and the impact of information technology enable changes in required competencies to be forecast.

Looking at many actual lists of competencies developed to cover management positions, I remain astonished at the diversity and find it impossible to extract any meaningful short list of the more common factors or headings. Not only is the range apparently diverse, but the language (the terms used) is 'company variable'. Perhaps this simply emphasises that the competencies which are felt to be relevant and found in effective managers do vary enormously between situations. Or it may indicate that there is scope for some serious research to develop and define a language of management competencies. At this time, the logical recommendation is that you determine a clear purpose for identifying competencies and then formulate a list which is relevant to your jobs and situation and intelligible to all users.

# III.4

## *Leadership*

### THE IMPORTANCE OF LEADERSHIP

Effective leadership is one of the fundamentals of gaining and retaining competitive advantage. Attempts by researchers to define universal qualities or the management style of effective leaders has shown that the personal qualities and competencies likely to prove effective vary with business objectives and environment, with corporate culture and organisation, and with the people in the supporting management team. Perhaps the nearest one comes to a universal ideal is in the concept of the 'transformational leader' who has the vision to see where the company needs to go and how to get there, and the charisma and communication sensitivity to convey excitement and carry a team with him.

The right leader can make an enormous difference to the effectiveness of the organisation and its capability to achieve superlative rather than 'ordinary' business results. 'Leadership ability' is a commonly selected competency, but is more in the nature of a general heading. For these reasons, the search to identify the qualities of effective leaders has run for a long time. If you can identify those qualities, you can search more knowledgeably for young future managers of high promise.

### QUALITIES OF LEADERSHIP

To lead is defined as 'to show the way', to guide, to direct, to persuade, to precede'. The search has concentrated longest on enlarging this set of traits or competencies, initially in the hope that there might be a universal set of characteristics. While there is acceptance that no universal set exists, many organisations appear to continue a narrower search for factors which are relevant to their own situation and industry.

All the evidence from these searches seems to indicate that leadership qualities which appear to be essential have some relationship with the whole cultural and environmental situation in which the individual leader operates. If a successful individual is to be transplanted and continue to be effective, it is likely that this new situation will need to have sufficient elements in common with the old to enable his means of achieving performance to be largely unaffected. If he were moved to a radically different cultural situation, he might find it very difficult to function so effectively.

Blake and Mouton's managerial grid attempted to identify effective *styles* of management during the 1960s. They provided a basis for people to analyse and understand their own styles, but no universal agreement evolved as to which style of leadership was most effective. Once again the broad conclusion appears to have been that there is a relationship between the qualities and style of the leader and the demands of the business environment within which he operates, and with the corporate culture and people being led. What works in one situation may be unsuccessful in another.

## Flexibility

It seems evident that no one style is appropriate for every situation, for the issues which arise and the ways they may need to be handled may be quite diverse. Thus, an effective leader who is required to deal effectively with a wide variety of situations will need real flexibility in his personal style, as a single approach will not always be effective.

Neider and Schriesheim give particular emphasis to this requirement for flexibility, and to the need for a leader to pay attention to the needs of his supporting staff. The leader should provide the obvious motivation of linking remuneration (and other 'rewards' such as promotion) to achievement of high performance standards and, in parallel, ensure that difficulties are cleared away to facilitate achievements, and generally provide support so that subordinates can achieve high performance standards.

## Vision

Leadership is much more than 'enabling', however. The concept of *transformational leadership* uses words and phrases like 'charismatic', 'inspiring', 'stimulates intellectually', 'acknowledges individuality', to indicate the personal qualities of a leader who has a vision of where he/the company/the department needs to go, and how to get there; and he can communicate this to his 'followers' in such a manner that they accept his vision and direction, and go with him enthusiastically.

This process of *envisioning* may be fundamental to good leadership, in that it provides the 'grand design' as a framework for all shorter term strategies, decisions and behaviour. It influences not only the broad direction of the organisation but also its culture, and provides the concept which conveys to followers an excitement and 'dimension of vision'. For the leader himself, the envisioning process is a rewarding intellectual stimulant, indicating, perhaps, the single universal quality of leadership – reasonably high intellect. However, even that is not quite universal, for there is ample evidence which suggests that particularly high intellect can be a *dis*advantage in a leader, especially where there is a significant difference between the intellectual level of the leader and that of his followers. A moderate differential, on the other hand, seems to provide a positive advantage.

## Recall

Another attribute which appears common among successful leaders is an exceptional memory. As part of their charisma, the ability to remember faces and names, and to recall and use large volumes of detailed knowledge, suggests formidable understanding and gives the impression of a powerful intellect which followers may respect.

## Communication skills

A number of exceptional leaders have emphasised that their demands for very high standards of performance from subordinates have been a key factor in their success. By challenging good people to achieve, they have attracted a strong response and the results sought, where other teams of competent people have been less stretched and have achieved less.

In all this, the sensitivity and skills of a good communicator, which includes being a good listener and keeping an open mind prior to decisions, seem particularly important.

### Ability to delegate

Good leaders tend to be good at delegating. The chief executive has a range of activities and responsibilities, and needs to ensure that he does not get bogged down in operational commitments which should be delegated; that he retains time to think and time to lead. If he delegates well and allocates time to being a teacher or mentor, and if he holds unswervingly to his values (and is generally seen to be right), then he puts his personal stamp on the cultural values of the company and on its business objectives and achievements.

### Interpersonal skills

A leader has to be accepted, not just appointed. He may be accepted because his is the dominant personality – the 'bull which can see off all challenge'. (Some 'leaders' have that quality, but little more.) More normally, he will be accepted for a wider range of relevant qualities.

He needs a further quality as a leader of a team if he is to extract full value. He must avoid domination and endeavour to draw out the wisdom and experience of all team members in a positive fashion, to explore all the angles of a problem and determine the optimum solution. It is for the leader to summarise the discussion productively, without damaging egos as some ideas are rejected, and guide the team to a solution its members can jointly 'own' and support. Perhaps the outstanding skills are interpersonal – listening and sensitivity, open communication and encouragement, negotiation and persuasion.

## LEADERSHIP COMPETENCIES

Leadership can be broken down into a series of competencies in specific situations. First it is necessary to be clear on the task and role of the leader, defining the business objectives and environmental setting; the performance standards expected; the corporate culture and organisation; and the qualities of the management team which is to be led. Only then can the person specification take shape and the competencies critical to effective performance and leadership begin to be identified.

Leadership includes an essential intelligence factor, as the intellectual capacity of the leader should at least match, and preferably exceed, that of most subordinates if he is to retain their respect. That relativity continues the pattern of linking competencies with specific leadership situations.

I cannot trace the origins of a quotation that leadership means "constantly furnishing the means for people to find in their daily work the stimulation and satisfaction that contributes to long-term meaning in their lives", but it does provide an attractive summary.

Looking at some actual lists of competencies developed to help identify potential leaders, there is no obvious list of half a dozen common elements. Below is a selection, in alphabetical order, from some lists which are in use:

Achievement motivation
Business acumen
Coaching
Collective working (teams)
Communication
Conflict management
Creativity
Decision-making
Delegating
Energy
Flexibility
Integrity
Interpersonal skills
Judgement
Knowledge (professional/technical)
Listening
Managing change
Maturity
Meetings (leading)
Motivating
Negotiation
Organising
Planning
Political
Pro-active
Problem solving ability
Rational
Self-management
Strategic
Team building
Technical/functional knowledge
Time management
Thinking capacity
Visionary
Will to win

Each of these, taken in isolation, appears to have some relevance to leadership to varying degrees, according to situations. You should identify factors which appear relevant to your own situation, and relevant to the application you intend.

## SUMMARY

Effective leadership is fundamental to gaining and retaining competitive advantage.

The competencies required in a good leader are closely related to business objectives, environment, performance standards, corporate culture, organisation, and the people to be led. Competence factors probably vary widely as a result, but leadership invariably includes a specific intellectual requirement and high interpersonal skills.

The charismatic and inspirational qualities of the transformational leader are widely sought, but some highly effective leaders operate in very different ways and could never be called 'charismatic'.

Flexibility is required, as a leader may need to adapt to different styles when facing different situations.

In the end, the task is to match the individual with the situation, to find leaders who are flexible, sensitive, have a realistic vision of where they need to go and what must be done to get there, and who can inspire their followers by their ability to communicate clearly and enthusiastically.

# III.5

## *Teams*

Much of the time, management 'teams' operate as a collection of individuals with largely functional or operating responsibilities. For a small proportion of time they must come together as an integrated force to determine broad strategies or policies. At these times, the ability to slip out of operational and into strategic roles, and the ability to work together on complex problems and contribute at a new level towards shared goals and to reach difficult decisions is vital.

Team building has been a popular activity for consultants and trainers, and some elaborate jargon has developed. While some of this may help people to understand the complexity of team working, or provide a basis for analysing why some 'teams' are incapable of tackling issues or reaching decisions, there are also some basic guide-lines which show how a good team can be put together, and on the culture which will support effective team work.

### ROLE OF TEAMS

A management team is likely to consist of a leader (the chief executive) and between five and ten directly supporting managers with functional or operational responsibilities. For most of the time, the activities and objectives of the members are largely independent and individual. To varying degrees, they co-operate with one another on operational issues. For example, the heads of marketing and manufacturing will agree priorities and schedules for the delivery of orders; and the finance director will talk with each of his colleagues about the financial impact of matters under their control.

They may meet regularly for broad reviews of the business and to consider wider ranging business issues, but most of these meetings will have a straightforward operational flavour and the team relationships will not be under any pressure. However, where decisions begin to become much more complex and longer term, and where the uncertainty is greater, the *nature of the problem* and the *way it must be tackled* will change. It will no longer be possible for individuals to sit inside protective functional boxes; they must come out into more exposed generalist roles and contribute on that much wider ranging basis.

In these situations, mutual trust and openness between the team members is crucial, and any atmosphere of 'point scoring' or political infighting is dangerously destructive. Further, the quality of leadership in drawing out the widest range of options and contributions, and steering towards a conclusion of considered logic, is vital, and the barnstorming approach is ineffective.

Without doubt, many so-called teams are never able to achieve effective team work. Apart from the factors indicated in the preceeding paragraph, there may be simple limitations within the team membership, such as poor leadership, narrow specialists incapable of appreciating wider issues and simply unwilling to contribute, or intellectual limitations.

In such situations, the inadequate 'team' is likely to fall back on some mechanism to 'resolve' the problem, such as forming a working party or project group to examine and recommend a course of action. If an inadequate team defines the problem to be addressed by a working party, there is a high probability of oversimplification with caution or political factors involved, which makes real consideration of much relevant material difficult or impossible. An inconclusive result or operational solution is likely to result where a major rethinking of strategic direction may have been required.

In the business environment which can be envisaged, it seems inevitable that there will be more questions on strategic issues. Shortcomings on the part of decision-making teams will adversely affect retention of any competitive advantage.

## TEAM LEADERS

Leadership is covered in the preceding chapter. However, the importance of a leader in a team situation requires further discussion here.

Belbin made a specific study of team leaders in his research into teams and team effectiveness, and identifies several 'classifications'. A chief executive, or any other manager, tends to be selected for a variety of reasons, and the ability to lead a team effectively would be no more than one of the considerations – although an important one. However, he would be selected against the background of the team in place (of which he may already be a member), and in the light of his overall abilities in relation to the direction of the business or task of the department.

As noted previously, the chief executive (or the manager) must delegate well and then act as mentor to ensure his people can cope with the responsibilities assigned. As a part of encouraging and developing his people, he will need a high level of competence in a full range of interpersonal skills.

## PERSONALITIES AND TEAMS

In his research and publications on team building, Professor Belbin identified a range of personality types and suggested that in an experimental environment the most successful team was the 'classic mixed team', in which a group with varied personalities and competencies could usually underpin any weakness on the part of its members, but that the balance could easily be upset by changing one member. Such teams are rarely found to occur naturally in industry.

Belbin suggests that good teams can be built up of team-orientated stable extroverts, well disciplined, and with reasonably good mental abilities. In large organisations, this allows easy movement between teams, and generally fits well with participative management.

He also drew attention to teams led by single outstanding people. Although these individuals are inclined to be dominant and authoritarian, the teams can still be effective.

I would refer readers to Belbin's book *Management Teams* for details of the personality types and mixes he suggests it is useful to have in teams. This is based on the evidence of watching many teams at work, including close study of temporarily formed teams in management training environments. The main application may be to provide insight which may be valuable in stimulating a team which is otherwise of limited effect. I would be cautious about using personality as the key factor in assembling a team since, given a team consisting of a varied selection, the specification for any replacement could become uncomfortably narrow.

Other writers and consultants have since developed various approaches to 'classifying' members of management teams, with the objective of achieving a reasonable balance of member types and avoiding the narrow outlook which may result from dominance by a single type. The objectives of most of this specialist consulting work is 'improvement of team performance' and avoidance of team conflict. There are certainly many teams which can be assisted by clarification of how teams work and an improved understanding of the roles of the members, but effective team working seems to involve corporate culture and the intelligence, experience and breadth of view of the participants.

## CULTURE AND TEAMS

Teams are more effective when people openly share goals and values and work together, and less effective in climates of mistrust and political infighting. Effectiveness is reduced by 'them and us' attitudes, and by all influences or attitudes which restrict the free flow of information within a team. This short paragraph says enough. Given that there is great variation in corporate culture, there must be many situations where the ability of a team to be effective is severely restricted by the attitudes noted, and others where culture strongly supports effective working.

In any analysis of corporate culture, or of the extent to which any elements in that culture restrict the ability of the company to achieve business objectives, the issue of team effectiveness should be covered. Many of the questions which teams should tackle (as distinct from individual managers) concern longer term issues which may not affect profitability immediately, but which are on a scale where their potential influence can be enormous. In such situations, the significance to longer term business objectives should justify high visibility being given to team effectiveness in resolving future strategies.

It is evident that culture can have a particularly powerful influence on team effectiveness, and be particularly inhibiting where the management style is not open and participative. In these latter cultures, there is a further probability of authoritarian rule with domination by one individual (or a small group) which so inhibits freedom of speech and action that any teams or committees are hollow shells. I recall an extreme case where the managing director of a subsidiary was called in to rewrite the minutes of his board meeting to reflect the subsequent decisions of the group chief executive officer.

## TEAM BUILDING

Teams build largely from within, shaped by leadership and by the developing personal relationships within the team, and less by changes to membership. Most of the team building work carried out by consultants, or OD people or trainers follows on from recognition somewhere that the existing teams are not as effective as they need to be, and attempts to improve that efficiency.

The consultants, trainers and OD interventionists generally see themselves as catalysts, helping management groups to function better. Their efforts frequently concentrate on analysis of team members so that closer working relationships may be encouraged, but if there are fundamental weaknesses in the make up of a 'team', or in the calibre of its members, it may be impossible to achieve any real advance beyond some increased awareness of how a team *should* operate and of the limitations which currently exist. Ultimately, it is the design of the team which is important.

## EFFECTIVE TEAMS

The range of personal qualities (competencies) to be sought in an effective team could be very broad, and would vary for business situations and culture and between structures, but a number of key elements may be universal:

- The chairman or leader must be able to draw out the best contributions from all members of the group, and should not dominate proceedings. The effective leader will be a mentor and coach to encourage paths of thought and debate before bringing the team to summarise, and then conclude on, agreed strategy.

- The team members can be expected to be qualified and experienced for their individual jobs and should fit in comfortably with the corporate culture. In addition, they must be able to step up into a broad team role in which they stand outside their operational or functional responsibility and contribute strongly.
- The team members must be able to share goals and values and pull together; recognising and adjusting to the strengths of their colleagues; contributing, not competing.
- They must communicate readily and openly; to share information and have mutual trust; to be mutually supportive; to be persuasive.

Teams are rarely built from lists of requirements such as these. Rather they evolve from series of appointments to operational jobs. In the specification for such posts at senior level, operational knowledge of a single function may be the only requirement, but an appreciation of the fit of that function into the total business and the intellectual capacity to think broadly enough about the new or unusual are essential. For example, when working on a SWOT analysis, attention to opportunities and threats may reveal an individual's capacity to think in sufficient breadth and appreciate the full implications, and therefore to contribute fully at executive team level.

Teams of such high ability individuals will work well if the culture is right and there is good leadership, and these abilities become critical elements in position specifications, to be filled by careful selection following planned development.

## SUMMARY

Effective team work is essential at the top level of any enterprise or sizeable unit, but needs to be recognised as a relatively small part of most senior managers' activities. These individuals work predominantly within their own function or area of operational responsibility, and to varying degrees in co-operation with colleagues on issues of mutual interest. Team work involves a different type of activity, which brings together the total abilities and resources of the team members to address major business uncertainties or requirements for radical strategy change.

Effective teams tend to consist of groups of people who are excellent at their individual jobs, but who bring an added dimension of broader knowledge and intellect to wider issues, plus a willingness to communicate freely and to work together towards common goals without recourse to political actions. Probably corporate culture is a significant influence on whether a team can exist and work effectively or not.

# III.6

## *Future requirements*

'Manpower planning' is a term with widely differing uses, and is therefore avoided here in order to be more specific. The purpose here is to forecast requirements for all levels and types of managers over the duration of the business plan, in order to establish targets for the management development programme. If management development is to be integrated successfully with business objectives, it is more or less essential to have a reasonable measure of the requirements for management at a series of points into the future, so that planning and development activities are directed to preparing people for real opportunities.

### THE 'MANPOWER PLAN' OF MANAGEMENT POSITIONS

#### Introduction

The pace of change in environment and in organisation, plus company mergers and rationalisations, make these forecasts particularly difficult to achieve for the longer term. Even the shorter term forecasts may have to record reservations, yet the best available estimates seem essential for meaningful development actions. As business managers, you are obliged to predict the future. As the assumptions you make will be recorded, reappraisal of forecasts can be rapid following any change of scenario.

The alternative approach to management development would be a universal programme of *ad hoc* development to provide 'flexible people' able to manage any situation which arises (or be 'outplaced' if not required). This seems an expensive and unreliable option, and would need a contingency back-up arrangement consisting of a highly geared recruitment machine to mobilise consultants and search agencies to instant action when an unfulfillable need arose. Hardly a main stream planning approach.

Earlier chapters examined the development of the organisation plan, determination of future competencies, the relevance of culture, and how changes in organisation and culture might be planned and implemented. It is the further *detail* of those plans which provides the picture of the managers and specialists required to run the planned business in the future.

## Details of the plan

Organisation sets out ideal groupings of activities and the top structure of management jobs expected to exist, plus a statement of the general concept of organisation expected to apply (which may differ from the 'now') and any changed cultural factors. Additionally, there should be competency profiles of the types of managers expected to exist, based on planned responses to environmental and other influences and the expected 'way of managing' – the types of people expected to be most effective. Finally, there will be job specific data covering the functional and general skills necessary for each post.

It is unlikely that all this data will be assembled for every job at each of a series of points in time, but the format should be sufficient for the range of requirements to be reasonably specific. For lower levels of management, the same sorts of data are relevant and are capable of projection on a similar basis, but such data will tend to be progressively more numerical within functions and categories as the numbers of positions increase, and less specific to individual posts.

In rough form, sketches of anticipated 'ideal' organisations can be developed covering the whole management strata. These may be drawn for a series of times, say two, five and ten years ahead, to add a degree of clarity to the evolution. This will help produce some firm numbers and other data, thus providing some specifics for the 'change agents' to work on to help clarify realistic time scales for changes. In practice, it is useful to pencil in actual names on the shorter term charts to add a further critical dimension and realism to the plan and to establish the individual development required. This may identify some of the 'hard' things to be addressed (such as problems of excess or obsolete managers) in the Review process of linking the management needs of the organisation with the deployment and development of managers.

## The plan itself

It is not practical to include an example of a total plan of projected management requirements here. The relevant detail will be drawn from various parts of business objectives and strategies, and their anticipated scenarios and assumptions. The core material will be the detailed business objectives through the period to be covered. If greater detail is concentrated on selected years within the business plan, such as years 1, 2, 5, 10 and 20, then the same years (or a selection of them) should be used for these organisation and manning projections.

Note should be taken of statements of alternative scenarios, related to various aspects of environment, and alternative major strategies designed to enable the plan variations to be achieved. These are crucial, in that they add information on the work which may need to be done, which may require significantly different organisation and manning standards. This should be covered by contingency plans.

The basic organisation plans will have been developed against this total picture, and some assumptions will have been included in the business plans about the scale and costs of the management structure. The further task is to use this information about each part of the structure to develop a detailed forecast of management requirements.

This example is a composite, drawn from two similar situations, both in international groups with medium to high technology product ranges. The product is otherwise immaterial for the purpose of the case, which concentrates on the sales and marketing organisation.

The *present structure* is associated with a strong home market which produces two-thirds of the total sales (all manufactured in the UK). There is a home sales force under a sales manager, plus a small marketing team concerned with market analysis and strategy.

Exports are well established, partly through three small distribution companies in key territories and a network of agents elsewhere, backed up by a small team of regional sales people. Example 6 shows the existing structure.

The *business environment* projections are fairly typical. There is expected to be steady technical development, but no revolutionary change is anticipated. Some new competition is expected, mostly from the Pacific basin, and the competitive scene is expected to become more aggressive and international everywhere, although there is confidence about the ability to continue to dominate the home market. While there will be more competitors in the 1–5 year period, some reduction is expected beyond that time. Price pressures will be associated more with improved productivity than with price wars, so that productivity achievements will be important for profitability.

Design is currently becoming much more influential; quality is already established as highly important; customer service will become more significant quickly, while the additional factor of the maintenance needs of planned future product ranges must be met. Finally, the home market is seen as critically important as the long-term design and management base.

*The business objectives* show a doubling of real volume over the first five years with equivalent profit growth and assume a similar pace thereafter in a growing market. They plan to concentrate initially on protecting and developing the home market, as any severe reduction there might destroy the company.

In parallel, it is planned to create two additional key territories overseas and to concentrate growth efforts in all five. In the longer term, these are scheduled to develop local manufacture, and ultimately to become the focal points for regional marketing in a network with the home parent. Agents and the field sales team will continue to press for growth, but will withdraw to niche markets (to be identified) where their markets are attacked and cannot be defended. Total withdrawal from any market will be avoided if possible.

No acquisition or divestment is planned, but small acquisitions to widen the product range are thought possible.

*Strategies* designed to achieve these objectives include the development of a full marketing activity, both at the home location and progressively in the five key overseas territories, to ensure the systematic gathering, analysis and response to the market place. One strategy defined will require all sales staff to

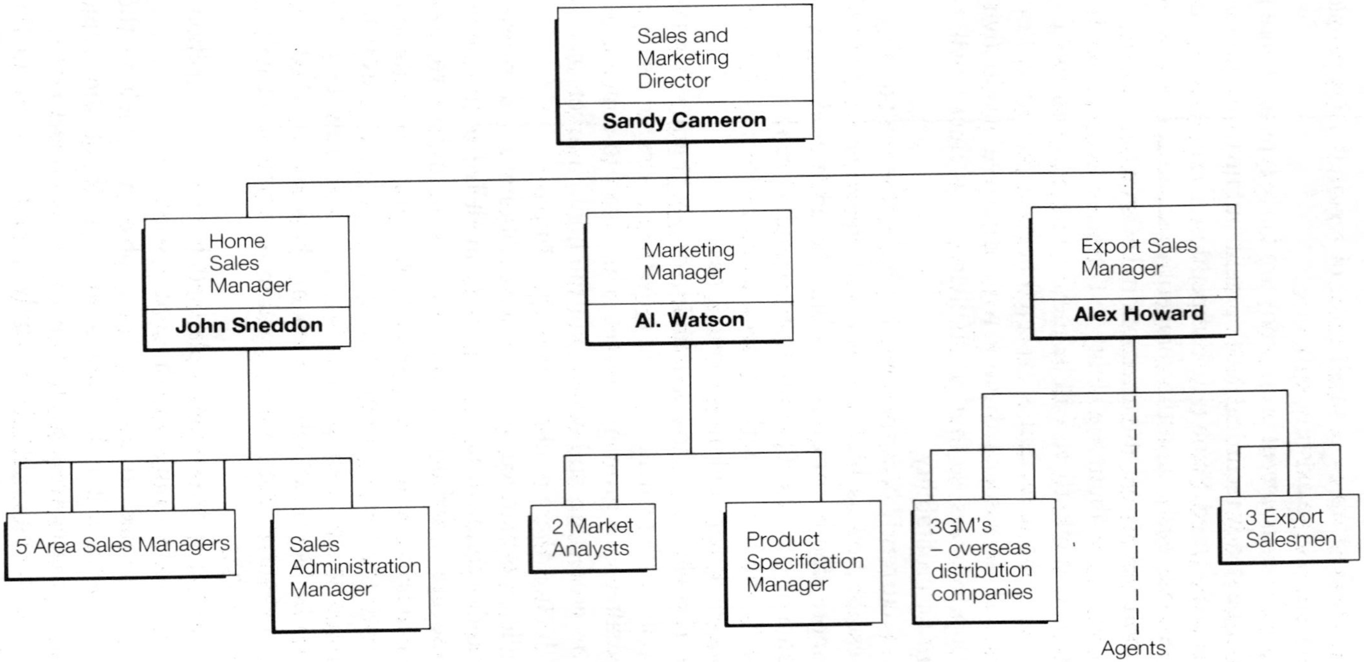


**Example 6** Organisation – current *Note:* Excludes clerical and secretarial grades.

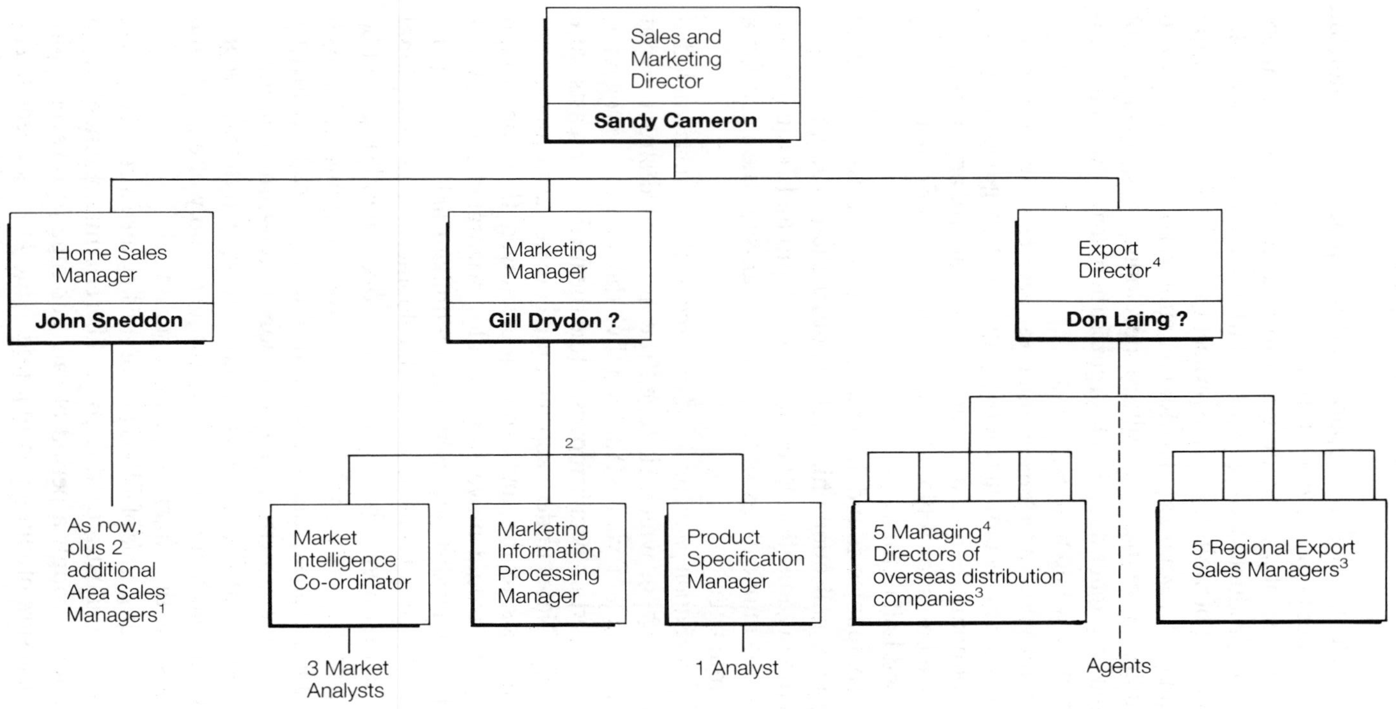

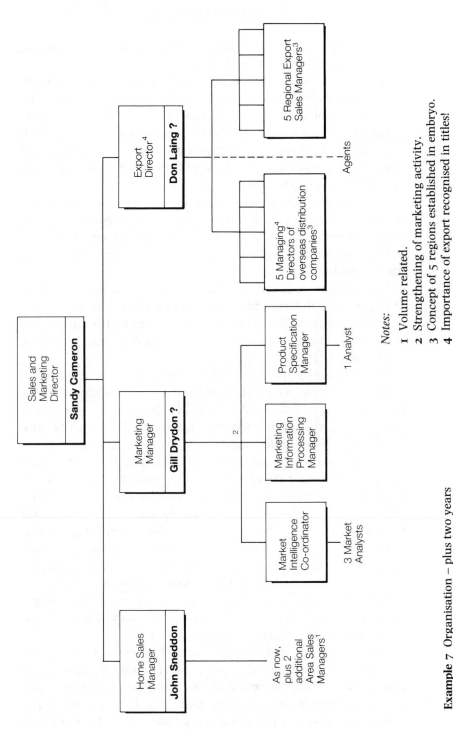

**Example 7** Organisation – plus two years

*Notes:*

1 Volume related.
2 Strengthening of marketing activity.
3 Concept of 5 regions established in embryo.
4 Importance of export recognised in titles!

prepare field intelligence reports and will link a proportion of bonus payments to implementation.

A further strategy was designed to link marketing staff more closely to product development – but does not anticipate the development of multi-discipline project teams within the duration of the plan. Development of better customer relations and concern for quality were part of culture development strategies, not expected to impact directly on organisation structure, but influencing 'how we do it' in some jobs.

The embryonic overseas companies were expected to develop dramatically; to become far more significant; to begin local manufacture of home designs and later some local product variations; to become bases for regional management of world sales during the second half of the plan.

The companies found it difficult to evaluate the impact of changing organisation philosophies, other than to adopt a policy of keeping organisation levels to a minimum, and could identify no cultural implications other than recognising the need for a quality manager.

The *organisation plan* consisted of three further charts, included as examples 7–9, which sketched the anticipated structures at two, five and ten years. Additionally, the two-year projection anticipated certain people moves, while the further forecasts were less specific. Notes under each plan indicate key assumptions.

An analysis of the top export job showed that the person specification would move from a sales orientated requirement towards a generalist one, with the incumbent able to direct the growth of a major international development. The provisional view was that a very high potential young generalist should be appointed within two years, on a three-year assignment; followed by an older, top ranking and proven director to lead the further rapid overseas growth. In terms of job grading, the changes in that job might justify an upward move every two to three years. In contrast, the home sales job might justify only one additional notch at some time later in the plan period.

The changing *scale* of jobs is one of the key measures of change. (Example 10 illustrates this in a different management team progressing through a period of rapid change.) However, more than a *measure* of change is required – the *form* is needed. The companies on which this sequence is based were able to outline

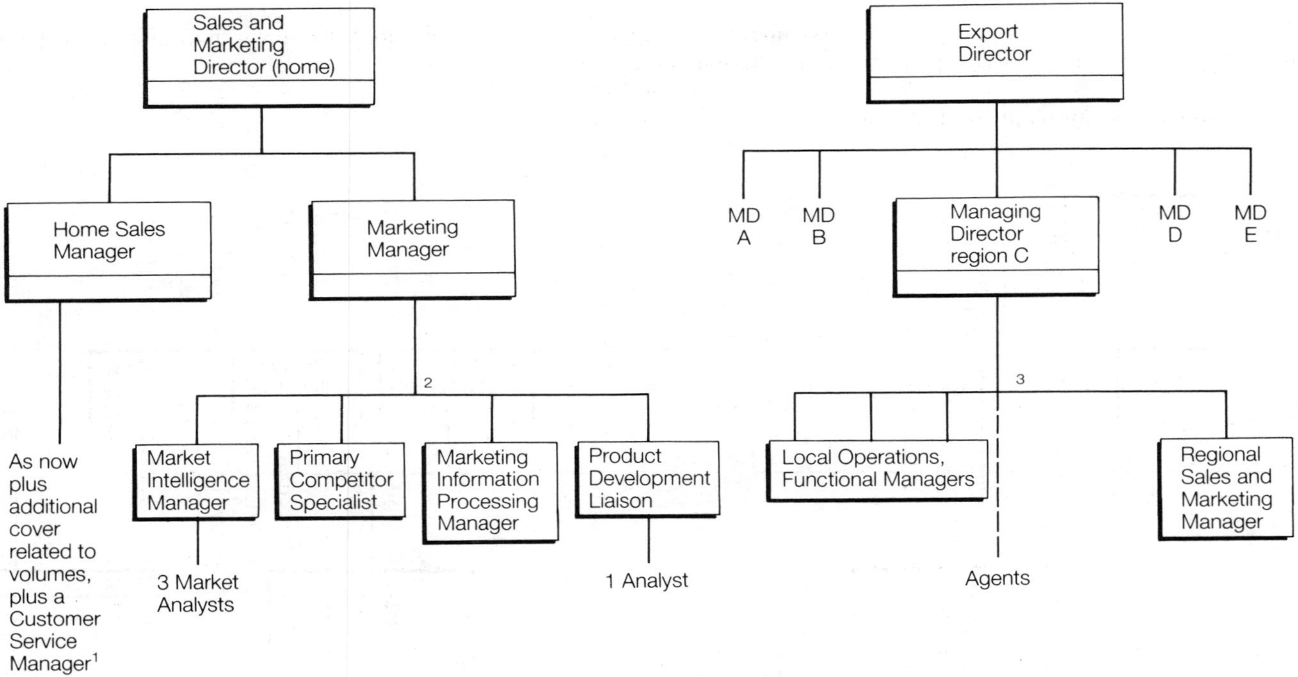

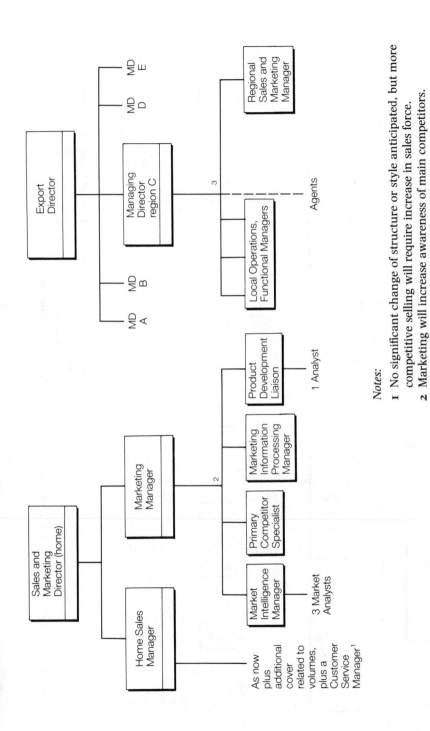

**Example 8** Organisation – plus five years

*Notes:*

1 No significant change of structure or style anticipated, but more competitive selling will require increase in sales force.
2 Marketing will increase awareness of main competitors.
3 Regional structure planned for year 5, but could be earlier.

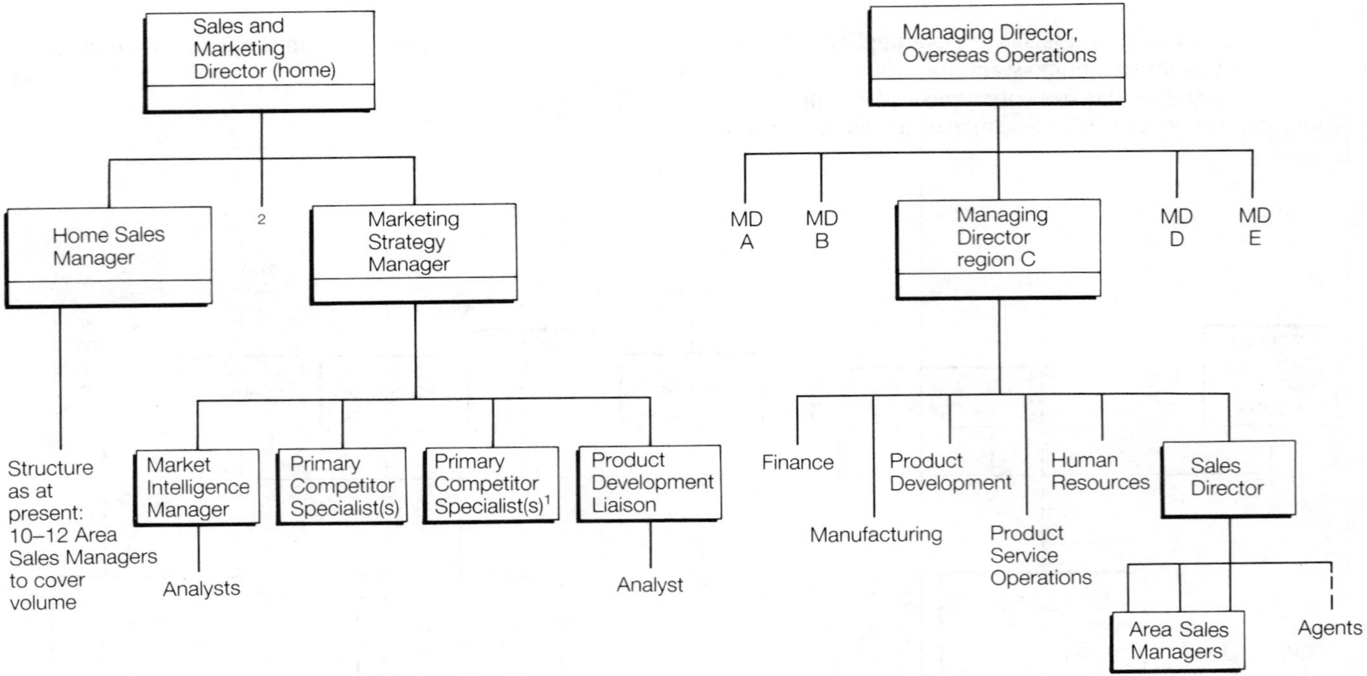


**Example 9** Organization – ten-year projection

*Notes:*

1 Marketing information should be fully integrated into management database.

2 Possible appointment of a Product Service Manager (related to future generation of products).

| Grade levels | Present establishment | 1-year forecast | 2-year forecast | 5-year forecast |
|---|---|---|---|---|
| 18 | – | – | – | 1 |
| 17 | – | – | – | – |
| 16 | – | 1 | 1 | 2 |
| 15 | 1 | – | – | 2 |
| 14 | – | 3 | 3 | 3 |
| 13 | 3 | 2 | 2 | 7 |
| 12 | 2 | 6 | 8 | 14 |
| 11 | 7 | 11 | 13 | 18 |
| 10 | 11 | 12 | 18 | 29 |
| 9 | 14 | 21 | 32 | 35 |
| 8 | 25 | 23 | 36 | 41 |

**Example 10** Forecast of manpower requirements by grade from a rapidly growing company

many of the jobs in the structure and consider the changes likely in the competencies required. From this data they were able to feed realistic future requirements into the next stage, the Review process, to influence the preparation of their future managers and the provisional matching of individuals with specific positions. The plan made no allowance for any acquisition, although the company planned to look for small ones which would supplement the product range. Nor did it develop any contingency plans. It assumed that any acquisition would run in parallel for a minimum of one year, during which time the relative strengths and cultures could be examined and logical plans developed to achieve integration, which it did not expect would divert it from its 'grand design'.

In general, I find this detailed picture of greatest use in continuity planning and for overall management development, where it is vital to see the future structure for which people are being prepared. Beyond this detail, broad numerical analysis gives some order of magnitude to the scale of recruitment and development required, although experience suggests that additional demands are constantly underestimated.

Example 11 shows such an analysis from a group of building companies. This has limitations in that it does not cover the evolution in the content, objectives and specifications of positions which retain established titles, but it does provide a clear summary of the scale of the recruitment and development tasks.

## SUMMARY

Analysis of the numbers and categories of managers who will be required to fill the organisation in the future involves 'exploding' the planned organisation to develop a forecast of the detail. This is possible, drawing on the full detail encapsulated within the business objectives and associated strategies and scenarios. While the result is unlikely to be particularly accurate in the longer term in companies undergoing substantial change, it will provide guidance on the management development programmes necessary and on the level and type of graduate intake and other recruitment required.

| | Totals | | | Losses | | | | Supply | | |
|---|---|---|---|---|---|---|---|---|---|---|
| | | | | | | | | | External Recruitment | |
| Category | Now | 5-year forecast | Increase | % PA | Over 5 years | Promotions out | Total requirements over 5 years | Internal promotions | Total | Annual rate |
| CEO of subsidiary | 5 | 8 | 3 | – | 2 | – | 5 | 3 | 2 | – |
| Branch VP | 1 | 7 | 6 | – | 3 | 3 | 12 | 3 | 9 | 2 |
| Contracts VP | 4 | 8 | 4 | – | 2 | 1 | 7 | 5 | 2 | – |
| Contracts Director | 13 | 22 | 9 | 10% | 8 | 5 | 22 | 20 | 2 | – |
| Contracts Manager | 18 | 32 | 14 | 10% | 13 | 20 | 47 | 5 | 42 | 8 |
| General Foremen | 38 | 76 | 38 | 20% | 57 | 5 | 100 | 50 | 50 | 10 |
| Foremen | 26 | 60 | 34 | 20% | 43 | 50 | 127 | – | 127 | 25 |
| Surveyor-Director | 5 | 8 | 3 | 10% | 3 | 1 | 7 | 6 | 1 | – |
| Surveyor-Manager | 12 | 22 | 10 | 15% | 12 | 6 | 28 | 24 | 4 | 1 |
| Surveyor | 16 | 30 | 14 | 20% | 23 | 24 | 61 | – | 61 | 12 |
| Director-Estimator/Planner/Buyer | 12 | 24 | 12 | 10% | 4 | 1 | 17 | 12 | 5 | 1 |
| Manager-Estimator/Planner/Buyer | 18 | 32 | 14 | 10% | 12 | 12 | 38 | 30 | 8 | 2 |
| Estimator/Planner/Buyer | 28 | 50 | 22 | 15% | 30 | 30 | 82 | – | 82 | 16 |

**Example 11** Forecast of management and specialist staff requirements in a construction group

# PART IV

# Bringing Needs and Supply Together

# *Introduction*

The first half of this book has emphasised that management development can only have purpose if it is totally integrated with overall business development, and has examined the very many influences on future management requirements which affect not only the number, but also the categories, levels and competencies concerned.

The second half of the book will be concerned with the provision of those needs, but first it is necessary to bring together in a single process a matching of all the detail of future management requirements with the evolving inventory of managers, in order to plan the resourcing of the organisation most effectively now and into the future, while facilitating the optimum growth and development of all these individuals.

Part IV is about that process.

# IV.I

## *Review process*

### WHAT IS THE REVIEW PROCESS?

The Review process, bringing needs and supply together, is *the single most important part of this whole management development process,* although it is frequently given insufficient time and attention. This may be because bringing all the data together can seem complex and difficult to grasp, but any reduction in complexity can be achieved only by discounting some of the data or taking sections, so that the full potential for effective resourcing and optimum development is reduced.

Example 12 summarises the total process in simplified flow chart form, reinforcing 'integration'. This is the bringing together of business and people data to ensure that the management requirements of the business are being met properly, both now and into the future; and at the same time, the abilities, growth potential and preferences of all the individual managers are taken fully into account so that each can develop as fully as is practicable. Example 13 is an expanded version, which enlarges the resourcing and development aspects.

It must be emphasised that this is a 'complex piece of machinery', so that any flaw in any one part can bring down the efficiency of the whole machine.

It is a process which can absorb a lot of time, and cannot be undertaken every time there is a decision to be made about a single appointment or attendance at a training course. The purpose of the Review is to provide for comprehensive consideration of all needs, business and individual, across the total scene, so that a complete pattern of decisions can be taken about all anticipated resourcing and development actions required over the months ahead.

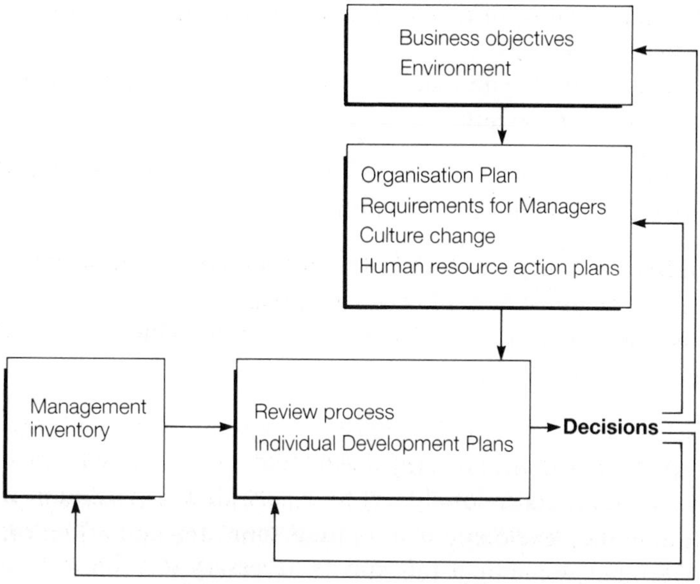


**Example 12** The Review process in perspective: demand and supply

This comprehensive Review provides the preliminary decision on all actions which follow. There may be sound reasons for a change of decision, but then the options and alternatives which were considered in depth in the Review itself should provide the starting point for any fresh assessment. If some new requirement emerges, the considerations in the Review should help define the options quickly, and the implications of alternative actions. Should the scale of unplanned change be extensive, a fresh review cycle might be initiated, at least locally, to re-establish planned evolution.

## SCOPE OF THE REVIEW PROCESS

In the Review process itself, the management task is to balance the many competing and sometimes conflicting elements. Some examples might be:

- the 'ideal' candidate who is not attracted to an opportunity or to the career direction involved
- competition for an individual who could fill any one of several openings

- uncertain timing of developments, which affects the timing of deployments
- varying pace of individual development so that people become ready early or too late.

The Review process cannot plan for events which develop at short notice, but should be flexibile enough to cope with:

- sudden needs which occur following an acquisition or new business opportunity, not allowed for in plans
- retention actions to avoid the loss of key individuals, conflicting with established plans.

The Review process is the 'master programme' which integrates management resourcing and development activity with business planning at an operational level to ensure that organisation structures and the development of management resources are aligned with the management requirements necessary to achieve business objectives and to respond to a changing and possibly hostile environment. In parallel it should optimise the utilisation and development of the management and other human resources available. The emphasis in most Reviews will be on the short-term, one to two year actions, but there must be a longer term three to five or five to ten year horizon for much of the associated planning, addressed under the management continuity heading, although using the same Review process.

The Review process is designed to bring together all the relevant information at regular intervals, and to use this data to re-examine, at every level:

- the clarity and relevance of present and planned future organisation and the competencies which will be required
- the effectiveness of the organisation and the deployment of the people within
- the relevance, suitability and implementation of individual development plans (IDPs).

Outputs from each Review should include:

- decisions on early organisation changes and on all anticipated appointments through to two to three months after the next scheduled review

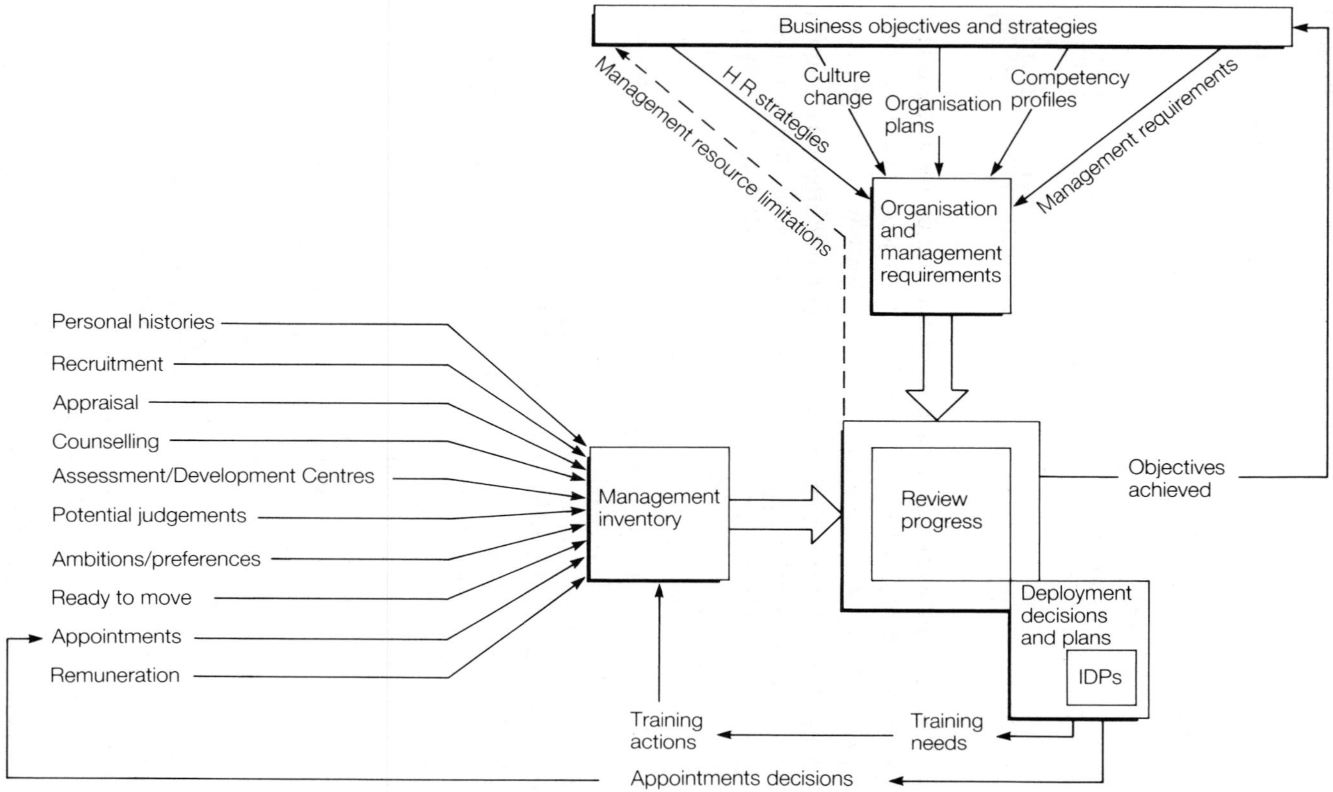


**Example 13** Management development: the Review process in perspective

- approval of all IDPs as a basis for all short- to medium-term development and training actions
- decisions related to longer term organisation, culture, appointments and development plans
- confirmation that business requirements can be resourced (or not).

All management development activities should stem from the Review process which is a process of continual reappraisal to identify problems, respond to new or changed needs, and then to implement actions or monitor progress towards action. It is essentially the means of driving the process for making management resourcing and development work within the business, and of involving management at every level in a network of associated decisions and actions. In addition to concentration on meeting the management needs of the business, it seeks full utilisation and optimum growth of management talent and, for example, will draw particular attention to the readiness of high potential managers for development moves, or to other priority issues.

## OPERATING THE REVIEW PROCESS: PERIODIC FULL REVIEW

### Comprehensive involvement

The way the Review process operates is likely to vary enormously from one enterprise to the next, but the principles should be more uniform. The most critical of these is involvement. All of the management group should participate, with the lowest levels contributing their parts first, and progressive reviews forming a 'reverse cascade' up through the structure (see example 14), finishing with a review of overall management development effectiveness, and of management continuity at the very top.

At the beginning of the process, a manager should discuss privately with each manager who reports directly to him, issues which are relevant to them and which are within the scope of the Review process. Subsequently, he should meet with his subordinate managers as a group, to consider issues of common interest, such as the development of high ability people who need to broaden by movement between functions, or organisational issues affecting more than one manager. Only when he has completed these Reviews

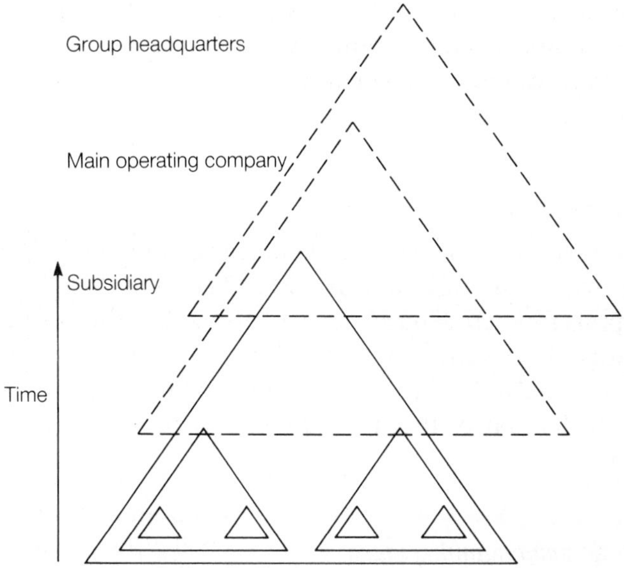


**Example 14** The Review process: an 'inverted cascade', building from small, local reviews up to the central board

with his people can he prepare for the Review with *his* boss. A reasonable target time for each level might be three weeks, if planned early into business diaries.

As Reviews progress up the structure, they should concentrate on the immediate two (or three) levels in the organisation, progressively dropping off those at lower levels. However, individuals thought to have high potential should remain visible, regardless of present level, as they should be seen as a corporate resource.

## Paperwork

The supporting paperwork will vary, with much being prepared as working notes for the participating managers, but it is sensible to assemble and retain some basic record of discussion and agreements to enable progress to be monitored later, or as the starting point for fresh consideration if an unforeseen development should occur. There might be four sections in the notes:

1 Business and environmental changes.
2 Organisation and manning reviews.
3 Human resource action plans.
4 Updated IDPs.

*Business and environment changes*

This first section should record the business situation and assumptions on which the Review was based. The notes might include a brief appraisal of actual business progress against the business plan, and changes in the environment which differ from the assumptions in the associated environmental scenario; followed by updated views and an evaluation of the implications for human resource management

*Organisation and manning plans*

This section should concentrate on the immediate organisation structure, including any fresh thinking on its evolution, and the filling of all management positions – both currently and into the future, including preparatory development. Example 15 shows how discussion was summarised by one manager for his unit, the format being much the same as would be used for formal management continuity planning (which is effectively what he is doing).

*Human resource action plans*

This section is a smaller scale replica of the human resource action plans detailed in chapter II.4, and will include reference to major human resource strategies associated with the achievability of business objectives. There should be notes on progress against the 'milestones' in current action plans, plus details of any new plans triggered by new business or environmental developments, and the human resource implications.

*The Individual Development Plans*

The final section of notes should record progress in implementing existing IDPs, noting additions and deletions resulting from fresh appraisals and counselling (or changes to individual preferences), as well as those resulting from altered business and environmental influences. Identified needs for action at a higher organisational level or on a wider scale should be passed up the line; for example, where career progression of an able manager is blocked locally, or where a transfer to another function is required.

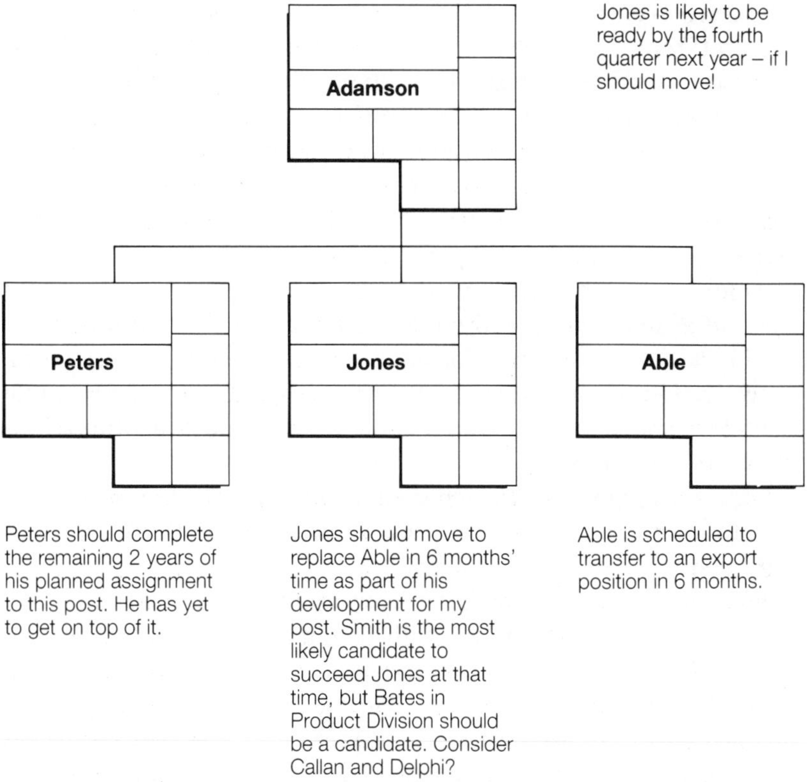
Adamson
Jones is likely to be ready by the fourth quarter next year – if I should move!
Peters
Jones
Able
Peters should complete the remaining 2 years of his planned assignment to this post. He has yet to get on top of it.
Jones should move to replace Able in 6 months' time as part of his development for my post. Smith is the most likely candidate to succeed Jones at that time, but Bates in Product Division should be a candidate. Consider Callan and Delphi?
Able is scheduled to transfer to an export position in 6 months.

**Example 15** Section of a departmental review summary

## Frequency

The frequency of this process should be determined by need. A company in a rapidly changing high technology sector might properly run through it at quarterly intervals, and have strong line management support for what it sees as a sensible discipline which keeps its organisation and utilisation of managers finely tuned. In less dynamic industries, a major annual review, plus a less formal but ongoing mid-year update, may be sufficient. If the frequency is only once a year, attention to the career development of the younger high potential managers will need some separate attention at the half way stage.

## Incentive to contribute to the process

The drive to carry through the Review process must come from the top and from the line managers, who must recognise the value to themselves and to the business or they will not spend the time! The human resource function may need to provide some of the drive plus some strong administrative back-up. Reviews are competing for allocation of management time and can only succeed if they demonstrate their contribution to business development and profitability; not by traditional personnel argument.

Line ownership of this activity is properly stressed. This may operate at two levels, as there is some logic in sharing ownership in the career management of small numbers of high ability people between their immediate managers and corporate management, as development may need to be on a wider scale than immediate managers can provide.

Local management is generally supportive if the process is working properly and they can see value for their efforts, but even then resistance to Review activity may arise around operational issues. The classic difficulty is that experienced by the line manager who has a high performing, high potential subordinate manager who is clearly ready for his next career step, but who will leave a substantial hole when he moves. The line manager is acutely aware of the danger to his own performance, and seeks to retain his key subordinate, particularly when offered a young and unproven successor as replacement.

There is no perfect answer to this situation and the line manager's conclusion that 'The only thing that comes out of these Reviews is that I lose my best people'. It is vital that a manager giving up an excellent individual should be sympathetically supported and provided with a replacement of similar calibre (even though less experienced), *particularly if he has proved to be a good developer of subordinates.* It does not take long for a manager to become known as a good developer, whose staff are invariably in demand and move on well, and then he is able to pick from the excellent people who wish to come to him.

Inter-functional moves may be difficult to arrange without senior management involvement, but these are primarily for the exceptional people, expected to go far and for whom multi-functional experience is a prelude to more general responsibilities (as a generalist, or back as the top man in his function). Usually, these moves need to capitalise on knowledge of the immediate business and be 'local' to business areas the individual knows well, so that his fast learning is limited to the new functional area. In the same way intercompany or divisional moves should generally be within functional disciplines, so that the fast learning is limited to the new business area.

## Application to individual decisions

The periodic in-depth Review establishes a scenario or framework of 'preliminary decisions', following which there will be many day to day actions to take a final view and then to implement the Review decisions. For example, a chain of individual moves and appointments may be planned in detail to follow a retirement. These should be under scrutiny as the implementation time approaches, and they would normally be implemented in a straightforward fashion.

However, one of the links in the chain may 'fail'. Someone may resign, or performance may falter, or a range of other circumstances may arise, causing the plan to be reshaped. If this occurs, the obvious starting point for fresh consideration should be the notes from the previous Review supporting the original intention, which may record the options and contingencies considered. It is logical to go over this ground in detail, starting from the original Review. It should not be acceptable to take a fresh *ad hoc* decision which is quite unrelated to the careful and wider ranging considerations which took place in the Review process.

All other actions requiring change should make the same reference back to the comprehensive discussion. For example, a decision to send someone on a training course is likely to have been planned as a part of his longer term development plan; secondments may occur to meet an emergency but are more likely to have been planned ahead to broaden experience; a proposed change to an IDP may have arisen on the basis of one incident, but should be viewed against the full assessment and track record; and so on.

Perhaps the most serious unscheduled action occurs when a key person resigns, or when an unplanned business opportunity requires an immediate appointment. The Review process may have considered these possibilities and noted contingency plans, but more often the necessary actions will disturb the plan. One such appointment recently was followed by a chain of seven others down the line, severely disturbing the entire plan. If that happens, a fresh Review of that sector of the business becomes a necessity. Indeed, any event which triggers a significant volume of unscheduled deployment change should be followed by a full Review to assess the degree of weakness caused and the actions which can be taken to reinforce the reserves of management.

## SUMMARY

The Review process integrates human resource development and deployment plans and actions with the evolving needs of the business. The process operates on an ongoing basis at every level of management, with periodic total Reviews from the bottom up to the top levels of the business.

Decisions about deployments of people are closely integrated with IDPs, which detail career development direction, possible appointments, and development and training preparatory actions.

The process is 'fluid', in that evaluations of the business are progressive (the environment and the development and deployment of individuals are changing continually) so that the Review takes place against a 'current position' which is ephemeral rather than fixed. Options and contingencies require the process to be continuous to enable current decisions about organisation and people to be well thought through, but always provide a basis for re-examination before implementation.

PART V

# The Supply of Managers

# *Introduction*

The earlier parts of this book examined the ways you can determine the future direction of business development, and recognised the extent to which inadequate human resources might limit that ambition. They went on to show how the Review process brings all business and management resource considerations together to establish the human resource strategies and actions necessary to implement business plans.

Management development is a complex activity of many parts, each contributing one element to the preparation of your future managers, and each existing for a specific, business related purpose.

This part examines these many elements; comments on the way they should contribute to a business individually or jointly; and examines what you can realistically expect from them, and practical applications which should contribute to gaining competitive advantage.

# V.I

## *Management resourcing and development*

### IN GENERAL

Management resourcing and development should be seen as a mainstream tool for developing business performance. It is the *total process* of preparing and providing effective managers, and refining their performance now and for the future.

This is not a 'single activity', as it requires a range of associated activities to be going on in parallel, related and interdependent. It will not be fully effective unless it is a complete process which addresses all the relevant issues and where the parts work together. It is not unreasonable to liken the process to an organism in which every part affects the others.

### Potential shortcomings

Many of the shortcomings in management development result from:

- activities not being followed through, which may occur even where the system elements are excellent
- activities not being designed to meet the needs of the business
- insufficient recognition of the impact of environmental change on the business, its future organisation, culture and management competency requirements.

Typical examples of the first of these include a good performance appraisal scheme not followed through with counselling discussion between appraiser and appraised; systematic assessment of potential not followed through with appropriate career planning and development; career development well thought through and planned but poorly implemented; remuneration policy objectives not associated with management development objectives. These, and many other discontinuities, can cripple the effectiveness of otherwise excellent schemes – and are surprisingly common.

## Designing the process

The design of management resourcing and development policies and practices must stem from the needs of the business rather than simply be idealistic. These needs should be readily apparent from the evolution of achievable business objectives, in which human resource strategies are embodied as an integral part of what must be achieved to enable the overall objectives to be reached. Non-achievement of the human resource strategies would place the overall plan at risk.

Not everything will be fully defined in these strategies. For example, the organisation and management plan will have been developed subsequently, but failure to provide the numbers and types of managers who will be needed would have an equally dramatic adverse impact on implementation.

The process of management resourcing and development must ensure that no key element is overlooked; that the coverage is comprehensive and the interdependence of the parts is clear. Also, it should incorporate a monitoring activity to ensure that requirements are followed through from each activity to the next, as failure to complete things may provide the greatest vulnerability. There can be little more misleading than formulating a full and convincing management development programme and then realising much later that the component parts are operating in isolation and ineffectively.

The final component in the process, and ultimately the most important, is the Review process, which brings the contributions of all the management resourcing and development activities together to generate a series of objective resourcing and development decisions and plans, which in turn provide the backcloth for the many individual resourcing or development plans and actions. This Review, and indeed the entire management development procedure, can be driven by a series of principles with great flexibility or variation in detailed practice. No standard procedure and culture are demanded, as long as the principles remain absolute.

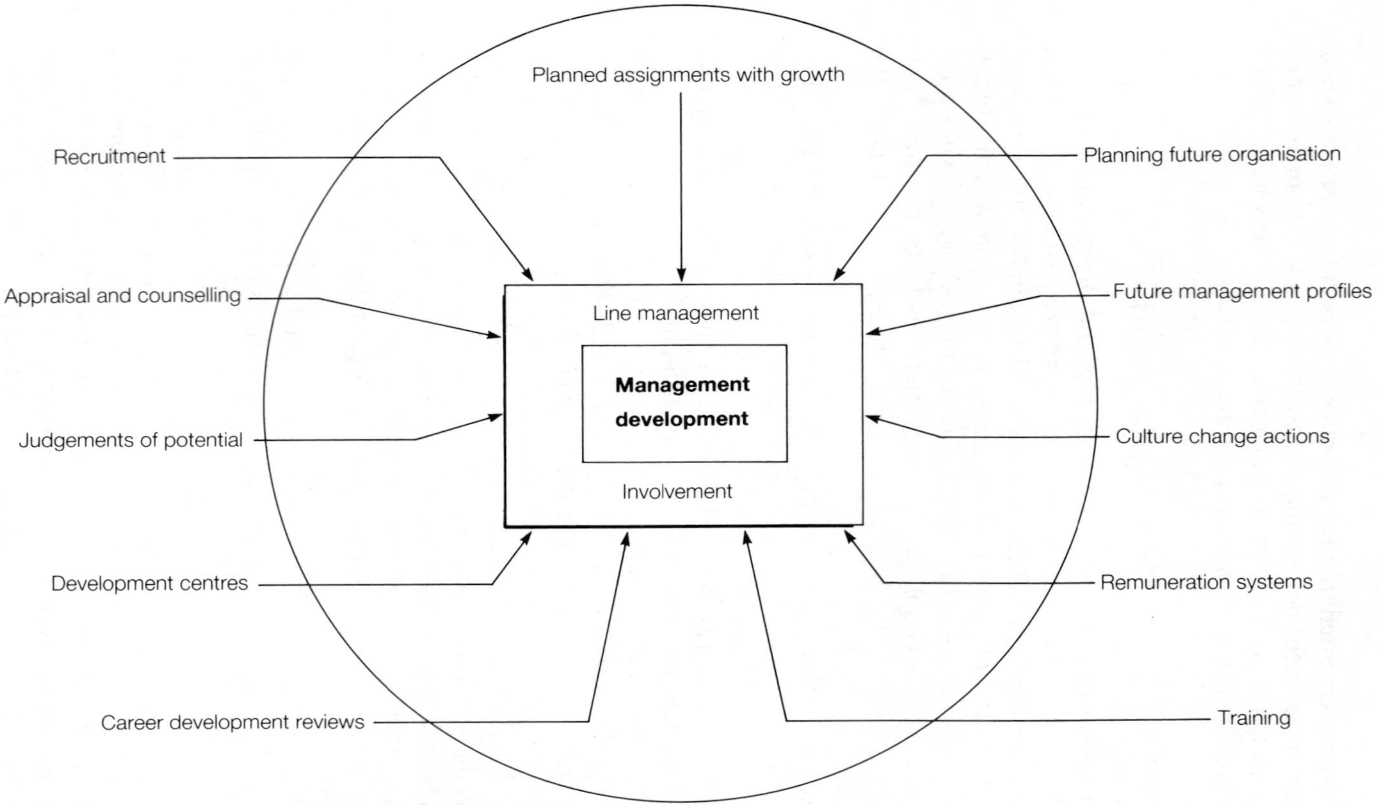


**Example 16** Management development: the contributing activities

Example 16 shows management development as a complex activity contributed to by many separate parts, which in turn are linked as they also contribute one to another. It is necessary for all these parts to be properly designed, used and linked for the total activity to be fully effective. All the mass of detail assembled about the people side of the business, which provides the basis for all people decisions, comes from these various components of the management development process.

## Establishing the needs of the business

Management resourcing and development must be driven by the needs of the business, for none of the various activities have any purpose in isolation. Of each part, you need to question 'What is it contributing to the business?'. For example, resourcing is concerned with providing the people necessary to run the business, but is dependent on contributions from other activities – for example, to clarify the competencies required now and in the future. Judgements of potential contribute to the provision of future management, and to the retention of good people in the shorter term. Appraisal is concerned with improving current effectiveness, and also with optimising the outlay on remuneration.

*This business linkage is further reinforced if line management owns the process*; if the line manager is deeply involved in determining how the activity is to operate. The human resource specialist is advised to contribute from a general business standpoint (and in that language), and to build systems around the understanding and preferences of his operational colleagues. This requires the specialist to ensure that his line colleagues properly understand any specialist/technical human resource contribution which may be necessary, such as the use of psychometrics, and to support its use. He cannot insist on a technical mystique which comes to be regarded as 'black magic'. In the end, the system may not always be perfect in professional terms, but if it works and is used because the line people feel it is 'theirs', that *is* perfection!

### COMPONENT PARTS

The parts of management resourcing and development, the ways they contribute to business performance and how they interrelate are outlined below.

## Database of personal information

This involves the collection and assembly of all relevant data about each individual and provides the authoritative source of reference for all reviews and decisions. It will be continuously evolving, with an in-feed of new information and with some data becoming out of date. It is essential that they are kept up-to-date (incomplete data quickly reduce the credibility of the entire database), and it is vital that the inputs are valid and objective, with proper qualification attached to any recorded 'snap judgements'. Finally, the database must be easily accessible for managers with the right to access the data.

## Management inventory

The raw database needs to be analysed to provide an 'inventory' of management which can be set against overall needs and provide a basis for policy judgements of the adequacy of the 'present stock'. Analyses of the 'flows' of people along normal career paths can be particularly valuable in assessing future supplies.

## Resourcing and recruitment

The quality of staffing at every level can have a real impact on business efficiency. Many management appointments need to be planned to last for periods of one to three years, as the appointees will need that time to develop and become ready for fresh opportunities. This suggests that there will be appointments to something around one-third of all management positions each year.

Every vacancy is a development opportunity to be filled internally if possible. The requirements for the post must be clearly determined, and the search to find the most suitable candidate must be thorough. The quality of judgements covering both internal and external candidates needs to be excellent, and a range of techniques for finding the right person is available.

## Appraisal of performance

Appraisal programmes have varied objectives, but the primary need is for a means of improving the performance of managers in their present jobs to improve overall efficiency. Secondly, appraisal contributes to the database on which individual development potential can be assessed. Appraisal will also influence decisions on remuneration, but care needs to be exercised to distance this application from the primary purpose.

Counselling, and the understanding and development of the interpersonal skills involved, are key elements in making appraisal work properly, as well as for the effective managing of people generally.

## Judgement of potential

Identifying people with the potential to advance to the higher levels of management is immensely important to the long-term management continuity of the business.

The potential to do a different or higher level job is always difficult to judge. It is necessary to understand what potential is, and how judgements can be made or improved, using a range of analyses and projections of data on performance, plus other techniques such as assessment centres and psychometrics which can add substantially to the reliability of judgements.

## Preferences, ambitions and mobility

Planning career development can prove wasteful of time and money unless the basic preferences, ambitions and mobility of individuals are known and factored in. This important contribution to the database should be obtained and updated regularly by managers from discussions with their subordinates.

## Individual Development Plans

Optimising individual development does not just happen but requires great care and planning on the part of both individual and company. However, satisfaction with personal career development may be the strongest single influence on management retention. The varied components of how individuals develop or may be developed provide the building blocks. From these the vitally important IDPs evolve, recorded in some straightforward way. These enable all development plans and actions to be monitored, to ensure they were realistic and logical in that they prove effective; that no key factors were overlooked; that they were successfully implemented; that development plans achieve the required preparation for the next appointment.

## Development: high fliers

'High fliers' may be seen as an elite group, a corporate resource which is the most likely source of future top management, and, as such, justifies top management interest and involvement. The extent to which high fliers should be an 'elite', the special attention they require, and the reaction of other managers to elite treatment for the few, need to be considered in each organisation or culture.

## Development: Self-development

Personal ownership of career development has become very important. This is frequently recognised in corporate culture, which should encourage individual development initiatives, even where these do not appear to involve personal development of immediate and direct relevance to the company. Individual self-development should be blended with company initiatives and opportunities wherever possible, but excellent value may be obtained from an able manager during a development phase leading towards a different career.

## Training needs

Before training begins, it is necessary to concentrate on establishing training *needs* systematically. These needs arise from both the individual and the organisation; from the demands of current activity, and from personal and business development in the future. Training can absorb enormous volumes of cash and time resources, so that priorities need to be determined.

## Training actions

Training *actions* must be designed to meet defined and agreed priority needs, but as they can still be expensive in money and in management time, they must also be seen to have clear purpose and to add value. Where possible, training activity should be designed and linked to visible impact on the bottom line. Provision of the required human resources in future is likely to become more dependent on training and retraining, particularly for some categories of specialist managers whose knowledge is in short supply.

## Continuity and succession plans

Management continuity is a vital responsibility for present management. Although ongoing, it tends to be subject to annual audit in the form of statements of succession plans which can be reviewed. These are a valuable part of assessing both the current and long-term effectiveness of the management development process, in that the provision of an adequate supply of suitable candidates at every level of management, as indicated by continuity planning, is a primary purpose of management development!

## Remuneration issues

Remuneration practice provides an important supporting role. It can be a valuable aid to, or have an inhibiting effect on, influencing behaviour and culture and on practical management resourcing and development. 'Reward management', of course, is a much wider concern, with actual career advancement being the primary reward.

### SUMMARY

Management resourcing and development covers all the activities involved in ensuring the preparation and supply of the managers required now and into the future, and in enhancing their abilities and opportunities to achieve high performance standards.

These various activities contribute independently to business needs and performance, but they also link with and contribute to one another. For optimum effectiveness of the management development process, it is necessary for all the various linkages to operate smoothly – there should be no discontinuities.

The Review process, in whatever form it takes in a particular enterprise, is the single most important element, in that it brings the contributions of all these activities into a single focus on their ultimate objective, which is measurable in terms of the adequacy of the provision of prepared managers (from internal and external sources) to meet all business requirements, and the competence of those managers to achieve the required business results.

# V.2

## *Management inventory and analysis*

### SOURCE AND DETAILS OF THE DATA

The supply of management to meet requirements can come from internal or external sources. The preferred source for most positions is internal. You need to know in detail the extent to which you can meet current and future requirements for managers from the people already employed. If it is concluded that the full requirement cannot be met internally, it will be necessary to plan to recruit from external sources, which may have long lead times. If it is found that there are numbers of people in certain categories who will become surplus to requirements, then time to plan retraining, redeployment or redundancy will be essential.

To assess the adequacy of your management resources, a comprehensive inventory of the 'stock' and the ways it is expected to evolve is required. This inventory should be in the form of a database, continually updated, from which meaningful analyses can be developed. It must, therefore, incorporate detailed information on all managers and potential managers, including the following:

- Complete personnel histories and track records, maintained fully up-to-date and including new or changed information on appointments, appraisal, potential assessments, ambitions, preferences, and mobility, training, and readiness for the next move.
- Imminent or planned changes of deployment, including assignments, projects or terminations.

All the data you require about people for organisation and management reviews, forward development and deployment planning, and so on, will come from this database.

MANAGING THE MANAGEMENT INVENTORY

The database has two main applications. It will be used to identify individuals with relevant skills and experience against specified needs. Also it will enable some assessment to be made of the overall internal supply position in relation to overall forecasts of management needs.

## Internal search

Within the Review process there is a frequent need to comb the full inventory for individuals who meet specifications for urgent or new or changed needs which have not previously been part of the forecast requirements. These specifications may be applied to immediate appointments, or to identify individuals who may be prepared within a given time frame. A degree of priority may be stated which may, for example, exclude people who are new in post or who are in exceptionally important positions and difficult to replace.

Once such a person specification is produced, a rapid search can be conducted to identify people who match it, following which a slower process examines their present and planned utilisation to determine which individuals might be best suited and most easily made available. From such a process, a short list of 'probables' may be produced for further discussion with their present managers and the managers 'owning' of the vacancy. All unexpected vacancies should be handled in this manner to determine whether internal resourcing is practical.

In the Review process, a large number of such examinations may be conducted as part of the process of exploring development options and establishing the optimum utilisation of the total existing management resource. The objective is to maximise the range of internal sources for future appointments and, in the process, to widen the range of career options for individuals. Inevitably, there will be some conflicts arising about the preferred utilisation and development of high ability people, and decisions to make, influenced on the one hand by corporate priorities and on the other by individual career preferences. The adequacy of time spent in the present job should also be a factor, to minimise ultra-short periods from which there cannot be adequate learning or contribution.

## Forecasting the supply position

Managing the inventory may be particularly important in situations of exceptionally rapid change, where projections of business and organisation appear to have an excess of uncertainty and the corporation needs to achieve maximum flexibility in deployment. Usually in these situations, it is the timing of change which is the greatest uncertainty. The database is then used to assist identification of possible candidates for positions at a series of points in time spread over the anticipated time limits. This approach will enable an assessment to be made of the ability to meet likely managerial requirements across a series of time options and enable realistic contingency plans to be developed.

### ANALYSIS AND STATISTICS

The inventory can provide a great deal of general information on overall management strength. Knowing the total number of employees is not particularly useful, but a breakdown of headcount into the main employment categories begins to be so. Jobs group naturally into a number of families or functions, which in turn sub-divide. For example, the personnel function breaks down into resourcing, development, training, remuneration, employee relations, and so on. A straightforward job coding system is generally useful if this sort of analysis is required.

Analysis of managers by function is likely to reveal some categories with quite small numbers, even in fairly large organisations. These specialist categories may offer very limited career scope in the company, and need to be marked out as categories where career development must be between units within a group of companies or is likely to be to and from other employers. While some of the individuals in these categories will be content in 'isolated' situations, many will prefer the option of joining organisations (or professional firms) with larger teams in their field, so that the attractions and rewards of a one-off post must be considered carefully. The head of the company medical function provides a good example.

## Age distribution

There is a view that age should not be treated as a limiting factor in employment and development issues, and demographic developments will further encourage an open mind. Even so, in general terms, younger people have the ability to learn and develop at a faster pace than their elders, so age is relevant to your considerations here, particularly where new skills are required. For example, the age profile in computer applications is still relatively young – and even more so in genetic engineering.

Analyses of age distribution, both overall and for various facets of the business, can identify potential problems such as the clustering of people in an age group which creates a blockage to the career progression of younger managers.

> A study by a large organisation revealed an age distribution at variance with the national pattern (apparently resulting from peaks and troughs of company recruitment activity). The board favoured action to 'improve the pattern' by 'favouring' recruitment of people born in the trough years, but, operationally, this proved unworkable and was dropped.

Such corrective action needs to be restricted to attention to real problems. There is no value in trying to achieve an ideal while the actual situation is perfectly workable. Indeed, in the case mentioned, the problem identified by the company was attributed to a business growth surge some ten years earlier which had resulted in numbers of overpromotions which eventually became serious blockages. In a similar situation, another group found that it had to 'outplace' a number of senior managers in their early forties who had advanced rapidly and become locked into posts seven to ten years earlier. They had become stale and had generally 'run out of drive', while younger, more able people were being blocked.

The national demographic pattern is going to present future age related challenges so that the internal age mix will need to be monitored. Through the early 1990s, the number of people reaching normal university entrance age will continue to decline, and the mix of ages of those graduating will be altered. The availability of 'young graduate' entrants will be reduced, and allowance for the entry of 'mature graduates' will need to be made. The effect of this on normal career progression profiles of graduate entrants and the supply of future managers will need to be monitored.

Two further age related analyses are worthwhile from time to time, both linked additionally to grade or job level. A straightforward analysis of age against grade, perhaps in the form of a scattergraph with a dot showing the age and grade position of each manager, will give a clear view of the distribution pattern, and highlight those people on the fastest rising tracks. A second analysis showing, at each job level, the relationship between age and time in a job or in the grade, provides a valuable means of spotting individuals who are becoming 'stuck' and whose career plans need reappraisal.

## Performance appraisal data

Unless there is some scoring procedure, statistical analysis based on appraisal data is difficult. However, if an internal search is carried out against a person specification, where high performance in the present job is one of the factors to be used to select possible candidates, it is useful to have some indication in the database of relative performance.

Generally, it is not necessary to have a precise gradation of relative performance. The concern will be to locate the best (or worst) performers, who can be identified in some way from the general bulk of less exceptional performers. An analysis of the best performers against the time they have spent in their current job may correlate with lists of high potential people becoming 'ready for a move'. An established manager with five years or more in his job should be on top of it, while high performance after only two to three years or less suggests rapid progress worth a closer look, not least because high ability people on top of a job begin to look for their next challenge and are very mobile.

## Potential ability

The same difficulty of measurement applies to potential, so some assessment of the extent of potential may be attempted. For example, the potential to rise one, two or three levels in the organisation within a set time frame might provide a useful measure.

One of the more valuable summaries can be extracted from continuity planning, listing, function by function and level by level, individuals considered as 'potential successors' and their degree of readiness. Analysis may show that a small number of names has been repeated many times over, revealing a thinness in continuity cover not previously obvious. Alternately, it may highlight the extensive cover available for, say, financial management, but a sparsity of future marketing and general managers.

There is a tendency to extract lists of individuals believed to have 'high potential', and this rating may be included in the database, together with forecasts of the expected extent and pace of possible advancement, for analysis of forward cover against anticipated management requirements. While somewhat crude, it does give an indication of how adequate or otherwise the cover may be, early enough to enable other actions to be taken to offset deficiencies.

Psychometric tests and assessment centre data can contribute rather more precision to judgements about apparent potential, but analyses of test results should be restricted to determining company norms, while individual scores should be viewed and interpreted professionally.

## Individual Development Plans

IDPs are a most important part of the database, particularly when managers are being matched against requirements, but they are even more difficult to analyse than is 'potential'. They are, of course, the product of all considerations balancing corporate needs with individual abilities and preferences, and consist of notes on career and deployment options and intentions, and specific development and training plans. It is possible to use the database system to monitor progress or implementation of specifics, but little more. Rather, the database itself is critical in contributing to objective career development planning.

## Turnover

The rates of loss of existing staff are contributing factors in management planning. The fact of loss is important to the company, in that each individual who leaves takes a knowledge of the company and of his job which can rarely be acquired ready-made from outside. The impact of leavers is invariably some reduction in full efficiency, at least for a period, even when a new internal appointment is made immediately.

However, a situation where *no* losses occur may be just as serious and should raise a number of questions. Is the management quality such that it is not employable elsewhere at comparable levels of responsibility and remuneration? Do managers feel 'locked in'? Are blockages restricting the career opportunities for high ability younger managers?

A company should monitor its staff losses and watch for changes in pattern. For example, an increase in the loss rate of recently hired graduates could have a serious impact on the future supply of potential managers. Graduate intake is a key programme designed to provide managers in the long-term, worthy of close attention to minimise losses and consolidate 'membership' of the company. Analysis of graduate departures frequently shows a peak loss rate after one and a half to two and a half years and completion of the second job. This links with the view held by some graduates that they must acquire experience in more than one company (a view which can be offset by positive career planning policies), and also with a tendency for some large employers to do some weeding out once performance and potential begin to be clear. Graduates who stay on beyond the three to four year stage are significantly less likely to leave (see example 17).

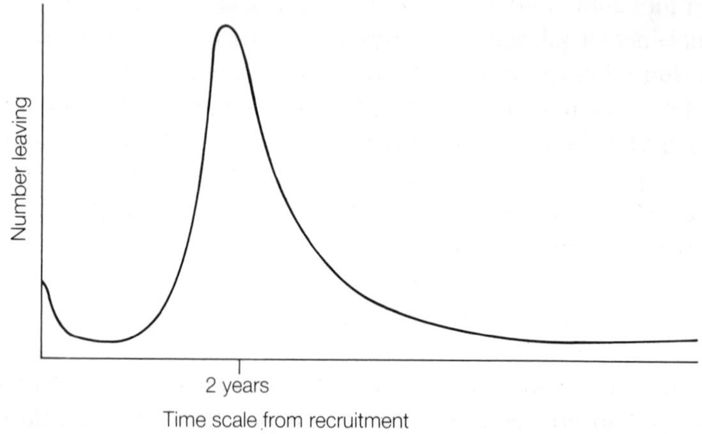


**Example 17** Losses from graduate intake and length of service

Another way of analysing turnover for categories such as graduates who are recruited in waves is to look at *survival rates*. Of the cohort recruited in, say, 1988, how many are still with the company and how does that compare with other years? Survival rates have a positive aspect (where losses or turnover sound negative).

## Promotion 'flow' patterns

The flows of individuals through jobs or grades or functions tend to form statistical patterns which are valuable as an aid to forecasting manpower supply and intake requirements. The analyses should cover several years if possible, so that any abnormal events are visible and any trend in flow patterns can be identified. Flow patterns are most valuable for forecasting flows from graduate or professional staff intake levels through to middle management. It is essential to look at the technical stream separate from the accounting stream, and so on.

At each level, record all the personnel movements which take place, to quantify the scale and form of the flow. Example 18 shows the flow through an engineering department (covering a single year). Example 19 covers a supplementary analysis to identify 'probability of promotion' norms for one of the engineer grades, based on data over a three-year period. A further analysis of lengths of service in the various engineer grades indicated that, in spite of a fast flow through, a number of individuals were getting stuck at each level, and these numbers had increased over the three-year period. Blockages could be expected to become a problem over a further two years of accumulation unless some action was taken.

Further analysis of flows will differentiate between people in 'fast streams' as distinct from those achieving average or slow progress. It may be relevant to consider administering career development separately for these streams, to pay particular attention to the future utilisation of people reaching their ceilings, as well as ensuring fast progress where it is justified.

As this study of flows moves beyond groups of similar managers into the zone of individual posts at the top of the management pyramid, statistical analysis ceases to be relevant; but a scheduling of succession moves in similar format may focus attention on the adequacy of cover or the amount of preparation still to be done. As flows become meaningless, the concern is with individual progression to specific posts. Example 44 in chapter V.13 on succession planning shows a summary page covering the top management of a company. An update of this summary is required by the group

| Category | Strength 1 January | Promotion from (1 grade) | Promotion from (2 grades) | Transfer to other divisions | Leavers | Total movement | % of total | Promotion to (1 grade) | Promotion to (2 grades) | Transfer from other divisions | Recruits | Strength 31 December |
|---|---|---|---|---|---|---|---|---|---|---|---|---|
| **Managers** | 6 | 1 | – | – | 1 | 2 | 33% | 1 | 1 | – | – | 6 |
| Senior Engineer I (Supervisors) | 8 | 1 | – | 1 | 1 | 3 | 37% | 1 | 1 | – | – | 7 |
| Senior Engineer II | 10 | 1 | 1 | 1 | 1 | 4 | 40% | 2 | 1 | – | 1 | 10 |
| Engineer I | 21 | 2 | 1 | – | 3 | 6 | 29% | 8 | – | 1 | 2 | 26 |
| Engineer II | 37 | 8 | 1 | 1 | 6 | 16 | 43% | 8 | – | – | 10 | 39 |
| Assistant Engineer | 14 | 8 | – | – | 1 | 9 | 64% | – | – | – | 8 | 13 |

*Plus further analyses by age groups, qualification levels, years of service in grade, etc.*

**Example 18** Analysis of manpower movement in engineering department board at six-monthly intervals as the plan unfolds, to provide reassurance that the continuity is developing. In practice, most plans get modified to some extent as judgements of individuals mature.

| Service in grade | Age | | | | |
|---|---|---|---|---|---|
| | 21–23 | 24–26 | 27–30 | 31–40 | 41 and over |
| Up to 1 year | 12% | 15% | 9% | – | – |
| 1 year and up to 2 years | 21% | 30% | 28% | 15% | – |
| 2 years and up to 3 years | – | 38% | 30% | 10% | – |
| 3 years and up to 5 years | – | 12% | 18% | 16% | 8% |
| 5 years and up to 10 years | – | – | 7% | 12% | 8% |
| 10 years and over | – | – | – | 10% | – |

**Example 19** Engineer I: probability of promotion within one year

## Other analyses

A range of other data and associated analyses may be valuable.

*Language ability*

In Europe in particular, the languages which managers can understand or speak are very important, and an inventory of who reads and/or speaks which language is virtually essential. Apart from providing a key element for short lists to European and other overseas posts, the ability to help with a translation or with an overseas visitor may be sought at short notice. The extent to which language skills are available in an increasingly international business scene suggests that an analysis which reveals limited availability should trigger action. It is noticeable that some companies consider competence in a second language as essential in their graduate recruits.

*International experience*

International experience is a comparable factor. Individuals who have lived and worked abroad for a period and have come to understand a different national culture at first hand will tend to have a better appreciation of overseas business and other overseas activities. (But beware the dullard who came back having learned nothing, and the liberal who came back wanting to change the world!)

*Industry experience*

Industry experience may be relevant within a group of companies which requires searches for people with experience related to other parts of the group, or for individuals with multi-industry experience. However, experience can be enormously diverse, and any attempt at coding the total range of possible experience to simplify computerised sorting out of particular combinations is unlikely to be worth the effort.

*Education and training*

Education and training are essential elements when analysing the inventory of human resources. Analysis of the graduate population by type and level of degree and against career progress can be informative. Other qualifications should be covered comprehensively for the same purpose, and a record of major training courses attended is necessary. Progression through core training programmes, related to present level and expected pace of progression, should identify individuals who should attend further training.

Analysis of the qualifications of those individuals progressing fastest through the management structure may provide indications of the best sources for the future supply, who will not always be graduates.

There will be variations in career progression patterns between functional areas, and other variations which may be due more to a bias on the part of a senior manager rather than the clear abilities of people in a particular stream.

*Planning ahead*

If the database is very good, it is always valuable to 'flag' *individuals who are ready for a next career move* or expected to become so within the next 12 months. To this can be added indications of whether the next move is already agreed and a date specified, or whether the individual appears to be blocked or have no obvious means of achieving the required next posting. This latter group needs to be listed regularly as urgent action will be required until an adequate plan has developed.

## SUMMARY

A sound database incorporating information on all managers, including how they are expected to develop, is of fundamental importance to any management development scheme and to the workings of the Review process.

This database will be used to help identify individuals capable of meeting all the diverse requirements of the enterprise, so that utilisation and development of people can be given the greatest flexibility, and deployment can draw from the full management resource. In this way, the management database is a major contributor to the overall Review process.

Analyses of the database against the requirements of the business provide pointers to some of the needs for human resource strategies on which achievement of business objectives will be dependent. In particular, analysis should indicate the adequacy of graduate intake volumes and the adequacy of career 'flows' to junior and middle management levels to meet the numerical requirements – overall, and by function. A sufficient supply of individuals with the potential to advance, with appropriate skills and, for example, with the right language abilities, etc., should be identifiable; and the data must be analysed early enough for any corrective action required to be initiated in good time.

The database must contain *all the information likely to be required in the management development process* to enable all decisions or options related to individuals to be determined as objectively as possible.

# V.3

## *Resourcing and recruitment*

### RECRUITMENT STRATEGY

Every vacancy provides a career opportunity for an existing manager. Decisions to go to the external market when it is not essential can lead to serious demotivation of existing staff. Resourcing strategy therefore needs thoughtful evaluation. The strategy should be long-term and incorporate systematic intake of graduates and other appropriate people to be developed up through the structure to meet the majority of planned needs. It is unlikely that *all* needs can be met internally, but the strategy should ensure that *the internal option is always considered first.* (At times when an organisation is reducing in numbers every effort should be made to avoid recruitment, but where the essential skills required are simply not available internally, it is better to avoid excessive compromise and initiate recruitment.)

Recruitment strategy should be designed to meet present and future management requirements by bringing in calculated numbers of potential future managers, such as young graduates and professionally qualified people, who are capable of moving quickly into junior management ranks and being developed up through the structure. External recruitment to more senior positions should be tightly controlled. It will always be necessary to bring in some people to specialist positions where numbers within the company are small and career opportunities limited. For other management positions, there is value in bringing in 'new blood' from time to time to keep an organisation from becoming 'in-bred', and to inject new ideas or fresh ways of looking at a subject. This may be associated with some cultural change programme, or to rejuvenate a function when the environmental demands are becoming more challenging.

If decisions to recruit externally are evaluated to see whether the development process is failing to meet company needs, there is an adequate safeguard. For example, few plans seem able to identify all the new skills required as an organisation grows and evolves, and some intake can be healthy. If the proportion of placements made from external sources becomes excessive, however, then the company is either not picking up impending environmental change, or the planning and development processes and development of individual careers are not effective.

Flexibility is a necessary competency in many specifications for management positions. Forward organisation design may require future management specifications which will be difficult to match 'from stock' if the new competencies cannot be developed quickly. In such an event, evaluation of any possible flexibility in structure and specifications to utilise the strengths and accommodate the limitations of available people, rather than resort to external sourcing, has to be explored.

Lastly, the filling of any position involves fitting an individual into an established team situation. Unless it is decided that the team style or culture is to be changed, then the matching of candidates should be both to the requirements of the job itself and to the team. If the previous incumbent had brought a particular quality to a team, finding a fresh team balance may require some shuffling of influences, as well as finding a competent performer for the vacant position.

## PLANNING RECRUITMENT ACTION

All recruitment action, indeed all action of any sort which leads to the appointment of an individual to do any job, is handled best through a series of logical steps:

1. The organisation in which the job is located, and the purpose, content and objectives of the job should be clearly defined and approved, and should have been reviewed to ensure that they are all current and valid. The ongoing need for the job to exist for at least a year into the future should be confirmed.
2. The job should be planned and budgetted, or similarly authorised.

3 There must be visible effort to fill the post from internal sources.
4 In the event that no internal candidates are suitable, the external market should be assessed to determine the availability of suitable candidates and the financial package likely to be required for successful recruitment.
5 The degree of flexibility acceptable in meeting the person specification should be clarified.
6 Recruitment and selection actions should be initiated.
7 Applicants should be evaluated.
8 The selection process should lead up to a decision and formal offer of appointment.

## Establish the vacancy

"Jones is leaving. Replace him!" or, "Get another person to manage the design team."

Simple enough instructions admittedly, but why is Jones leaving? Could it be that the organisation is changing imperceptibly and that the change in work has unsettled Jones? Throw in one doubt of this sort and it becomes worth checking carefully on the real vacancy before steps are taken to fill it. It is essential to know what the vacant position involves.

The review of requirements is best done by interview with the preceding job holder, where one is available, or with the immediate manager. If a job description and objectives exist, they provide the starting point, and the review should determine if and how these have changed. However, lack of an earlier description is not critical, as it need not take long to obtain a complete outline of the post. If the post is a new one, its requirements and duties need to be adequately defined.

More important at this stage is an evaluation of the particular tasks and problems which the new person will have to face; the objectives, and the competencies required. For example, a marketing manager may have to be prepared to cope with rapidly growing and undefined new competition; a personnel manager may have to create a special retraining programme to prepare for impending office automation. The person specification will be influenced by the particular skills needed, the degree of difficulty faced, and the performance standards expected. Remember that the higher the position, the more unique the role and specification.

Once the job content, objectives and person specification are confirmed, the job level can be checked and a recruiting salary range determined. Within a grading structure, the overall salary range will be immediately available, but occasionally special factors may apply to the particular market group, so a proper check on values should be automatic. Additionally, the precise person specification required will influence the commencing level; for example, someone having only the minimum experience required to meet a specification would justify the minimum salary, or a higher rate would be appropriate to take account of the substantial experience and track record of another candidate.

## Establish that the vacancy is budgetted

However clearly the job is established and urgency stressed, it should not be possible to proceed with filling the post until it is clearly established that the position has been budgetted for and the expense is expected. At any time a variety of smooth-tongued managers can justify recruiting additional people, but if these additions were not taken into consideration in business plans and budgets, what will be the impact on the bottom line? If the job does result from a post-budget reappraisal, it takes little enough time to set out a brief supplementary plan to justify the action and show the expected financial impact, as an essential discipline in manpower control.

If the position is budgetted or covered by an approved supplementary plan, take a final confirmatory look at the requirement to ensure it is for essential work or necessary discretionary work.

## Internal sourcing

Only when the vacancy is clearly established and approved should any sourcing activity begin.

Outside recruitment of any sort is expensive and takes time, so that, apart from all the other reasons, the need to examine and make use of the 'existing stock' makes economic sense. Sometimes the decision is not clear cut, and it may be decided to include internal people on a short list, in competition with external candidates.

*Possible approaches*

The search within a company can take one of two main approaches. It can leave the initiative to the individual, after letting staff know what vacancies exist; or it can make use of all available information on staff and endeavour to match the job requirement with suitable candidates and provide an opportunity to progress an individual's career.

Taking the former case first, this approach may overlook the best candidates as they may not apply for a variety of reasons. These may vary from simple lack of adequate understanding of the vacant post or underrating their own abilities, to not applying due to straightforward pressure from a selfish manager. Where the 'employee initiative' approach is adopted, I prefer a back-up internal search as a cross-check to identify candidates who have not responded.

Where the company adopts the second approach and searches its database for candidates, there is no reason why internal advertising should not be used as a cross-check. Internal advertising also serves a useful purpose in drawing attention to previously unknown potential transfer and promotion prospects within the organisation, and in emphasising an intention to develop staff from within rather than to replace from outside. Further advantage comes from identifying staff who are unsettled, or who are known to want to move for any reason. These potential leavers may be retained by taking action to deal with their concerns.

*Identifying potential candidates*

Where a company assumes the whole responsibility for internal selection, it must ensure that it has the facilities to identify all employees potentially able to fill a vacancy, and can select the best choice with a minimum of employee participation. If it adopts this course, it should seek appropriate publicity for its procedure, which must be visibly effective, and be prepared to answer staff who ask whether they were considered and rejected when an appointment is made!

Many vacancies are known well in advance, so that the situation may be examined at leisure and each appointment planned as a potential career step for an individual, with sufficient time available for training up or otherwise preparing the selected employee. Not least in importance is the feasibility of the new appointee sitting alongside the previous job holder for a period, in order to pick up the reins at first hand.

The management development process will have assembled detailed information on all managers, their potential and IDPs, providing a valuable guide to available and suitable talent within the organisation. This database can be accessed whenever a vacant position has not been anticipated, possibly arising from a termination or from a new situation.

*Tailoring the job to the candidate*

Not all internal placements will necessarily be perfect matches to a specification. Occasionally, the only person available with sufficient experience or knowledge must be appointed, even though he lacks some of the qualities specified. On these occasions it is advisable to modify the job content, specification and performance expectations to fit the appointee in order to reduce any appearance of a poor choice, and build up to the desired standards gradually.

Such a situation might arise in a technical department, where the available 'deputy' is a brilliant specialist who is hopeless at administration. The activity might be restructured to support the new manager with a good administrative deputy, so the strengths of the new man are used fully and his weaker areas are protected.

This leads on to a further aspect of internal selection, that of finding a job for a person, rather than a person for a job. This is an important requirement for high potential employees who are ready for a move but whose advance is blocked. It applies also to competent people who have lost ground due to organisation change but who retain the abilities to manage larger tasks.

A list of 'readies' (people 'ready now' for promotion) probably rests on the majority of management development managers' desks, and the search for suitable places for them is constant. Opportunities may be anywhere but may need to be opened up. Chain movement may help to solve a problem by shifting a series of people and opening a position required for a key person in the process. The first stage must be to identify the special requirements and a possible 'target' job, in terms of man and job specifications, grade level, working relationships and so on. From this first point, the means of achieving the opening can be studied and planned.

## External sourcing

*The market*

Assessment of the external market is essential before recruitment is begun, as the skills you require may not be freely available on the market. It may show that you will need to recruit people who will require training to meet your requirements, which will require sufficient lead time. Knowledge of the present and probable future of the employment market is essential, for if that market is very tight and requirements cannot easily be met by recruitment, you may need to reconsider the achievability of some basic commercial objectives.

Knowledge of the availability of various categories of individuals or skills is therefore important, together with assessments of the way availability is likely to change. The first part can be provided with some accuracy by most recruitment staff, who acquire an excellent 'feel' of the current market place. The second is more difficult. The analysis needs to be as specific as possible on questions of when, where, and why change may occur, and the likely impact on the calibre and price of future candidates. For example, good managers may be available from another industry but need some retraining before becoming fully effective, but this will be temporary. The supply situation will influence the method of recruiting, and the market place is yet another element of an environment which is continually changing.

*Flexibility in the specification*

Faced with potential difficulty in locating and attracting the ideal candidate, it is as well to know how much flexibility can be tolerated in the specification. For example, tight age preferences can usually be relaxed, but if the company is wanting to fill a senior position for a fixed period until a designated rising star can fill the post internally, a precise age restriction may be essential. Normally, age qualifications, ideal target companies and the experience specification should all be open to some variation, as also should be the remuneration package.

*Initiating recruitment action*

The basic process is too well known to require detail here, but there are some essential points to be covered. There are a number of options to be considered when recruiting senior managers, but no perfect answers. Whether it is better in a particular case to advertise, to use consultants or search people, depends on several factors. For example, a common reason for using consultants is less for their skill than to buy their time handling a great deal of the detail of recruitment!

When to search? If the target population is quite small and it is possible to identify the places they are likely to be, then search is the most precise way of 'getting the message' to most of that population. Beyond that, the search process places you in a selling situation, and you will need an attractive job and an equally attractive package to land the person you seek. If the population is larger, or more dispersed, or cannot be so easily located, then search is less effective than a large, well presented advertisement in the right medium. If you can attract the interest of your potential target and give him an 'independent' to talk to first, this is as effective as search.

The briefing of the consultant will have to be extremely thorough, and you will want to feel absolutely confident that you will be properly represented. I prefer search consultants to accept some penalty if the assignment is not completed because they cannot satisfy the client, although this is against their normal fee structure. Whenever external people are briefed to handle a recruitment or search assignment, it is advisable to get them to provide a detailed written statement of your requirement, so that you are reassured that the precise message has been received and understood.

*Applicants*

Where an external organisation is handling an assignment up to short list, much of the initial grind is avoided. If all applications are to be direct to the company, systematic handling is essential. For example, applicants deserve a courteous response, even if it is only a brief 'regret' letter to a non-conforming hopeful.

Most advertisements are likely to produce substantial numbers of applicants, so that a 'booking-in' list to check off subsequent action is reasonable. An extracted list of those of interest after the initial sort can follow. The initial selection requires reading all applications to weed out those which do not conform to the specification, that is, most, but not all, non-conforming replies. It is invariably worth looking twice at good candidates who do not fit age or qualification ideals, and considering the implications if they should be selected.

For example, there are always excellent technical managers who have come up the sales and marketing route to general management, and who possess the intellect to absorb and utilise an immense amount of technical knowledge, though not degree qualified. And there are frequently experienced older-than-ideal candidates who retain their drive and originality as a supplement to experience, who are in the market following an acquisition or a similar upheaval.

Initial interviews in-company, or short listing externally, produce the short lists of people who fit the requirement reasonably well.

## Selection

As the final selection process begins, it is essential to be clear on the process to be used – who is to be involved, and who is to take the appointment decision. For example, precisely who will interview candidates; and is the appointment decision to be made by the immediate boss, or is he recommending an appointment for decision by *his* boss?

The selection process will generally involve interviewing, and most managers require training in interviewing skills at some stage. The five point system designed by Munro Fraser asks interviewers to assess:

- Impact on others – physical make-up, appearance, speech, and manner.
- Acquired qualifications – education, vocational training, work experience.
- Innate abilities – natural quickness of comprehension and aptitude for learning.
- Motivation – the kind of goals set by the individual, his consistency and determination in following them up, his success in achieving them.
- Adjustment – emotional stability, ability to stand up to stress and ability to get on with people.

The art of interviewing involves structuring and controlling the use of interview time, establishing rapport with the candidate, steering the direction of the conversation by precise questions, and listening very carefully. At management levels, listening includes 'hearing' what is *not* said, and probing why: establishing a full picture of the candidate. While the most effective interviews (by a good interviewer) are on a one-to-one basis, group or panel interviews are still widely used. These need to be managed to be effective, so that the interviewers agree who will take various initiatives to avoid conflicts of interest developing.

Some group selection situations may be developed along the lines of an assessment centre, particularly for selection of graduate entrants where interpersonal skills provide an important factor in selection, or to cover aspects of work which can be observed in role-playing type situations. These group sessions may also be supplemented by use of psychometric tests.

For senior managers, the use of an external psychometric assessment can provide an invaluable cross-check on all other data, and influence the ultimate decision. For example, it is not unknown, even today, for individuals to claim qualifications in excess of those actually attained, and test batteries may 'flag' that the claimed first class honours are 'unlikely', or that the claimed track record would be difficult to achieve, given the candidate's vulnerability to stress.

The test battery, selected using an informed understanding of the position concerned and the qualities needed, will 'take a reading' of the overall intellectual strength of a senior candidate, which can be vital, given the range and complexity of decisions he may have to take. The battery may also give an indication of stress tolerance. A reasonable level of stress may be expected in most senior management jobs, so that tolerance may be taken as proven; but a few individuals do manage to build up an excellent record through a series of low stress appointments, but are extremely vulnerable if they chance on a high stress situation.

Of course, test material is available to all psychology graduates, but this does *not* imply a competence to use and interpret the results meaningfully. Also, some psychologists will admit that management psychology is at much the same stage of its ultimate development as medicine in the middle ages – but there are a few gurus who can work miracles.

Once the selection is made, it should be confirmed by making a formal offer, subject to medical and reference checks, which should be cleared quickly. Many employers leave negotiation of the package to this late stage and, particularly where search is involved, this can lead to expensive solutions. The package on offer should be presented early and resolved early, so that there is a clear agreement on that key issue before the talking begins.

## QUALITY

The balance between internal and external candidates should be evident enough for an enterprise to have a clear view of the forward career opportunities for recruited staff. With few exceptions, the demand should be for individuals who have the ability to progress beyond the initial post, and most applicants of stature are likely to seek placements which offer scope for further advancement.

A high percentage of future managers are likely to come from the intake of graduates and young professional staff. They may join directly from university or after a few years' experience elsewhere, or they may be people who achieve university entrance standards and then elect to go directly into professional or vocational training. This intake needs people able to make an early contribution, who have the personality, ability and drive to progress into managerial positions in their middle to late twenties. Graduate recruitment specifications should stress the requirement for potential managers, although there will be other qualities required for many vacancies offering functional career progression. Attracting a proportion of the very best is important, and you must seek some measure of the relative quality of those you recruit.

## SUMMARY

Resourcing strategy must fit the requirements of the business and should be adequately detailed. The priority should be to advance internally developed people wherever these can match the specifications required; to use every vacancy as a career development opportunity.

Recruitment strategy must be similarly defined as it provides the source material for all internal development and resourcing in the long-term. For example, it is likely to emphasise intake of graduates and other young people of similar calibre in sufficient numbers to meet most of the future requirements for managers and senior specialists. As not all these needs will be met from internal development sources, specifications for recruits at a later stage should be individual, based on the anticipated forward requirements and supply, as well as the immediate need.

Recruitment is a process with a logical series of steps which should be followed or checked off. To recruit without establishing the need clearly, or without checking the availability of internal candidates, can be potentially damaging to morale; while considered action to attract, process and select from good candidates should ensure optimum recruitment results and supplement the corporate management inventory.

The selection process should make use of all aids available to ensure a good decision, recognising the limitations of interviewing by many managers, and using psychometric aids were practicable, in the long-term interest of both the candidate and the employer.

# V.4

## *Appraisal of performance and counselling*

Performance appraisal and associated counselling can make heavy demands on management time, which need to be justified by applications which are business related.

### PERFORMANCE APPRAISAL

#### In general

The main purpose of appraisal is likely to be to improve individual performance. The appraisal process should help identify performance weaknesses and suggest how they can be overcome, leading in due course to improvement in performance by the individual and probably some improvement in overall business efficiency.

There are a number of other uses. For example, if the objective is to identify training needs so that training investment is properly directed, these needs should be business related. Another application might be to identify who does (or does not) achieve personal and business objectives – and why. Where the application is to be remuneration, appraisal should help to identify the relatively more valuable employees at every level, influencing how best to motivate achievers by directing the distribution of salary budgets, or indicate achievement of commercial objectives which determine bonuses.

Appraisal looks backwards in time for objective data on how the individual has performed, but then looks forward to establish agreed actions to improve performance, to establish new objectives for the next appraisal cycle, and may seek to identify the need for new skills in the job as environment changes and priorities are altered.

The appraisal process primarily concerns the individual and his immediate manager, and involves an interchange between them regarding the individual's job attainments over the last months or year. The prime output from the appraisal should be a set of agreed actions to be undertaken by the manager and his employee to improve job performance: a basis for each manager to 'coach' his subordinate. The manager at the next level may have a contribution to make, but he is not likely to be as closely involved and able to make such a positive contribution. Only where there is a degree of disagreement between individual and manager is involvement from the next level necessary, to counsel or arbitrate.

Appraisal is a natural part of the wider and ongoing management development process. As such, it is important that both manager and subordinate prepare for each appraisal discussion, and that agreed actions are followed through. Appraisal should not be concerned with penalising people for mistakes. Remember the old adage: "If you have never made a mistake, you have never made anything." But we should expect people to learn from each mistake.

Because the word 'appraisal' is emotive, at least one large organisation has dropped the word from its vocabulary and describe much of the activity as 'counselling'. Indeed, much that is valuable in appraisal comes from the communication, the talking about performance, and the agreements to do specific things to develop people.

If appraisal is to be effective, the users (the line managers) need to feel that they 'own' the system; that they have been deeply involved in its development; that they understand it, believe in it, and use it because they get value out of it rather than because human resource people push them to fill in reports which they do not understand and from which they get no value.

## Purpose of appraisal

Human resource management cum management development will require information about individual performance for a variety of purposes. Some common uses are as follows:

- To help improve individual performance, by analysing performance in the recent past to identify problems, achievements/failures, strengths/weaknesses, so that agreed action can be taken to help the individual to perform better.
- To assist in identifying further potential.

- To contribute to identifying the direction of a next career step (while performance and track record can be indicators of potential ability, there is no direct correlation).
- To identify training needs (as part of the above or as the primary objective).
- To use overall performance on a comparative basis for salary purposes.
- To appraise achievement against agreed personal objectives, or again commercial objectives or priorities for bonus purposes.
- To appraise existing managers against the profiles expected for future management, or against the criteria of other jobs/person specifications/Hay points, etc.

This list is unlikely to be comprehensive, but all these applications are in use and some are potentially conflicting. In an over systematised multi-application situation, a line manager may be tempted to judge what he needs to do to gain best advantage from the system rather than use it openly; for example, justifying a desired salary adjustment for one of his people may be more important to him than other possible applications.

Other situations might require acceptance that high achievement against the narrow commercial goals specified for bonus purposes does not automatically correlate with impressive performance over the demands of the total job, or noting that recognition of some weaknesses in last year's performance does not imply 'failure' or even poor performance. The purposes of appraisal determine the aspects of performance which need to be appraised to give relevant information, and this will vary with the intended applications.

*Performance improvement*

Performance improvement will require information which is directly related to the job being done or to its objectives. Appraisal will need to concentrate on what the job holder has done particularly well, or not so well, and analyse why. From this data it will be possible to see where and how performance may be improved, and to identify development or training needs related to current performance. However, managerial performance can be very difficult to measure because individuals will vary widely in *how* they set out to achieve their goals. As part of the appraisal, the senior manager should try to see his subordinate as a 'whole person' and to understand his approach to the job in order to assess his abilities to make a unique contribution to the organisation.

*Aiding decisions on remuneration*

If the application is to be concerned primarily with influencing decisions on remuneration, some measure of performance against standards used when setting salary structure levels will be required, i.e. how well does actual performance relate to performance standards associated with levels in the salary scale? In parallel, it should be asked how performance or contribution compare with those of other managers at the same job level. If bonus is involved, there may be some separate short-term objectives with payment directly related to achievement.

It may also assist judgement of the rate at which salary should progress, but appraisal should *not* be designed to provide a basis for mechanical conversion of appraisal into pay. Some organisations require supplements to the main appraisal which show the translation of detailed observations into an overall judgement of each individual's performance against that of other people in jobs at a similar level. This may involve a forced ranking, with the objectives-based appraisal as background supporting data.

Line managers tend to recognise the two distinct appraisal requirements and tend to agree with separate ranking for salary purposes as a 'ranking of overall contribution and value'. Where small groups of managers can discuss each other's departmental rankings and discuss the integration of departmental rankings, their ownership of the process ensures it is taken seriously and that individual bias is minimised.

*Judgements of potential*

Appraisal may also contribute to judgements of potential. This may be a secondary aim of the scheme, with pointers being sought from performance on project work, standing in for a more senior manager, non-standard activities, personal initiatives, or understanding shown of higher level responsibility. These are all factors which are possible indicators of any ability to do other or higher level jobs. Straightforward performance of the normal elements of the present job gives relatively few clues to potential, of course.

*Aiding decisions on career development planning*

Finally, information from appraisal may influence decisions on the career development planning for the employee, as it provides indications of the extent to which he is on top of his present job, and of his readiness to tackle some other role.

## Appraisal format

*In general*

The format used for appraisal can vary enormously and no 'standard format' is proposed. However, the process must:

- be based on criteria which are objective and relevant to the job
- involve face to face discussion between the manager and the subordinate being appraised
- focus on the individual's performance and his development needs.

A typical format would include:

- Identification: employee's name, job title and organisational position, identification of his manager as the appraiser.
- Objectives: the tasks, priorities, standards, timing agreed between the manager and the subordinate at the beginning of the appraisal term, possibly modified by agreement mid-term when events which would not have been foreseen have occurred, or where the company plan is changed.
- Achievements against objectives: at the end of the term, with 'how and why' notes.
- Identified strengths and limitations: (the limitations may be the more important, as they can place blocks on some career routes, and need to be overcome for others).
- Agreed actions: to improve performance and to prepare for future opportunities.
- Final notes: by the appraisee, by the manager, by his manager.

No single approach to appraisal has universal acceptance, and some variations are noted below to supplement the earlier material which concentrates mainly on the *appraisal of management performance against objectives.* For those involved in running a business, achievement of the business plan numbers will be critical, and these provide the primary objectives, but a *balanced* end result will be expected! Achieving sales targets by selling at too low a price and failing to meet profit targets will not be acceptable: neither will achieving profit targets but producing a disastrous cash flow position.

Not all objectives will be short-term and financial. Longer term objectives to open new markets or launch new products can be equally critical, as can maintaining time and cost schedules towards a new manufacturing facility to be ready two years ahead. And all sets of objectives for managers should include quite specific aims related to their responsibilities for developing both the present and future management staff under their control.

### *Performance ranking*

Performance ranking is one of the more effective of the simpler forms of performance appraisal, and consists of asking managers to rank subordinates on the basis of their relative performance. The simplest ranking plans make no attempt to determine the factors to be considered, but complex schemes can be developed.

Rankings will generally identify the outstanding performers and poor performers with reasonable accuracy, and probably indicate that members of the middle group are sufficiently similar in value to the organisation for further differentiation not to be worth the effort. This sort of ranking is mainly relevant to salary administration and can be a useful supplement to a full objectives-based procedure.

### *Forced distribution or paired comparison systems*

A variation on simple ranking is found in forced distribution or paired comparison systems. In the latter case, managers are asked to take a series of pairs of people and say which is the more valuable contributor of the two. Where the numbers are large, a forced distribution may be used to identify, on the basis of the whole performance, the best 10 per cent and the worst 10 per cent, and then the next best and worst 20 per cent, leaving a residue of 40 per cent as the middle block of 'average' performers. These relatively simple methods have the advantage of being reasonably fast and, if more than one appraiser can be used, of being acceptably accurate. Again, the only application of this approach is to remuneration.

### *Linear appraisals*

Appraisal schemes using linear scales may attempt no more than a single overall assessment of performance, or they may require a series of reviews against separate factors or traits. They may use a scale from 'good' at one end or 'bad' at the other, with no defined intervals or guides to intermediate values, or they may use words to describe standards for numbers of points along each scale. These may help establish the appraisal concept in a relatively unsophisticated company, but are obviously very limited in scope.

### *Appraisal against job profile*

Appraisal against job profile is more than usually valuable for obtaining some measure of suitability for a different post rather than of performance in the present job. The profile is likely to consist of a range of competencies and standards relevant to the job in question, and the appraisal is concerned with establishing the closeness of the match between the would-be incumbent and the ideal specification.

If a common set of basic factors and a common vocabulary have been used to cover a variety of management jobs, it becomes possible to match performance strengths and limitations against a variety of job profiles, and to obtain guidance on the most suitable future appointments for an individual. There is at least one widely used management development database with this profile matching facility built in as a selection tool.

A similar process uses a factor and points based management grading system where, in addition to evaluating management jobs, it is possible to evaluate individual abilities on the same scales and then to match job and person points profiles. In theory, this seems an excellent approach, but I would use it only up to the stage of acknowledging identification of any individual who might be considered as a 'possible' for a vacancy.

### *New forms of appraisal*

New forms of appraisal may be demanded in the future, influenced by radically changed organisation and the impact of information technology. As managerial and specialist roles evolve, and the volume of 'digested' and freely available data increases, it will become natural for individuals to be more aware of performance on a day to day basis, with self-appraisal reducing the need for more formal systems. Performance improvement pointers will always be in evidence and personal performance 'targets' will be self-imposed.

Involvement of the manager will become negligible on performance feedback as it becomes 'self-regulating', and he will concentrate on improvement of personalised job design and organisation change modification to assist individual performance and contribution; constructive elements beyond the direct control of the subordinate.

Should a situation arise where performance failure is developing, the individual concerned (and his colleagues) will be acutely aware of the facts, and some form of corrective action will be participative. Indeed, future appraisals may stress appraisal of team or 'community' effort and results rather than isolating individuals.

## The appraisal process

Appraisal involves far more than a simple form-filling exercise performed once each year. Properly done, it involves a year long cycle, as set out in example 20.

### *Development of appraisal skills*

Individual managers tend to appraise with widely differing standards, from generosity to harshness. In order to minimise variation in standards and ensure common levels of understanding of purpose and content, practical training of all appraisers is necessary – not only at the time of introduction or modification of a system, but every year, in advance of appraisals, as a refresher. Attention to the required counselling skills is especially important. Managers, and any other appraisers, must understand the system and its purpose in order to make their appraisals objective, and to appreciate how they can involve, communicate with and counsel those they are appraising. Appraisal must be participative and involve two-way communication or it becomes restricted in its value. The development of counselling skills is covered best by role playing, using real examples of anticipated difficult situations. This is frequently a confidence building exercise for managers expecting difficulty in appraisal of a poor performer, and can improve the effectiveness of the process.

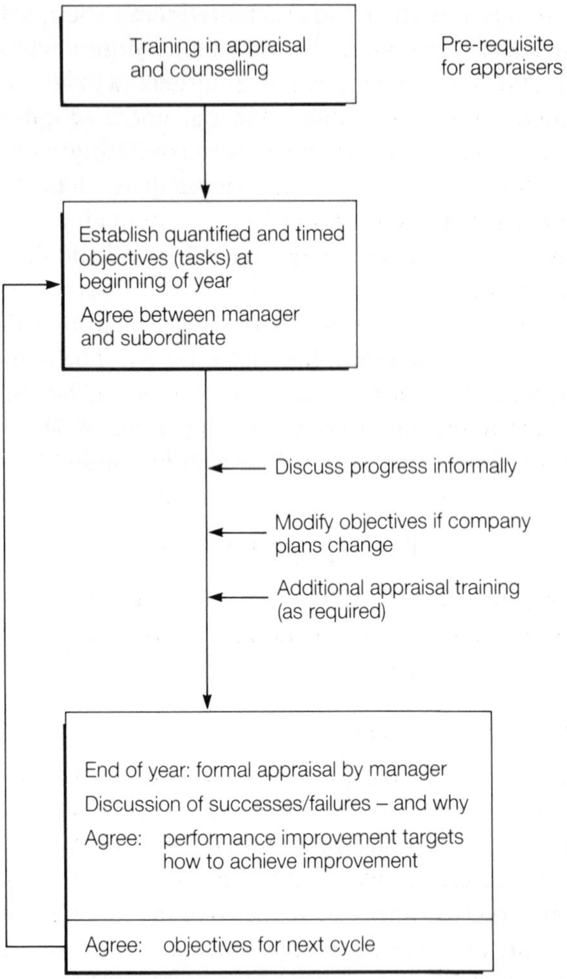


**Example 20** Appraisal of current performance in present job: sequence through the year

*Appraisal against agreed objectives*

By far the most meaningful approach to performance appraisal, particularly for senior staff and executives, is appraisal against agreed objectives. This approach recognises that the main purpose of appraisal is to provide guidance and support in helping the individual to improve his performance. That requirement dictates the procedure, which requires the manager and subordinate to work closely together, first to establish and agree a set of objectives, projects or tasks for the review period – usually the next 12 months. These objectives need to be specific, quantified where possible, and to have completion times stated for the separate elements. The requirement for the manager and subordinate to agree these objectives in detail ensures clear communication and mutual understanding between them.

At intervals through the year, progress should be discussed, generally informally, and some changes may be agreed to objectives where new and unforseeable influences have developed. Notes on the changes and on achievements to date should be made when they are discussed.

At the end of the year, the original objectives and the subsequent progress notes should be gathered together for a more formal overall review. How well has the subordinate done? What did he do outstandingly well? What did he not do well – and why? From the discussion should emerge agreement on achievements, plus agreement on areas where the subordinate could do better and a programme of action designed to achieve that improvement. In parallel, the objectives for the next cycle should have been established.

In the following months, it is essential that the points agreed in counselling discussions are followed up on schedule, or value will be lost. This can be tied in with the informal progress reviews through the year.

*Self-appraisal*

Self-appraisal is becoming more relevant and important. The individual being appraised is the most aware of his own performance and generally is critically honest about it. Some of the most valuable discussion and counselling arises from encouraging the use of the individual's self-appraisal as the discussion basis, rather than using that drafted by the manager. If corporate culture and personal relationships allow this approach, it can be extremely powerful.

## COUNSELLING

### The value of counselling

Talking to subordinates about performance, career development or remuneration can be very time-consuming if it is done thoroughly, even after careful preparation. The pay-off for this use of expensive managerial (and subordinate) time must therefore be convincing in business terms.

This should be achieved as a direct result of clarifying communication between managers and subordinates at every level, which ensures that everyone knows what is expected of them and is working efficiently with a clear common purpose. In parallel, it should be evident that individuals are working to improve agreed aspects of their performance, are reasonably confident about their forward development, and feel properly motivated and rewarded – in short, that they are not distracted from their prime organisational purpose. While no-one will measure the effect on the bottom line with any precision, effective counselling should certainly be contributing to organisation efficiency.

'Duty counselling' – counselling done as an unavoidable but irritating duty – will have little positive value, and almost certainly a negative effect in raising expectations and providing nothing. Badly handled counselling may lead to great damage in terms of worsened relationships or conflict, which may require subsequent intervention from a higher level or by independent human resource people.

## The counselling process

### *The need for some formality*

Effective counselling requires managers to become trained and sensitive counsellors, ideally enthusiasts who take the trouble to prepare carefully for each individual session. Preparation begins with clarifying the purpose of each counselling session, arranging it with some formality, and ensuring that there is adequate private time to complete it without interruptions. By 'some formality', I mean that the session should be prearranged and the purpose stated, even if it goes over ground previously covered informally. It is a curious fact that many individuals appear to feel that informal counselling is 'not part of the system', and only accept that they have had any appraisal feedback if the meeting is set up with due formality.

### *The scope of counselling*

The most common objective of most counselling will be directly limited to appraisal, but there will be occasions when counselling will be appraisal-related but the real emphasis will be on remuneration, or on individual career development (or exceptionally for a reprimand). Usually discussion will flow into the second area, and there is no need for rigid boundaries. If a performance improvement related appraisal discussion moves onto the question "... and what will the effect be on my salary ...?" the response has got to be convincing, even if the appraisal process under discussion is not directly linked to remuneration.

Because counselling is essentially two-way communication, it is acceptable to encourage the subordinate to take the initiative, particularly where self-appraisal and self-development is encouraged. It is far more effective to draw out self criticism or identification of limitations than to point out failings, and the message is then evidently received and understood, while the individual may close his mind or reject what he is told. Positive progress is obviously much easier after reaching the point of acceptance of an issue. The personal relationship enabling the subordinate to feel confident in self-criticism is not easily achieved, and must be nurtured.

## Counselling format

Counselling does not respond to a standard approach or set of rules, but there are some 'do's and don'ts' which justify some guide-lines. For example, it is always advisable to consider the *value to the receiver* of any contribution you make. If it will be impossible for the subordinate to achieve any change of behaviour, it will be of no value to discuss a limitation. As an extreme example, a stutter or a limp or twitch might be viewed as a 'limitation' in some circumstances, but is permanent. The objective should be to address areas where performance related improvement is achievable. Also, do not raise things which are irrelevant. Nothing can be gained by pointing out that someone is 'not creative', if their job and career plan do not require creativity.

In opening a counselling session, *praise first* is a useful guide, setting a positive note on the discussion. Coverage of any criticism also needs to be positive, best achieved by *planning the structure* and *concentrating on essentials* (and not too many of them) rather than detail.

The appraisees' view of events is critical, so that leading into a subject with *questions rather than comments* may draw out background and explanation for observations previously not seen in context. When comments are made, these should state the behaviour observed, or the event, factually, and the appraisee should be invited to comment on how this might be perceived. If the purpose is to *help* the subordinate rather than reprimand him, increasing his understanding of how others have perceived and reacted to him may lead into discussions of how improvement may be obtained.

Finally, *the session must end positively*. Repeating some comment on successes and strengths can be blended with the actions agreed upon to deal with any problem situations or behaviour.

## SUMMARY

Appraisal is about evaluation of current performance of the current job, and associated communication between manager and subordinate.

Every appraisal system must have clear purpose, and should not be arbitrarily used for other purposes where it may mislead. Each system should be designed for its purpose, preferably involving user participation to encourage ownership.

Various forms of appraisal are in use. Again, the format selected should be based on the intended applications. It must be job related and objective, and it will be influenced by corporate attitudes to appraisal and corporate culture.

Performance *does* influence pay. When proposing salary actions, each manager must be influenced by the performance of his people, together with factors such as grade, level of present salary, etc. The manager will need to tell the individual what action has been determined, and take full responsibility for that action. For this application, one of the performance ranking techniques may help.

Appraisal of present performance provides one of the main sources of data from which judgements may be made of potential to do other or higher level jobs, but appraisal does *not* directly assess potential; neither does performance correlate with potential.

Counselling is a vital activity, based on personal relationships between manager and subordinate which enable uninhibited discussions to take place, designed to improve performance, guide career development, and cover remuneration. It is an important element in corporate culture. Properly handled, it can contribute positively to the efficient running of the organisation.

# V.5

## *Judgement of potential*

### INTRODUCTION

Identifying people with the abilities to become the future generations of senior management is essential to the continuity of the business. However, the majority of managers at all levels have *some* further potential to do other, or higher level, jobs, and it is necessary to identify the form and direction of that potential in order to optimise the development of all employees. Subsequently, the preparation and development of these people will have a profound influence on the corporate future.

Appraisal is primarily concerned with performance in the present job, but for the future you require realistic *judgements of potential capability to do other or more senior level jobs.* This involves projection of the objective performance and other data against the anticipated demands of other job situations to assess the probability of success in a new situation, and of the personal development and support required to improve that probability.

Assessment of potential is inherently difficult – and increasingly so as the prediction spans a greater gap of seniority and longer periods into the future. Nevertheless, the effort has to be made, if only because the accumulation of experiences and challenges required to prepare and to test a well-equipped future director or senior manager takes a number of years and is unlikely to occur other than by a deliberate and sustained plan. For these reasons, regular reviews of the development of apparent potential are essential.

General predictions of potential are made for graduates and younger managers, based on intellectual strengths, aptitudes, qualities of leadership, drive, commercial judgement, etc., but these are tentative judgements which will need to be refined and tested to establish the direction for development.

Because potential is difficult to judge, you need to build up your factual data of pointers to potential, and then to supplement this knowledge in systematic ways where this is practical. For example, in-company programmes known as Assessment Centres can provide invaluable insights into the potential of young managers in their late twenties and early thirties. These programmes use a combination of structured and observed exercises which simulate a variety of managerial situations, providing pointers to likely behaviour and effectiveness; plus use of psychometric tests to measure verbal and numerical abilities, critical thinking, etc.

## INDICATORS OF HIGH POTENTIAL

### Progressive development of potential

A large proportion of managers at all ages will have *some* potential to do other or higher level jobs. The judgement you seek is of the *extent* of potential. Which are the individuals with *high* potential? In other words, which individuals appear *able to advance at a fast rate to more senior positions*? And which individuals appear to be exhibiting the qualities which may take them to the top? Ideally, you would like to pick out the individuals who are most likely to go 'right to the top', but in practical terms the reliability of these projections falls away rapidly as the period of the projection and the number of levels increase. It is far more effective to concentrate on realistic progression through the immediate level (or exceptionally two levels) and a period of no more than three years, with consideration of *possible* long-term development which is accepted as 'provisional'; and with continuing updating of projections and career development through that period.

Clearly, many of the facets and challenges of a top management role simply are not encountered in the work of a younger manager. Potential is developed *progressively*, as different and larger assignments are undertaken. Hence *assessment of high potential in young and inexperienced managers* must rely primarily on observation of those personal characteristics which can be judged even in a relatively junior job with restricted scope.

The following list is neither exclusive nor exhaustive, but these indicators do tend to be evident in younger managers judged to have excellent potential, and may assist those responsible for making what is inevitably a difficult judgement:

- Exceptional overall competence: sets own standards above those imposed.
- Learns rapidly: displays curiosity, does not repeat mistakes.
- Thinks independently: identifies problems/issues for himself, sees broader implications of possible solutions, adaptable.
- High energy/output: works persistently to complete tasks, withstands stress well.
- Good at communicating, persuading, influencing and negotiating. Can give and take advice in an acceptable manner.

With promotion to broader and more senior roles, it may become possible progressively, to observe other characteristics:

- Able to analyse complex issues, to isolate key elements, to take decisions on incomplete evidence, to make realistic action plans, to execute plans decisively.
- Assertive, profit-conscious, competitive outlook.
- Tolerant of ambiguity.
- Understands how to structure teams: delegates well, good at motivating subordinates, good at developing talented subordinates.
- Shows a grasp of strategic issues outside his own current area of responsibility.
- International in outlook: responds positively to the world outside.
- Physically and mentally resilient: calm and confident under pressure.
- Sensitive to and at harmony with company style.

As the career path develops even further, particular types of experience become important. Success in these activities may be regarded as 'qualification' for senior rank, or the activities can be seen as elements to be integrated into a career plan. Some examples might be:

- Direct profit responsibility in a front-line general management role.
- International experience.
- Success in a variety of businesses.

- Involvement with strategy formulation and with public/political issues.

Many companies claim that they want their managers to be entrepreneurial, but this is an attitude of mind rather than a skill, and needs to fit in with corporate culture. Entrepreneurship involves doing new things, or doing the old things in new ways. It involves responding creatively to opportunity, with flexibility and drive. The entrepreneurial manager thrives on and capitalises on change; he sees change as an opportunity rather than a threat; all qualities one might also expect to see in a manager of high potential. But entrepreneurship requires a supporting corporate culture, and some of the organisations which claim they want entrepreneurs have cultures which rapidly destroy any entrepreneurial tendencies!

## How to identify potential

An athlete whose times have been improving steadily might be judged capable of some further improvement as a logical projection of results to date. To an extent, judgements about managerial potential are also influenced strongly by track record, but closer analysis of an individual should look for more fundamental indications of abilities to do different or higher level work.

Example 21 shows how that analysis might function, building judgements partly as extensions of known job performance information, and then utilising data about personality and intellect to judge the likely ability to absorb and cope with new experience. Pointers from the lists above can provide encouraging indicators, but these identify aspects where it is necessary to 'test and stretch' capabilities to build a fuller understanding of the strengths and abilities which go beyond the demands of the present job.

Performance at a particular level will have involved dealing with a wide range of problems and situations, taking decisions from available data, and working with a set of colleagues. A higher level post may involve dealing with *similar* problems and situations but require a *different perspective* right across the board. Assuming that the manager has sufficient professional knowledge for a prospective next post, does he show sufficient breadth and vision to indicate his likely ability to handle the higher level demands?

In practice, you set out to minimise uncertainty. Project work,

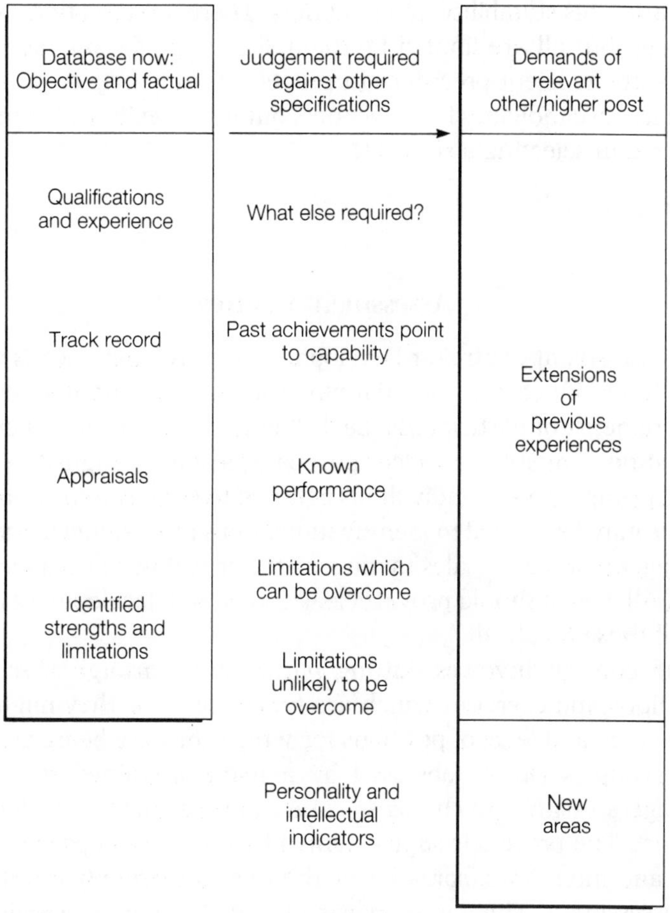


**Example 21** Judgement of potential

assignments or 'standing-in' can give brief exposure to a range of situations relevant to a possible career move. These increase the range of factual data from which projections may be judged and they narrow down the areas where some provision of extra support from senior management may be required. It is, after all, in no-one's interest to let an appointment fail.

Some organisations have developed full 'libraries' of management profiles – of the qualities and skills required by managers in each of their senior jobs. They use a personal profiling system which produces a profile of each manager using the same criteria, for matching the individual against possible future assignments and indicating his suitability and readiness. There are variations on this concept, but all are limited by the ability to profile managers and jobs with sufficient precision. In practice, it may help to produce a 'long list' of candidates for a vacancy, but more flexibility is generally required in selecting a short list.

## Assessment Centres

The Assessment Centre (or Development Centre) approach is widely used to clarify career potential plus the training and development requirements of participants. Each 'Centre' – an event rather than a location – must have a clear purpose. Most are designed to assess small groups of 8–12 individuals believed to have potential, and the events may be slanted to identify individuals most suited for general management (or for sales management, or technical management, etc.). All events should provide clear career and development advice for all those involved.

The concept involves putting participants through a series of situations and exercises which are typical of those they might face in the type and level of positions for which they are being assessed. The group is closely observed by a team of trained senior line managers with psychologist and management development support. The process is supplemented by a battery of psychometric tests and interviews, spread over the two to three day duration of the assessment. The observers spend a further day assembling the detailed conclusions on each participant and are personally involved in providing feedback.

Every Assessment Centre programme is designed for a purpose, usually to identify from within a group of individuals already believed to have potential which of them will best meet a particular specification. The results are not win-lose type conclusions, although some individuals will have positive and others negative conclusions about their suitability for the particular requirement. All members of the group should emerge from subsequent counselling with a much clearer view of their optimum development paths, and the realism of their own preferences and ambitions. Individual development planning becomes more focussed and positive. With a 'Development Centre', as distinct emphasis from an

'Assessment Centre', the emphasis is on this last factor, without reference to specific job category.

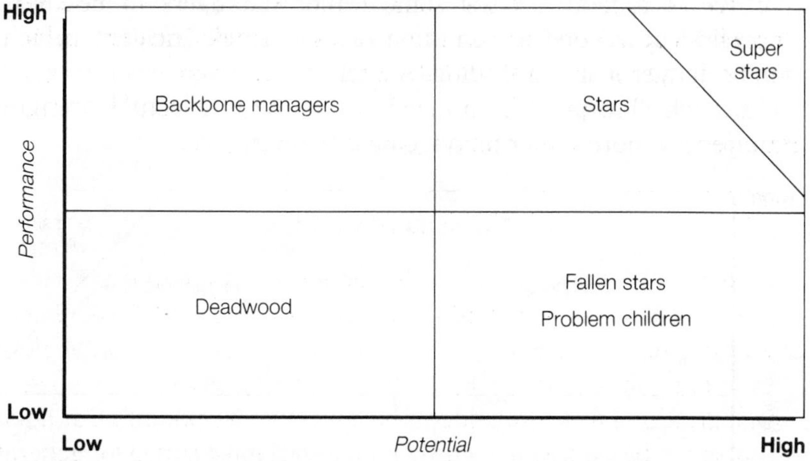


**Example 22** Matrix relating performance and potential

As Assessment or Development Centres absorb a great deal of management time, a variation is to commission individual assessments by highly skilled psychologists to provide comparable data, but these lack some of the 'ownership' which senior managers feel about Assessment Centre results in which they have participated as observers. The value of either of these approaches is that they provide a very much higher level of reliability on forecasts of the form and extent of potential than is achievable by more subjective management judgements.

It is notable that, without Assessment Centre inputs, line management judgements of potential are heavily influenced by track record, even where this provides no positive indication of any ability to work in different areas or at a higher level. The idea that someone who performs well should move on up is flawed. It simply does not follow that individuals who are high performers in their current jobs will also have high potential. The matrix presented as example 22 gives an interesting insight into that difference. It shows that some high performing managers have low potential as they are at their career limit, yet these people are invaluable as the essential 'backbone' of the organisation. In contrast, some high potential managers may be badly assigned and performing poorly, becoming 'problem children'. Another less serious version of the same chart, shown as example 23, does highlight the differences rather more vividly!

There is a tendency for some senior managers to be over-impressed by a good presentation or by a single incident, which can be dangerously misleading. A fluent tongue may ensure a good 'sales pitch', but provides no evidence of the intellectual strength required for more senior management performance.

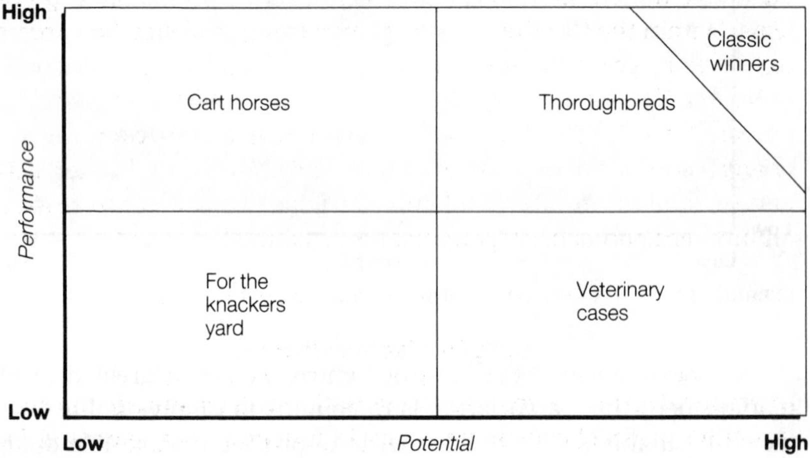


**Example** 23 Another view of the relationship between performance and potential

### POTENTIAL FOR WHAT?

## The broader outlook

Much attention tends to be concentrated on identifying 'high flying' individuals with the capabilities to become the senior line managers of tomorrow, but you must not forget that organisation development is likely to result in a requirement for increased numbers of specialised managers of high ability and broad horizons. It is important to identify managers whose potential is in that direction and ensure their appropriate development. This is only one of the changes likely to occur in the skills and abilities (competencies) we shall require of managers in the future.

Assessments should provide a general observation of potential to senior levels, supplement this with some measures of strengths and weaknesses, and an indication to career preferences, and then provide guidance as to the most suitable career avenues for the optimum development of each individual's potential. For example, some 'lack of toughness' may be career limiting in direct line management, but the other skills possessed by the individual may suggest development to become a potentially outstanding and influential director of a staff function.

Given the escalating pace of change, it is unlikely that anyone will be considered to have high potential unless they are also readily adaptable to new situations and able to deal with unfamiliar problems. Within the UK, there is still a very strong tendency for careers to develop predominantly within one discipline or function, although development of a 'business-wide breadth of view' is expected for senior functional appointments. However, future change and a trend towards greater adaptability may alter this pattern, and the question 'potential for what?' may come to require an answer approaching 'potential for anything'!

## Emerging 'generalisms'

In practical terms, increasing specialisation will encourage the continuation of development up a single function, supplemented by closer exposure to other functions and the workings of the overall business, gained by participation in small intensive project teams. Two distinct forms of 'generalism' will emerge. Some individuals will show the abilities and interest to lead and manage larger multi-functional activities and will tend to move out of the specialist stream, while others will become outstanding specialists but have a broad appreciation of the fit and contribution of their specialism within the whole business.

Every company evolves its own unique style within which the current management has norms and values likely to influence judgements and acceptance of new individuals. Inevitably, there is a tendency to perpetuate the existing style through selection of people whose characteristics fit the existing pattern. Because the world is changing fast, most organisations will need qualities of adaptability and flexibility of mind, and should take care not to reject people of high ability because their attitudes or style do not conform to the existing norms and culture. Evolutionary culture change is natural, and may be influenced positively by the addition of some very able but non-conforming characters who query the relevance of continuing past habits and become the next generation of opinion formers.

## WHO SHOULD IDENTIFY POTENTIAL?

Because potential is difficult to identify, you should encourage (or at least be willing to consider) 'inputs' from a variety of sources, so that all individuals with more than average apparent potential do get identified and then reviewed objectively. The prime sources are the immediate manager and his manager, but there are other people within the company who have contact and may recognise signs of potential which they should bring to the attention of the management development people and to senior management. By widening the sources of information, you may overcome any attempt to conceal able individuals from notice, or hold on to those who are ready to move.

## SUMMARY

'Potential ability' is the ability to grow into other and higher level jobs. Almost all individuals within a management population should be expected to have *some* potential, but judgements are required to identify those with the ability to progress more rapidly: those considered to have 'high potential', from whom the senior managers of the future are most likely to come.

It is important to determine the likely extent and direction of each individual's potential ability. This requires an evaluation of the likely *pace* of growth, and a clarification of the *type of activity* for which the individual's combination of skills and abilities best suit him. In particular, it is useful to identify those who will be most effective managing, as distinct from advising or consulting, and those with a generalist rather than specialist flair.

Potential is always more evident at the point where someone is on top of one job and poised for the next appointment, and tends to be less visible during the learning phase in the new challenge. However, it is important to retain visibility at all times of those regarded as having high potential.

Judgements of potential involve gathering comprehensive data, particularly about younger managers, which give indications of the *pace* at which they are capable of developing and likely direction.

Assessment begins with analysis of past achievements to extract pointers to abilities to manage other or more senior level activities. Assignments, projects and opportunities to 'stand-in' for a more senior manager all provide further information. So too will psychometric assessments of personal strengths and characteristics against those characteristics known to be associated with high potential.

Assessment Centres are widely used to expose small groups of people to a variety of situations and problems generally associated with more senior management positions, in which their behaviour can be closely observed. This process also uses various psychometric tests of intellectual qualities and personality which add to the validity of the process, helping to improve the quality of judgements and refine understanding of the form individual potential may take.

# V.6

## *Preferences, ambitions and mobility*

### INTRODUCTION

Career development is strongly related to abilities, but individual preferences, ambitions and mobility can have substantial influence (although they are liable to change). Knowledge of these influences is an essential ingredient in assembling realistic IDPs which set out the intended or most likely career paths for managers, detailing planned development and training actions, and probable career moves. Information on preferences, ambitions and mobility should avoid assumptions being made by senior management which are out of line with what will be acceptable to the individual or his family, and should save both the costs of wrongly directed development actions and the recruitment costs which can arise when a planned internal move is shown to be unacceptable at a late stage.

There is a joint responsibility on the part of manager and subordinate to ensure that the company has sufficient awareness of each employee's view of his future, which should be *on the agenda at most counselling sessions.* However, if there are some 'restrictions' of interest or mobility, the subordinate may be cautious about revealing his feelings in detail in some cultures in case there is a reaction against his 'lack of commitment'. The manager has the task of drawing out key information in counselling sessions or informal discussions, which is sufficient for acceptable job possibilities to be considered in management planning. Obviously, no final career decisions can be taken without more direct involvement of the individual, but there can be quite wide ranging 'what if . . .' discussions around company preferred deployment options before serious possibilities are put to an individual, so that the obvious 'no go' situations need to be understood.

## PREFERENCES

During the early years of career development, there are generally several avenues open for a next move, and many individuals have clear preferences which influence their selection of the vacancies they go after. One key consideration will be around the degree of specialisation. Those who aspire to top management may seek to broaden their experience through a number of diverse assignments to develop a 'generalist' curriculum vitae, while others may find their career satisfaction comes from growing in a specialist function.

Selection of preferred activities may be influenced by ultimate career ambition, but other factors are present. Preferred life style is increasingly influencing willingness to work in some of the more demanding 'workaholic' organisations, which attract individuals who are willing to make such a commitment but repel others. In this way, the culture of an organisation, as perceived from outside, has significant impact on employment image and the ability to attract able candidates from outside.

Willingness to move to a particular location to take up a promotion may be negative although the individual is basically mobile. If the job itself is not seen as being in the preferred activity and environment, or is not seen as potentially enhancing the preferred or visualised career, an opportunity for immediate advancement may be of little interest. However, if the individual's views are known, it may be possible to present such opportunities in a manner which is found attractive.

The manager needs to obtain as clear a view as the individual can provide of what his subordinate would prefer as further career stages, and of the sorts of assignment he would find most interesting:

- I want to get hands-on line management experience in an operating environment; not another staff job.
- I must get some experience in marketing.
- I could not work in that industry.
- I believe I need an overseas assignment with real responsibility.
- I need to be able to continue my studies to complete the MBA.
- I do not want more responsibility.

Get to know the reasons why, so that the preferences are understood. The comments listed above should be only the beginning of a discussion.

## AMBITIONS

You have to learn to live with the views and career preferences of your managers, but if you believe that the capabilities of an individual fall short of his ambitions, the disagreement may be serious.

High, but unrealistic ambition is likely to be associated with an equally unrealistically high expectation of rapid career advancement. This cannot be ignored, for such an individual will be demanding and will initiate discussion about why progress is not happening. Rational discussions of achievements and suitability for other opportunities should bring realism into the situation. If it does not, a move to test the subordinate under a different manager should determine whether the initial judgement of potential is reliable. If the assessment is confirmed and the employee's view of his future cannot be modified by counselling, it may be appropriate to part company as the relationship is unlikely to remain workable.

More frequently, the mismatch in view of potential is the other way round. The senior manager can see the way an individual could advance, but the individual 'doesn't want the pressures' of a more demanding job. His preference is to stay at a level, as the limit of his ambition. Frustrating though this is to the manager of an able individual, it is invariably a situation which must be accepted – for the time being. It is noticeable that ambitions change with circumstances and, for example, may rise in line with economic pressures at home, or change when domestic responsibilities are over.

Occasionally, participation in a self-awareness or a self-development seminar, where there is strong feedback from a group of peers, may lead to a change in the level of self-confidence and an upward or downward adjustment to greater realism in ambition.

## MOBILITY

When an opportunity arises for an attractive appointment involving a significant geographic move, at least one-third of the immediate 'yes please' responses seem to get reversed after the partner or family becomes involved. In most of those cases, the partner may have given a casual agreement to the concept of mobility, but react differently when faced with a reality. For the planning of potential overseas postings, the discussion has to be blunt from an early stage, and specific as early as practicable to ensure commitment.

Even within the home country, the willingness of a south-east manager to relocate north of Watford cannot be taken for granted, even after a declaration of mobility. Establishing the extent of individual mobility requires real probing to ascertain the acceptable limits. The willingness of a family to move to 'x' will be much more positive, for example, if there are family connections in the area, but nothing is certain until the real offer is on the table, the family have visited the location, and the offer has been finally accepted by all participants!

Career progression in some large organisations has been linked traditionally to mobility. Development required that an individual did not spend too long in one place, and was rarely promoted without a transfer. The banks and the church were good examples. This policy is changing, and large organisations appear to be seeking new and acceptable rules. Acceptability is recognised because individual attitudes to mobility are far less permissive than a couple of decades back. Company attitudes have been influenced also by the high costs of transfers and the difficulties arising from enormous regional variations in house prices.

Career mobility is still expected from high ability, intensely ambitious individuals, who are clearly heading for high positions where some variation in experience and working environments is seen as essential. These committed individuals are likely to accept the opportunities to advance which are offered, and the employer is likely to have strong views on the experience it requires in its top people. The cost factor is irrelevant where the number of people is small and their future vital to the organisation.

Below this 'elite' group, there will be many marginal cases of high ability people, perhaps slightly less able or less dedicated, for whom opportunities which require domestic upheaval will involve a wider range of personal considerations. Some individuals will choose to step off the 'high flier' track, accepting that reduced mobility may have some limiting effect on their ambitions. Some movement of these people will still take place, but it may be more to deal with emergency business requirements than to develop the individual, and a significant proportion of company requests to take assignments may still be turned down for domestic reasons.

A further group which requires mobility covers those managers who are following functional careers in categories employing relatively small numbers (such as legal, personnel, and perhaps finance). There may be only limited opportunity for local career advancement within a company, so that individuals are faced with developing their careers by changing employment or accepting slower advancement as they wait for 'convenient' opportunities to arise within the organisation. Career development and continuity planning are likely to assume and encourage mobility within the function and across the corporation, so that knowledge of the real extent of individual mobility is important.

Inevitably, there will be a number of individuals who seek career advancement and will accept a geographic move, but who appear to have little potential for further growth and will therefore gain little from such a transfer. Where the enterprise does not see any value in the expenditure required to transfer such an employee, it is unlikely to be willing to carry the full costs of the transfer. Where such individuals take the initiative and apply for internal vacancies which involve a domestic move, it is reasonable to treat them at least as well as external applicants for equivalent positions. If limited financial assistance with house movement must be given to make recruitment possible, a similar level of support should certainly be available internally.

## CHANGING ATTITUDES

One of the features of preferences, ambitions and mobility is the extent to which ideas change, sometimes dramatically. I recall the sales director of a major public company who was very evidently at his career limit until his last child moved out of the family home and his wife promptly took a full-time job. Suddenly clear of domestic ties for the first time in years, the sales director changed his work pattern and attitudes and speedily became the obvious successor to the managing director.

Change of domestic circumstance is the most common cause of changed attitudes. Marriage, the arrival of a child, buying a house, or, alternatively, divorce will alter personal priorities and reduce or increase freedom of action. Most managers will pick up a subordinate's impending change of situation and ask questions if the change may affect agreed development plans.

### SUMMARY

Knowledge assembled about individual preferences, ambitions and mobility must be taken into account in preparing IDPs if these are to be realistic. This should include the views of domestic partners where these may override the views of the employee, for example regarding acceptability of an expatriate posting.

Views of preferences, ambitions and mobility sometimes change sharply over short periods, so that it becomes important to check the current position before career decisions are taken.

If individual ambition is felt by company management to be unrealistic, counselling or participation in a self-awareness seminar may be required to minimise bitterness from unfulfilled expectations, and to encourage realism about potential.

# V·7

# *Development: Individual Development Plans*

## INTRODUCTION

### The value of development

The managers and future managers of any company are its most critical resource. They have the capacity to inhibit or enhance business development. The continuity of the enterprise and continued growth and prosperity is assured through them. It is through your management resources that you obtain competitive advantage. Development activity ensures that you encourage your managers to achieve their full potential; that you ensure they are prepared for the responsibilities they may have in the future, and are able to achieve optimum efficiency in the present; and that the best of them develop that 'edge' which will enable the company to gain competitive advantage.

The whole management development process progressively focusses on the development of individual managers. As the process is demanding and time consuming, the return on investment needs to be clear. Managers should ensure that they *add value* to their subordinates, and that they use them well.

### Alternative to development?

The investment in time and effort required to develop managers is sometimes challenged by senior line managers preoccupied with 'today', and the alternative course of action (not bothering to develop people) should be examined. As vacancies would presumably continue to be filled, with or without development activity, the justification for development lies elsewhere, and there are four points worthy of comment:

1 Recruitment is expensive; it takes time; it brings in people lacking company knowledge; and there are invariably some people in the organisation who could have filled the vacancy. Apart from the substantial costs of recruitment, there may be periods when a managerial slot is vacant or 'covered temporarily' so that errors or serious omissions may occur. Development, career planning and internal promotions generally encourage retention of good people and minimise serious gaps in management staffing.
2 The planned preparation of a manager for a new role ensures that he will be effective quickly and not from a point some months later. In an important new assignment, preparedness can make the difference between success and failure, as delays can enable competitors to react and diminish competitive advantage. The planning of development facilitates the achieving of optimum deployment of managers as jobs and people change.
3 Evolutionary job change has to be identified and allowed for. As the business objectives and environment change, the detailed content and objectives of each managerial job, the degree of difficulty and the person specification and competencies required will be evolving continuously. Maintaining high standards of performance in this situation requires ongoing development and training, without which the risk of getting out of touch with the demands of the job may become serious, and at worst lead to ineffective performance and managerial obsolescence.
4 When a manager leaves a company unexpectedly, normal succession planning may not provide a solution. If the position is a key one, emergency succession should have been identified, but the individual specified may well be being prepared for some other post for which he has a preference, and was suggested for the now vacant position only on the basis that it was a low probability. Wide-ranging development plans can take emergency possibilities in their stride and provide a choice of cover which is both adequate and allows for individual preferences by being flexible.

In spite of these arguments, some managers still believe that the increasing rate of change in the business environment and in the skills demanded of managers is making any long-term and systematic approach to development rather pointless – but this is nonsense. However, development does need to be thought out and made to work properly.

## THE DEVELOPMENT PROCESS

### How people grow

People 'grow' in a number of ways. Their level of knowledge develops from a variety of learning situations, ranging from reading or watching, through various forms of education and training, to work experience doing a permanent job or part- or full-time assignments or projects. In addition to the acquisition of knowledge, some of these activities build self-confidence and competence, and encourage the development of personality, visible through improved social skills. The ability to take good decisions from inadequate information while under pressure may be one of the abilities which a young manager develops from an operational assignment. Only by 'doing' can he get a real appreciation of the demands and complexity of higher level work.

Managers grow far more from 'doing', from exposure and response to changing opportunities, than by any other means, although the use of training to supplement experience and prepare for further assignments is also important. A planned sequence of jobs, selected to fit his developing abilities and his personal preferences, and preferably under development-conscious managers, will produce the fastest pace of growth towards becoming a more effective manager and reaching his ultimate potential.

### Development planning

Careful development planning should stretch the competence and personality of the individual continuously and steadily, without undue stress, and with support ready to hand if called for. It is likely to take an individual of high ability up a ladder which is initially functional, and may then interchange functional and generalist steps in the progression towards top management. This progression should encourage the growth of both wide-ranging business skills and judgement, and the development of broadened personalities.

The process of personal development should be designed to maximise the pace of relevant learning and personal growth by planning appropriate deployments, identifying the stage where learning opportunity will be exhausted, and acknowledging the need to initiate fresh assignments to maintain intellectual stimulus and challenge in order to keep people at full stretch. It can enable individuals to progress to high levels at a fast pace, while ensuring that they acquire the necessary breadth of experience and vision in the process.

The 'designing' and 'planning' of development must be emphasised for it rarely happens casually. Development assignments have been likened to planting out young plants from the greenhouse to open garden. The ground needs to be prepared, the seedlings must be brought to readiness; then they will need some protection, particularly at the initial stage, and need to be watched throughout the early stages in case they should become battered by the environment. The parallel with young managers is strong.

It is the development opportunity, far more than anything else, which enables the young managers to grow; to push out the boundaries of their experience and enable them to feel free to set their own limits as they develop their abilities. It is rare for undue conflict to arise from fuzzy boundaries in a culture that encourages growth; concern is with growing rather than protecting a tightly defined patch.

In the development of managerial competencies, every manager needs to know something of how people develop, for he has *personal responsibility for his own development*, plus active involvement in and contribution to the *development of his subordinates*. It is no joke that some managers can develop subordinates, while others can only think of training courses.

However great the organisation's involvement, the ultimate responsibility for development rests with the individual. The organisation can provide a supportive culture and facilities, and can formalise the process so that individual development is planned and can be seen to be happening, insofar as development is relevant to the organisation. The limit to this involvement is that development for activity which is outside the concern of the organisation, say for hobby purposes, may be a part of an individual's development plan of which the company is aware, but in which it is not involved.

Within the interests of the organisation, some agreement on development objectives and optimum career development should evolve between manager and subordinate. This should take into account any career preferences and ambitions, as well as personal strengths and limitations, and likely career opportunities within the enterprise.

The pace of individual development is determined by our judgements of growth in abilities, readiness for a next step, and, to an extent, on the needs of the business; and are updated at the periodic Reviews of actual deployments which should take place at intervals.

As with the seeds in the parable, people grow better in fertile soil than on stony ground or surrounded by weeds. Development will be more effective if the environment is encouraging rather than unsupportive. Talking on this subject, a former chairman of 3M is reputed to have said, "If you want the best from people, give them room to grow ... if you build fences around people, you get sheep."

## Mentors

To facilitate optimum growth, the use of a high level 'tutor' or 'grandfather' (not the direct line manager) to oversee each high potential individual, to talk with him periodically and influence the direction of his development, can be invaluable and should be encouraged. (This is not always practicable, particularly in smaller overseas companies.)

The mentor can be invaluable as a stimulant and guide to the developing manager, and also as a spur to the company to ensure timely actions to prepare for the next deployment of his charge or participation in relevant training. With more time to devote to development issues than a direct line boss, and more 'clout' than an adviser from human resources, the mentor can play a substantial and direct role in steering the course of development and ensuring that the right things are done. In this respect, he provides invaluable support.

In addition to mentors, some direct line managers are exceptionally effective as developers and motivators of their subordinates. These managers need to be identified and utilised as a vital resource. They deserve to be allocated the best of the high potential candidates, for they are likely to guide the growth of these people through any difficulties and to produce the best developed subordinates. (Invariably, they also produce excellent personal performance!)

## Development jobs

One of the best ways of developing experience is by assignment to carefully selected jobs. Many companies believe that some particular jobs are especially valuable for this purpose and specify identified positions as 'development jobs', which are reserved for the exclusive appointment of the higher ability younger managers as definitive steps in their personal growth.

These posts include, for example, the general managership of smaller businesses where an individual can get to grips with a full business for the first time and take profit responsibility. Certainly these posts can represent considerable career milestones. Another favourite is the business planner for a business, usually under the overview of a more senior corporate planner. Business planning, of course, involves integrating inputs from all functions and develops an appreciation of the working of the total business.

In practical discussion with top line managers, I find that the development requirements of their managers are very diverse, so that only a small proportion of their needs are adequately met by the designated development slots. It is only when the total range of jobs is considered as accessible for development that needs can be met fully.

Of course, there are people already in most jobs, but no-one should stay put for ever, and the need to clear the way for a 'rising star' may be just the trigger required to encourage serious thought about the next assignment for a manager who has become stuck and may be at his limit. It is curious how well some moves initiated in this way provide a resurgence of effort on the part of the moved manager.

Another way to open a particular slot for use in development is by a simple exchange of positions for a set period, where the slower progressing manager may return to his old post after a two year stint elsewhere, while the faster moving manager is assigned to his next challenge. Or the manager whose position is 'borrowed' may undertake a project assignment for his own further development.

While it is advisable not to shuffle managers too frequently, it is at least as important to make sure that no-one stagnates. Development planning should create real pressure for change wherever this appears to be happening.

## THE ELEMENTS OF DEVELOPMENT

There are a number of actions or elements in an individual development plan:

- Planned work experience
  - challenging assignments
  - moves when learning opportunities in a job are exhausted
  - projects and secondments
  - internal/external
  - full-/part-time.

- Training and education
  - training
    - knowledge and skills required in current/next/future jobs
    - bring 'technical' knowledge up to date.

  - education
    - further education
    - professional qualifications
    - languages.

  - other self learning
    - professional reading/reading lists

- Coaching, mentoring and counselling.

Most of this list is self-evident, but some comment on the value of project teams for development is relevant. It is already obvious in organisation structures developing along the lines suggested as the norm in the future, that there will be a great increase in the use of multi-functional project teams for an astonishing range of purposes, and that this provides great developmental exposure to other functions and to the workings of the business.

In one forward-looking organisation, I found teams looking at the more obvious business problems, and then others looking at such things as job restructuring to reduce the number of interfaces; to improve focus on customer issues; to reduce management layers and increase spans of control. Others were reviewing the perception of business sectoring, at expense control, at line management participation in human resource management, and so on.

Selection of people for project teams will be influenced by their ability to contribute to the problem in hand, but the obvious people may be set in their views, so that selection of high ability people who will be more open-minded and who *will have to learn* may provide the most productive contributors.

## CAREER PATHS

John Smith starts his career as a graduate entrant and management trainee, and finishes as managing director. The path he may have taken on the way has been the subject of a number of studies. His career may have unfolded within one company, or he may have been forced to move about in order to achieve his promotional steps. Increasingly, his career development will have been planned, a process variously known as 'career profiling/planning/pathing/mapping'.

### The career pathing process

Career paths are designed to encourage systematic development of numbers of similar individuals, such as the graduate intake, to ensure that each has the opportunity to participate in the full range of training and to gain experience in a planned range of relevant activities, and then to progress logically along the most suitable career development route.

These routes can be relatively simple for most people, for the bulk of the 'future manager' intake will enter a particular function, and through their early years will concentrate on developing their knowledge and skills within that area of choice. Most will seek a variety of experience to cover all aspects of their chosen function before concentrating on more general operating roles within the function, or a specialist aspect.

For example, young accountants will tend to want some experience of the various elements of financial management, after which some will want operating responsibility leading into full accounting responsibility for a small unit, while others will be attracted to financial analysis, or taxation, or to an audit practice. There is substantial interchangability at the early stage, but as people progress further along a career path, it becomes more difficult to switch to an alternative, due to differences between knowledge acquired and that required in a job.

This rigidity is in conflict with the needs at the higher reaches of management for both generalists and specialists. Some companies have clear rules that no-one may be appointed to positions above a certain level unless they have spent time working in two major functions in addition to their primary one. An accountant must have worked in a production or technical capacity and in marketing, for example.

There is real advantage in general managers having fulfilled this requirement, but I have reservations about the same rule being applied to top functional people. There is no doubt that they must have a full *understanding* of the interrelationships and workings of the complete organisation, but this can be acquired without trying to do jobs for which they may not be suited.

Inter-functional movement, and indeed inter-company and international movements can all be expensive, and each organisation needs some ground rules. There are two main justifications for authorising such movement:

- The movement is a part of planned development for the individual, who is believed to have high potential to progress to more senior positions, *and* the broadening is believed to be in the long-term interests of the corporation.
- The movement is required by the corporation to meet a particular business situation which cannot be achieved with a lower cost solution. The movement may involve a key individual (the only man for the job), or may involve a high potential individual who also meets the first justification.

Transfers to broaden experience which involve heavy expense should not be accepted where neither of these criteria apply.

Probably the bulk of career progression takes place within a single function, with only a relatively small number of people deliberately moved or casually moving between career streams. The company is likely to want a small core of high ability people to gain multi-functional experience as a preliminary to general management or a top functional post, but it would see little advantage from more widespread interchange. Similarly, for employees generally, their market values represent the sum of their knowledge and experience and ability to apply these, so that any move to a fresh function not 'subsidised' by management would involve a drop in value which would rarely be acceptable.

## Single function career patterns

The annual graduate intake is predominately into jobs with the expectation that, at least for the early years, progression will be into the junior management of the selected function. At the initial stage, only a small number of graduates are seeking to broaden immediately.

If the bulk of early career development is within a functional group, it is logical to define sensible stages and to encourage some systematic progression through them. Normal rates of flow should evolve so that requirements can be forecast, and the core training relevant to each stage should be clear. However, the rate of individual progress should vary with performance, as appraisals show how quickly an individual gets on top of the demands at each level, and assessments of potential show ability to cope with higher and wider-ranging assignments.

Example 24 shows a structure for the progression of manufacturing engineers through the ranks. At the beginning, graduate engineers undergo some initial induction, and then a period of two years of varied experience and training designed to prepare them to qualify as chartered engineers. At the end of that phase, they go on the first management programme in the core training structure, and move into a 'position of responsibility', based on preferences and strengths. In this job, they continue to participate in some production training modules, as well as further management training.

Further assignments would be considered at the six-monthly deployment reviews, where consideration of readiness to move and the best next step (at the same level or more senior) always precedes any review of vacancies. If individuals are ready for a move, then a means of matching readiness to opportunity should be found, if necessary by shuffling several people. In practice, some people might spend several years, and perhaps do two or three jobs, at that first management level, while another individual might move up after a single 18-month assignment, based on management's assessment of his readiness and ability to cope with higher levels of work.

As the manufacturing engineering career structure goes to higher levels, the numbers of jobs inevitably become fewer, and the length of time spent in each job becomes longer. Some individuals reach their personal ceilings at each of the levels, and the extent of this

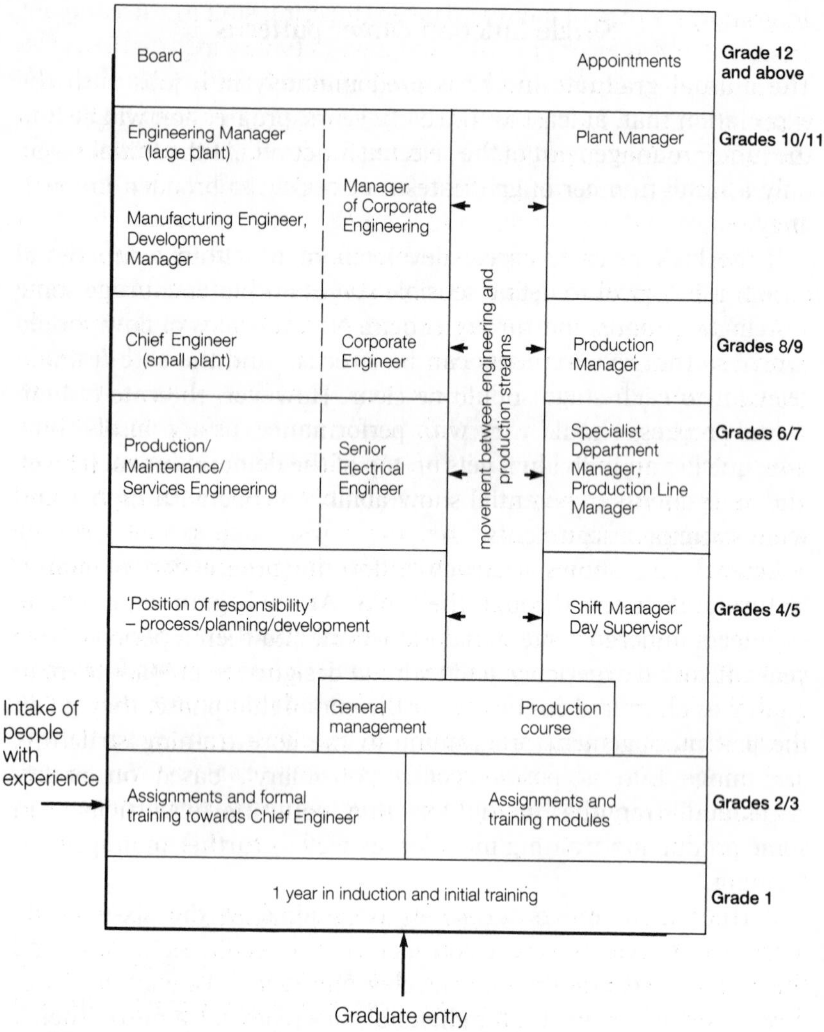


**Example 24** Career development structure: engineering and production management

needs to be monitored to ensure that the progress of younger able managers is not blocked. Some weeding out may be necessary if this begins to happen, to transfer out people who have run to seed.

For able senior people who reach their career limit in their forties, movement into a different post at the same level after five to seven years is advisable, to stimulate them with fresh challenges. One senior position not shown on the example (as it has some flexibility in grading) is that of mentor. The engineering staff in the company from which this example was taken always have a mentor to oversee the career development and counselling across the function: always a senior manager assigned for the last five years or so of his career, and selected for his past achievements in developing subordinates.

Similar structures and philosophies exist in that company, covering finance and marketing groups, for their information technology staff, and abbreviated profiles are used for functions with smaller numbers. They can be used in virtually any organisation.

Within finance, marketing and personnel, the corporate career streams divide between some of the specialist aspects and the functional generalists, with relatively little interchange between them. For example, taxation and audit people seem to have chosen their own paths and wish to retain their specialist knowledge. In personnel, the general personnel officer/manager stream is often separate from streams of specialists in narrower fields such as salary administration, which may be largely outside the area of involvement of the generalists.

Interestingly, patterns of market values reflect this separation and lack of flow, so that specialist posts within a function are frequently more highly priced than generalist jobs in the function with apparently similar personal specifications. A closer look suggests that person specifications may be different, with rather unusual personalities fitting naturally into some demanding specialisms.

## Multi-function career planning

In some organisations, it is still rare to find a manufacturing manager with some marketing experience, for career planning will have followed 'natural' lines of progression through a single function. This may have been perfectly acceptable for the majority of managers, with only a small number provided with any operating experience outside their primary function, but it has become essential for senior managers to have a total understanding of the business.

Where career development expands to include more than one career path, the pattern may develop as shown in example 25. This criss-crossing could be between the line and functional roles within one function; between the primary functions and assignments in

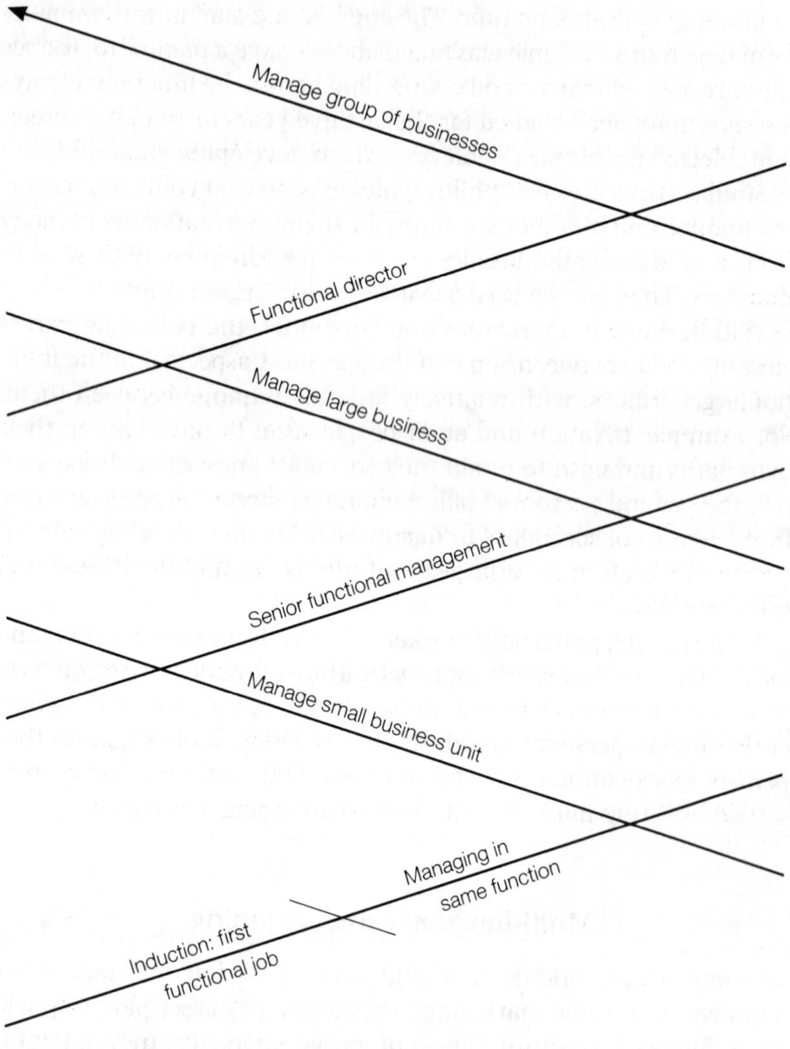


**Example 25** Career progression criss-crossing between functional and general management paths

other major functions; or between progressive appointments alternately in general and functional management.

Other companies make reference to 'spiral' career paths, where the progression is broadened to provide experience in additional functional areas to supplement the criss-crossing between line and primary function deployments.

The critical factor is that there must be a purpose behind career patterns of this type, a longer term intention which may not be evident from any single appointment along the way. Usually this will take the form of a long-term plan to develop a high ability individual towards a much more senior post, with a series of hurdles to be overcome in the process.

Such a career path has a distinctly higher than normal level of risk, although it may be associated with a similarly high level of potential reward! The risk element should be accepted as largely a company responsibility, in that it is taking the critical decisions to expose the individual to the appointment and will have assessed the form and extent of the risk in advance and judged that it can be overcome. If there is a failure (and there will be some), it must be handled sympathetically as a learning experience, and career damage minimised for the high ability individual who continues to be a valuable corporate resource. Frequently, the reason for failure will be unexpected change in the business environment which an inexperienced man could not be expected to handle.

## The future

Future organisations appear to require greater degrees of specialisation, but combined with even wider appreciation of where each contribution fits into the overall business, plus an understanding of the overall business operation. This will develop in part by the increasing use of project teams, which will tend to provide more extensive cross-functional exposure; and also by use of management training modules designed to set individual specialist areas in the context of the broader business.

As we evolve towards future structures, the manager who is a possible future managing director must be provided with the broadest possible range of experience, covering not only the various facets of his original function, say marketing, but also finance and ideally at least one other function. A key purpose of development planning is to prepare each individual systematically for anticipated future responsibility by arranging to fill in the experience gaps and overcome any weak points. Good people with the potential to move into wider spheres of responsibility should be given opportunities to get to know several functions at first hand. Even if they finish up as head of a functional area, they will need the understanding of how functions integrate in order to be fully effective. This is most easily achieved through some form of planned job rotation.

In the future organisation, there will be an end of the traditional hierarchical structure, with a grading structure associated with ranks and responsibilities, and promotional ladders by which individuals progress up the structure. There will be relatively few 'ranks', but far more significant will be the cultural differences which will change the career structure.

The structure is likely to develop with 'personal grading', in which career advance may take the form of a higher personal rating of knowledge level and ability to contribute to the business, without any apparent change in responsibilities. This may appear to be a move towards the pattern in the civil service and local government which appears to be qualification and service dominated; but the future industrial pattern will have to establish objective criteria related to value of knowledge and the ability to apply knowledge to business decisions, actions and initiatives. Some of this will continue to be single function or single activity linked and provide areas for the development of high level narrow specialists. Other individuals (and even the top level specialists) will use project participation to broaden inter-functional knowledge, and progressively develop multi-functional management experience. The leading edge of this change is already visible in high technology companies, new industries, and others which have progressed through major transforming change.

## INDIVIDUAL DEVELOPMENT PLANS

The management development system must cover every individual. An IDP should exist (however simple the format) *for every manager*, up to and including all board members. For an individual approaching retirement, the IDP may show no more than a retirement date and a note of the action to be taken at that time. Another may record that an individual will progress no further, but if he is 15 years from retirement, other actions may be called for to provide ongoing stimulation and job satisfaction to avoid deterioration of performance.

An IDP is relevant for *all* career staff. Based on all available objective information about each individual (including known preferences, etc.), plus future organisation and management requirement data, the IDP should record how you expect the individual to develop over the next several years (including alternative options where appropriate), and detail development plans, training requirements, and anticipated appointments.

*These are working documents*, continually added to and annotated as plans or moves are put into effect, and monitored to ensure plans are implemented. As such, they sit with the line manager as a reminder of *his* commitment to planned actions, but management development staff should monitor progress. Although these are working documents, the *quality* of the evaluation and decision-taking is of critical importance to the future both for the individuals and for the company, so that any limitations in the process must be corrected.

## Ready to move

Within the management development process, identification of individuals who are ready for fresh assignments, or for further stretching, etc., and then taking actions to move them on to their next assignments for further growth is vital, and must be followed through, *however valuable they may be in their present role.* To slow or block the growth of an individual ready to grow may damage or restrict the ultimate potential of that individual.

Periodic reviews of the abilities and readiness to advance of all senior and management staff are essential, and every vacancy provides a career development opportunity. The ideal next assignments for all managers should have been determined, together with provisional timing, so that moves can be planned ahead to ensure continuity (frequently involving a chain of related moves). Where no local opportunity is likely for an able individual becoming ready for a move, wider opportunities should be sought within the group. The current state of readiness to move for each individual should be evident on his IDP and is part of the overall management inventory.

## Individual Development Plan content

An IDP is a brief summary of the key information related to the individual's forward career plan. It is likely to contain the following data:

| INDIVIDUAL DEVELOPMENT PLAN<br>*(NOTE: SEE PRINTOUT OF PERSONAL HISTORY ON REVERSE SIDE)* | | **CONFIDENTIAL** |
|---|---|---|
| SURNAME | FORENAMES | |
| POSITION TITLE | COMPANY | LOCATION |
| PERFORMANCE ANALYSIS | | |
| POSSIBLE ULTIMATE POTENTIAL *(INDICATE SPECIFIC POSITIONS)* | | |
| DEVELOPMENT NEEDS | | |
| LIMITATIONS TO BE OVERCOME<br>PREPARATION REQUIRED FOR FUTURE APPOINTMENTS | | |
| TRAINING NEEDS | | |

| DEPLOYMENT PLANS | | | | |
|---|---|---|---|---|
| 19__ | 19__ | 19__ | 19__ | 19__ |
| | | | | |

| PREPARED BY | DATE |
|---|---|
| | |

Example 26 Individual Development Plan: format 1

| | |
|---|---|
| Identification: | Name<br>Job title/company/location/grade<br>Date of birth/age |
| Summary of career/experience: | Qualifications/major training courses attended<br>Dates/companies/positions/major achievements |
| Strengths: | Summary of major strengths relevant to future job possibilities |
| Limitations: | Notes on any factors which may restrict the scope or direction of his future development, or which need to be overcome by experience or training |
| Personal preferences: | Mobility<br>Job type<br>Extent of ambition |

Development action plans:

| | |
|---|---|
| (i) Job: | Ready for move when?<br>Next job/options/timing<br>Specific appointment planned |
| (ii) Other factors: | Training plans to meet agreed needs<br>Actions to overcome critical limitations<br>Experience needs to be met |

*Note:* Where Assessment Centre or current psychometric data are available, this should be indicated and any key information recorded.

Examples 26 and 27 show IDP formats developed by two major companies, and example 28 shows a variation which I have used, setting out similar information on a blank sheet.

## Individual Development Plan audit

Preparing an IDP may be the easy part, as implementation causes more headaches. As with any other plan, it represents the best effort at the time the plan is made, but the business situation

<table>
<tr><td colspan="2">INDIVIDUAL DEVELOPMENT PLAN</td><td>DATE</td></tr>
<tr><td>NAME</td><td colspan="2">TITLE</td></tr>
<tr><td>COMPANY</td><td colspan="2" rowspan="2">INDIVIDUALS RESPONSIBLE FOR MONITORING PLAN</td></tr>
<tr><td>LOCATION</td></tr>
<tr><td>IMMEDIATE SUPERIOR</td><td colspan="2">HUMAN RESOURCES</td></tr>
<tr><td colspan="3">POSITIONS FOR WHICH EMPLOYEE IS PLANNED NOW</td></tr>
<tr><td colspan="2">POSITIONS FOR WHICH EMPLOYEE IS PLANNED IN 1–3 YEARS</td><td>TIMETABLE</td></tr>
<tr><td colspan="2">POSITIONS FOR WHICH EMPLOYEE CAN QUALIFY IN 3–5 YEARS</td><td>TIMETABLE</td></tr>
<tr><td>DEVELOPMENT NEEDS (PRESENT POSITION)</td><td>PROPOSED ACTIONS</td><td>TIMETABLE</td></tr>
<tr><td colspan="3">DEVELOPMENT NEEDS (FUTURE POSITIONS)</td></tr>
<tr><td colspan="3">ASSIGNMENTS SHOULD BE PLANNED TO ENSURE THAT OPPORTUNITIES CAN BE REALISED<br>1.<br>2.<br>3. TIMETABLE<br>4.</td></tr>
<tr><td>MANAGER'S SIGNATURE</td><td colspan="2">REVIEW SIGNATURE</td></tr>
</table>

**Example 27** Individual Development Plan: format 2

and environment change endlessly, as do the pace of individual development, personal preferences and mobility, and the availability of managerial opportunities. Business change may cause opportunities for planned moves or assignments to disappear and require rethinking of a series of deployments in chain moves; the timing of a planned training course may prove difficult; business priorities may generate new and unsheduled assignments; and so on.

Any overall plan needs to be kept close at hand so that progress can be monitored and the Review process updated. Concern only arises when the plans agreed in an overall review begin to drift off course and are not being revised. Ideally, managers should audit the progress of development plans within their own area with some overview by the next managerial level. There should be sound *business* justification for changes, and evidence that the plan has been rethought and individual actions rescheduled. If this is not happening, it may be legitimate to ask why expensive management time is being wasted developing plans it is not intending to implement!

A periodic external audit, perhaps by a central management development person in a large group, provides a useful independent evaluation of progress. This should look beyond the implementation of planned assignments and training courses to review the success in developing the managers required in the business. For example, are management positions being filled internally by individuals of sufficient calibre as required; are people going into the positions planned for them, and on schedule; and are they being successful when appointed? This, after all, is the purpose behind all the effort, so if the end objective is not being achieved, you need to know, and to find out why. Any problems with the availability and preparation of candidates, judgements of suitability for preparation, or limitations in early specification of future job requirements, should be clarified.

## SUMMARY

The purpose of development is to optimise the growth and use of the management resources of the enterprise, both currently and into the future. Where orderly internal career advancement is visible, able people are retained in the business (and company knowledge is retained); employees tend to be motivated to perform

**Stanley Neal JACKSON**

**Born:** 12 August 1957 (33 in 1990)
**Married:** 2 children
**Qualifications:** BSc Economics

A short, stocky man, 5′7″, 170 lb, generally well groomed, quietly dressed, glasses for reading, mild Devon accent.

High intellect, high verbal skills – articulate, highly numerate. Warm, mildly extrovert personality. Good at social graces. Well balanced – stable, no evidence of psychiatric trouble, high stress tolerance.

**Education:** Plymouth Grammar School to 1976. London School of Economics to 1979 – pass degree in economics.

**Career:** Took a short-service commission in the RAF Education Branch and became a station education officer. Decided not to remain in the Service and sought an industrial education appointment in 1982.

Joined xxxxxx company as an assistant training officer and was transferred to assistant personnel officer at the end of the year. He was moved around to a number of assignments in the personnel department during 1983 and appointed personnel officer for a small factory (400 employees) at the beginning of 1984.

He was engaged on all aspects of personnel work, but under heavy-handed central guidance, and left to become personnel manager of xxxxxx company, a small independent engineering firm, in June 1985.

His contribution to this post was substantial. He developed a rational approach to all personnel matters and 'sold' this by formal and informal training at all levels.

Promoted to Head Office shortly after we took over his unit in November 1987, he became group training manager. He virtually created our whole supervisor and management training activity and is playing a part in planning development of individuals.

**Future:** Substantial potential evident. His work on specialised training courses has broadened him and an assignment on production planning from October next will be the first of three leading to appointment as manager of one of the smaller units in 2–3 years.

**Example 28** Career profile and Individual Development Plan well by the prospect of reward by advancement, and morale is high. Avoidable recruitment costs are minimised.

Development does not just happen. It requires careful planning, and discussion at several levels to balance individual and company requirements and preferences. As self-development gains greater recognition, 'joint ownership' of careers and increasingly open career discussion increase in parallel.

There are a number of elements in developments which need to be balanced. The major learning comes from doing; from taking responsibility; learning by experience. Selection of the right mix and sequence of job assignments and projects will enable the individual to grow fast, his development supplemented by relevant education and training, and guided by a sympathetic mentor.

IDPs appear to be crucial elements in the development process, in moving intentions from loose generalisations to recorded specifics. The format for recording is unimportant; the act of recording is vital. It enables each manager to follow up the development plans for his people and to question why plans were not implemented or were changed; an essential discipline if development is taken seriously. In chapter VI.1, this is taken further as a part of the audit of the effectiveness of development thinking and actions.

# V.8

## *Development of graduate intake*

### INTRODUCTION

The annual graduate intake is seen as the primary source of future middle to top managers in most companies over a ten to 20-year time scale. Candidates for the very top positions in that time scale are likely to come from the cadre of high potential younger managers identified during their early years and coming primarily from the graduate intake. The quality of selection to this elite cadre is improving steadily, and the career development of those on high potential lists is increasingly led personally by CEOs in discussion with their boards.

The task faced by most companies is seen as improving the quality of their total graduate intake, with particular attention to the flow of high ability candidates for the 'fast progression' cadre. Attracting and then holding people of the quality required involves attention to:

- clarifying *future requirements* – numbers, quality, profiles, etc.
- analysing *demographic factors*, internationally, and anticipating wider competition for graduates
- improving the flow of *able candidates* to the company and the attractiveness of opportunities
- improving the *quality* and suitability of those *selected*
- achieving full *utilisation*, and optimising *development* during the early years, with frequent objective reviews of ability and development
- personalising *individual* development
- progressively *identifying* those who appear to have the ability for

*'fast track'* progress, followed by in-depth assessments of potential after about five years
- additionally offering opportunities such as *MBA course* 'scholarships' for the very best, as part of the process of rapid broadening, and attractions such as financial assistance with relocation and house purchase to supplement competitive salaries
- *minimising losses* of people the company wants to retain.

## FUTURE REQUIREMENTS

It is recognised that future organisations will be different in a number of respects, and that companies need to make judgements regarding the numbers, types and competency profiles of the managers and specialists they will need for the future. Even by the year 2000, a number of changes are likely to be generally established:

- Developments in information technology will make much middle management administrative work obsolete, in that 'digested' data will be readily available through computer work stations, simplifying the supervision of subordinate operations and enabling control spans to be extended and management levels reduced.
- Business units may become larger, but there will be a great proliferation of multi-discipline project teams to progress action on many facets of the business.
- The 'command/obedience' mode of management will continue to decline, replaced by more participative and open leadership, again encouraging wider control spans and fewer levels.
- There will be greater diversity of specialist functions and greater individual specialisation; yet much collaboration between groups of specialists.

In summary, organisations are expected to be flatter, with wider spans of control, made up of specialist (functional) groups with more flexibility to form and disband teams as the business requires. Specialisms and specialist management will be more developed, but so will generalist skills in those who naturally lead teams or specialist functions.

It is necessary for each organisation to study those developments and make its own judgements of its probable future organisation and the types, levels and qualities of managers and specialists it will require. These may be 'translated' back to judgements of the sorts of graduates that should be recruited now. Future competency profiles are a prerequisite when defining the qualities to be sought in today's graduates.

## DEMOGRAPHIC FACTORS AND EUROPE

Demographic forecasts for much of the western world show some further decline in the numbers of people reaching university entrance age over the next decade, estimated as likely to reduce graduate output by 7–10 per cent in the UK over the first half of the 1990s. European data varies between countries, with Germany affected most severely. Variations in birthrate patterns are significant, influenced by such factors as the proportion of catholics or ethnic minority groups in the population (which have shown little or no change in birthrates) and the proportion of lower social groups with a high incidence of unemployment (which have shown the greatest falls in the level of birthrate). (See also the section on demographic change in chapter II.3.)

Demographic factors should not slow the graduate intake rate for most companies, provided that actions are taken to ensure recruiting success and encourage retention. However, given the added factor of the European market, it needs to be recognised that there should be some increase in UK recruitment from European universities, and that remuneration levels for graduates will escalate faster than general salary movement over the next five years. In parallel, the UK should expect some recruitment challenge from employers in mainland Europe.

There will be some change in the age mix of graduates as numbers of 'women returners' use degree courses as a route back into work, and more older people take degrees. As most graduate entry schemes are geared to the early twenties, the increasing number who fall outside those norms and have different career aspirations and potential will provide opportunities for employment initiatives.

Some *categories* of graduate may be in short supply. The area of most concern in the UK appears to be the supply of technical graduates, and there is great irritation in parts of industry that the output is not being increased at the expense of 'useless' archaeology and history courses, etc. The output of technical graduates through the 1990s is expected to be well below the requirements indicated by employers. Perhaps this will put sufficient pressure on the use and reward of these people to raise their status and their place in the pay hierarchy, and to generate the funding for more relevant university places. Alternatively, employers of technical graduates will turn their attention to overseas sources, and may need to transfer research, design and industrial engineering activities to continental bases.

## CANDIDATE FLOW

For most companies or groups, graduates are attracted by advertising, by distribution of brochures through campus careers offices, by 'milk round' visits and various graduate 'fairs'. The milk round remains the preferred recruitment source, as fairs rarely provide adequate opportunity to talk to good candidates and also attract numbers of first year students on 'shopping trips'.

Only a small number of companies are really well known at university level as 'good developers of young graduates'. The exceptions attract large numbers of applications, and can be extremely selective. Further, they do *not* have to offer high starting salaries if the norm of fast career and salary progress is established. Other organisations seeking 'the very best' but lacking attractiveness to graduates may offer premium salaries (50 per cent or more over the normal rates) to attract candidates, who can expect to be discarded after a year or two if they fail to perform.

Actions being taken to improve the flow of candidates include:

- increased use of high potential young graduates to 'front' recruitment in the field – particularly as 'campus managers' at their 'universities of origin'
- increased use of career success stories in literature
- more selective targetting of universities, plus the development of closer links with the careers staff at the universities
- increased use of carefully selected top managers to talk to graduates in the field, as well as when they come in for interviews
- increased attention to continental (and Irish) sources
- attention to MBA sources, and the offer of some 'MBA scholarships'.

Once the candidate flow is adequate, the urgency is to select and then clinch employment. The selection process is very much a two-way process, for while the company is sorting out the individuals who match its requirements, the candidates are selecting the organisations in which they will feel most at ease and which appear to offer the most attractive career opportunities.

Speed is important. The company which shows it can make up its mind and not get bogged down in administration – which can make the offer on the spot and hand over the formal offer before the candidate leaves the premises – is saying something powerful about itself as an employer. Most graduates are impressed by the employer's overall image and the career opportunities offered.

## IMPROVING QUALITY

Quality is singularly difficult to define. In general, most companies believe that they meet their own demanding quality standards, but most are aware of the high remuneration offered by some consulting and city firms, and the fast career development achievable in some organisations, and may ponder on the quality which has been missed.

The consensus seems to be 'try harder' to attract some of the 'very best' and, where individuals show high ability, to progress them on very fast tracks. To support this, reviews of performance, of pay, and of deployment are taking place at six-monthly intervals for the first three to five years, as a full year is too long an interval between progress reviews for fast developers. There is clear evidence that some of the most able graduates do not seek the highest starting salaries, but look for real opportunities to develop and to be rewarded for achievement.

Some measure of quality is possible in terms of psychometric test results against graduate norms (which some employers find a better guide to intellectual strength than degree class). Use of test results as a guide to quality assumes that the graduates are 'better' if their test results are above graduate medians. A variety of personality tests are also used in graduate test batteries, but unless some of the factors can be linked to required competencies, they may not provide much guidance, and certainly nothing measurable. Future competency requirements include the need to be highly articulate, excellent on interpersonal relationships, self confident, adaptable, able to cope with stress. Tests can add to the confidence in your judgements of most of these.

## EARLY USE AND DEVELOPMENT

A survey of current UK practice shows that the predominant form of graduate recruitment is direct into jobs; generally into the functions preferred by each individual, which then provide the early career paths towards middle management. Most graduate recruiters have numbers of jobs which must be staffed in this way. Research indicates that direct entry seems to be followed by faster career advance than starting as a trainee with a period of job rotation.

Development and training have a substantial part to play in the early stages of employment. Generally, they focus first on induction, and then almost exclusively on the function selected, but a number of companies provide exposure to several areas of the business during the initial months. A smaller number recruit graduates with a 'generalist' objective; provide an initial multi-functional exposure; and then agree a 'main stream' function for the initial few years, supplemented by wider training. There is little to choose between these options, as the spotlight is on all young graduates to pick out those with the apparent potential to progress very fast, but the 'generalist' induction may have attracted graduates who envisage a generalist career. (Others choose the generalist track to help them select a career function.)

It is the identification of exceptional potential which is the key to sorting out those who have the abilities and drive to progress much faster than the norm, and who have the intellect, interest and ambition to broaden, from whom some will rise to high levels. It is necessary to:

- 'test and stretch' all graduates
- ensure intense assessment of abilities and achievements during the early years in order to determine the varying rates at which they can progress, and to identify those with the apparent potential and the wish to broaden
- continue to recruit the bulk of graduates to fill necessary jobs, and expect them to progress in the initial function until they demonstrate exceptional ability and/or the interest and ability to broaden
- provide exposure to various functions during the initial months as a part of induction and initial development.

## ASSESSMENT OF POTENTIAL

There is logic in steady observation of performance and achievements of these young managers over a period of something like five years after university, before making a major judgement about long-term potential. Early judgements will have placed some individuals on a fast track, and these may well be confirmed in most cases. By the five year stage, young graduates have established an initial track record, their ambitions are clearer, and many companies consider that the timing is right to use some form of in-depth assessment which provides a very detailed picture of abilities and strengths to aid judgements on the next phase of career development. Detailed information is assembled on each individual for discussion at board level to determine which individuals justify inclusion on their young high potential lists. Those selected generally have their further career development through their early thirties planned, with some direct CEO involvement as they rise towards board positions. In big groups, this attention and progressive testing would continue through into their forties if they are candidates for the very top positions.

The selected cadre of those with high potential for development is of fundamental importance to the company – and should be visible on a regular basis. The board should safeguard the progress of this cadre, which can involve initiating moves to avoid the possible loss of individuals whose careers may be blocked, and broadening careers deliberately where this is thought to be in the interests of the company and the individual. It is not expected that all names will remain permanently on lists: continuing judgements will add and delete names periodically. The critical factor is that this vital resource will be visible, and the progress will be monitored to optimise development and value.

Top management attention must not be limited to this elite group, for the vast majority of the graduate intake will show potential, even though it may develop more slowly and to lesser peaks. Systematic and individual development for the whole of this cadre is essential to the future well-being of the company, and to ensuring its future competitive strength.

## MBA COURSES

With the rapid increase in the availability of good UK-based MBA courses, 'MBA scholarships' are being offered by some companies to the best graduates after three to five years' practical experience, where that form of broadening is seen to be in the interests of the enterprise. While some companies worry about their people not returning from these courses, there appears to be no problem where company development is known to be responsive and realistic.

It is likely that the numbers of MBAs qualifying in the UK will increase by a factor of ten through the 1990s, and that this qualification will become a significant element in the development of many high potential people destined for top management.

## REMUNERATION

It is not necessary to quote figures here, which would quickly become dated. Comment on variations in salaries is more relevant, and the ranges are surprising.

The 'fit' of starting salaries offered by any company must be such that the values of the levels of jobs and competencies achieved three to five years into the organisation relate sensibly to both starting salaries offered by any company and to the organisation's management salary structure. Some city firms and consultants appear to use starting salaries 50 per cent to 100 per cent above what appear to be competitive levels for similar abilities, and then to force very rapid development which results in a high fall out rate. Analysis of the sorts of people who survive this treatment suggests that they are the more mature graduates, who are quite clear about what they want to do and are highly ambitious A more 'average' graduate might reach this level of maturity in his mid-twenties rather than on obtaining his degree.

It is evident from other analysis that by no means all graduates are attracted by excessive starting salaries, and that many with excellent degrees and evident potential are attracted to accept 'ordinary level' salaries in companies where it is clear that personal development is excellent, that career advance can be rapid and is promptly reflected in remuneration. Some of the most effective recruiters use this approach and also achieve high retention rates (in a climate where many other graduates see company change as the only way to obtain varied experience and advancement).

A feature which has crept into many recruiting packages is the provision of various forms of assistance to get a foot on the home ownership ladder. As this is a popular ambition, and many graduates work away from parental homes, help with costs and subsidised mortgages can prove a great attraction – but it is very difficult to restrict such a benefit to a limited range of staff.

## SUMMARY

The graduate intake provides the primary source of candidates for future middle to senior management and is, therefore, of considerable importance to every company. The task is to attract and then retain sufficient graduates of suitable quality.

Demographic changes in the UK/Europe will have some impact on the availability and costs of graduates in the years to come. Mature graduates in the UK, and older graduates from the continent, will alter the traditional entry-age patterns (and perhaps career patterns) of graduates. Some categories (such as technical graduates) may remain in short supply, which may alter utilisation of graduate staff, and even location of high technology work.

Most graduates are recruited directly into jobs rather than training schemes and expect to stay in their initial functions through their early careers (and many permanently), advancing to middle management. Progressive selection of those with the potential ability to progress more rapidly, and to broaden, results in great flexibility in the pace and breadth of individual development. The most able form the 'high potential' stream, covered separately in the next chapter.

# V.9

## *Development of high potential*

The most important resource in the care of any board of directors is the present and future management cadre, which will ensure the continuation of the enterprise and its ongoing growth and prosperity, and provide the source for all competitive advantage.

Within this resource group, the most sensitive category is the select cadre of high potential younger managers, which will provide the primary source of candidates for senior management and board positions in ten to 20 years' time. The career development of this elite is increasing under the hand of the CEO personally.

### HIGH POTENTIAL PEOPLE ARE DEMANDING

High potential people are those with a combination of high ability and drive; people who make new things happen, anticipate and grasp opportunities; gain competitive advantage; and grow the business.

> At the point where we appoint a high ability individual to a new post, we (as his manager) have a tough task instructing and guiding him, but his learning curve is immensely fast. In a matter of months, he has a strong grasp of the job. He gets on top of it fast; innovates freely; develops his ideas and contributes to wider things. In all too short a time, he feels he has no more to learn in the post and feels ready for 'bigger things' and from that point his continuing employment is 'at risk'.

There may be an understandable pressure to keep such a person in his present post, for there is clear value to the company from his contribution and his manager will want some 'pay-back' from his own input to adding value to the man. But an individual with real potential will know that he is on top of his job and is increasingly aware that he could cope with something more demanding. If he is kept in the post too long, he may decide to leave, or he may become increasingly frustrated and become less effective until someone comments, 'Not the man he used to be – no potential'. Either way, you will have lost an individual with potential and, at worst, you may have a bitter man who is blocking the advancement of others.

The lesson is obvious enough. Where you have an individual of high ability, he is going to need extra attention and consideration. He is likely to get on top of his job 'too quickly', but once he shows signs of being able to handle bigger things and *begins* to look 'ready to move', then time is running out and you need to have that move identified and scheduled. If no opportunity is found within the area covered by his immediate management, and none can be created (by moving others, or in the form of a worthwhile project), it is important to 'flag' his availability up the line quickly to widen the search.

## FOUR AGES OF POTENTIAL

There is a great deal of difference between our view of the potential of a newly recruited graduate and our view of further potential of an established senior manager. Although significant potential can exist at all levels, and age should not be a bar, younger managers do learn and develop fastest. However, age provides an adequate basis for looking at different stages of potential.

### The mid-twenties

Up through the mid-twenties there is not likely to be any substantial track record to demonstrate evidence of potential. The judgements made will be based on intellectual strength, personality, and perhaps the degree of maturity evident. The first years of post-academic achievements are visible, indicating the ability to adapt to a fresh situation and make things happen. The embryonic track record is likely to look good, and early career plans have begun to test and stretch capability. This has been described as the exploratory stage of a career. At this age, the apparent 'fliers' tend to be those who appear more mature, are always quite certain of what they are going to do, and who are working hard to get there.

## The late twenties to early thirties

Age 28 to 32 seems to provide the critical decision-taking stage for most employers to assess potential. It is at this point that track records seem to be showing clear indications about which individuals learn fast, cope with new situations, and show a grasp of broader business essentials. All the available information is assembled to determine what is really indicated about future potential as distinct from past performance. The quality of thought and planning which has gone into career plans to test and stretch abilities now shows through, for those considered to have above average potential should have been placed in appointments and assignments which tested capabilities beyond their present levels.

At this stage, many companies supplement their data by making use of Assessment Centres, which provide more detailed information on the extent and form of potential, and then talk out detailed IDPs, which take into account apparent potential, individual preferences, and future opportunities.

It is at this stage that some very able people come to terms with not being ideally suited to general management (which in some organisations is curiously regarded as 'failure'), and direct their careers to high level functional or specialist management roles, or to non-managerial specialist roles which may become extremely influential and senior. As all these activities are essential to the direction of a well managed enterprise, this 'streaming' is valuable to all parties – and each stream is potentially as rewarding.

## The thirties

The thirties provide a period of great testing and stretching as individuals climb their chosen paths at varying speeds. Some will continue to show an astonishing ability to grasp the complexities of new situations quickly and make real contributions, while for others the pace is simply slower, or a ceiling is reached.

### The forties

In the forties the high potential stream has thinned out considerably, and now it contains only the small number of highly placed individuals who are thought to retain the potential for significant further advance. The testing and evaluation of this group to determine their suitability for the highest offices will be ongoing.

There are many individuals who will be assessed as having potential for further advancement well beyond their forties, and no cut-off point is implied here. In fact, most managers have some further potential at all stages of their careers, but 'high potential' implies the ability to achieve significant further advance in a short period of time, and that does become progressively more rare.

## DEVELOPMENT

Organisations which actively manage the process of development gain a significant competitive advantage. Research in the USA has shown a correlation between the most successful top managers and the breadth of their experience, showing that slightly less successful top managers in the same enterprise had rather less breadth of experience.

The development of high potential follows the same basic style and principles as the development of other managers, virtually all of whom have *some* potential to do other or higher level jobs. The 'peculiarity' of the high potential stream is in their ability to absorb new information and new situations at an exceptional pace; to complete the learning curve in a new situation and move rapidly into the contributing phase. The penalty is that such people can run out of learning opportunity in a job and become bored too quickly. Once they feel ready for new challenges, they may concentrate effort on finding them at the expense of their current assignment.

### 'Test and stretch'

If their development is to be managed effectively, such individuals' proven abilities and their needs must be comprehensively understood, and assignments found for the best which are marginally beyond their near-term capabilities so that they are challenged to the limit and must strive hard to cope. That can be a critical time if any unexpected development should occur, but the next level of management should be 'on alert' to provide support in that eventuality. In the process these individuals grow rapidly, but all too quickly they complete or get on top of the task, and once again begin to show readiness for the next. It is, of course, essential that the next challenge be provided, even if this means giving priority to young high potential managers when more proven ability is available.

Inevitably, not every 'challenge' goes smoothly, for there can be errors of assignment, or the business may conspire to produce an unplanned set of environmental changes! If 'failure' should occur, the probability is that it is not solely the responsibility of the individual appointed, particularly if there was a known element of risk in the project. There must be a commitment to watch and support any high potential individual who is placed in any 'test and stretch' position, for the probability of overstretching must exist, especially where the assignment involves extensive new or higher level responsibilities.

If 'blame' must be allocated for failure in such circumstances, it falls largely with those who created the opportunity and approved the appointment. The main objective in such a situation must be to recover the confidence and upward movement of the candidate by placing him or her in a fresh assignment with a high probability of success – and *not* recording a black mark. As one CEO noted, "When they stumble, they should be evaluated in a way that shows them how to succeed, rather than be shoved off the list of hot prospects."

This type of situation arises frequently in entrepreneurial style companies which are continually evolving new products and businesses, where the statistical probability and expectation are that a substantial proportion will need to be aborted. In such a culture, there is no shame in having projects which do not fly – only in not trying hard enough. However, some other managements have difficulty in accepting a share of the responsibility.

Some organisations make substantial use of 'development posts', which are specially identified as providing exceptional development opportunities and are reserved for high potential candidates. I find this excellent in theory, but rather mechanistic in practice.

It is, of course, always worth identifying positions which appear to be particularly valuable for providing developmental experience. Of overriding importance is identification of the development needs of *individuals*, and then matching those with the most suitable posts. Those positions are likely to have incumbents, but the point about development *planning* is that there should be sufficient lead time to arrange a series of moves without disadvantaging anyone. The availability of *all* jobs for development purposes provides maximum flexibility.

## Breadth of experience

A key demand from many companies is that all their high ability people must learn to run a complete business and that this involves doing it. If the company is fortunate enough to have a large number of small business units, and particularly if some are overseas, then these are ideal testing grounds and learning opportunities. Even where the manager in question is progressing towards a senior functional position, to have run a complete business with responsibility for the bottom line provides an opportunity to learn exactly how his function fits into the total business, which will remain invaluable.

However, I am not convinced of the value of insisting that would-be functional and specialist managers have to *run* a business in order to understand it fully. These people are generally highly intelligent and have the ability to grasp and fully understand business organisation and concepts without taking line responsibility.

There is much value to be gained from interlacing general and functional placements, in that an in-depth knowledge of the workings of more than one function gives added insight to operating in subsequent general or functional positions. Example 25 sets out such a career pattern. Also there is some evidence that individuals with the wider breadth of experience tend to achieve top jobs ahead of equally able but 'less broadened' executives. They learn to think a bit more strategically, rather than just analytically and as implementers.

## People management skills

One group of skills more than any other will be required by a future senior manager. The role of manager requires getting things done through other people. For some of these people, the manager is responsible; others will be his equals or superiors; others his customers and suppliers. His effectiveness as a manager and his ultimate performance will depend on personal relationships and his ability to get things done. As each manager exists within an enterprise, the task is to manage *through the system and structure*; to get things done through people within the organisation, systems and cultures in which they all exist.

In observing subordinate managers of high potential, the way in which they manage their staff (and other personal relationships) should be closely watched, to see that they develop a culture of open communication, that they are sensitive to others and handle people firmly yet compassionately, that they handle older subordinates well and gain their respect, that they develop their subordinates. If these things are going well, this provides another positive element in the growing track record.

## Training

Not all the development of the young high flier can come from 'doing'. There need to be injections of other learning to prepare for future assignments. Traditional management training in the form of 'receiving instruction' is unlikely to suit most of this impatient and fast learning group. It will be necessary for learning to be strongly project-based, preferably with live projects, with the potential to have a direct impact on company decisions and on the bottom line. This is not a place for the normal training establishment and staff. There is a need for access to a mentor; to high level expert knowledge in the form of business school linked consultants, and to senior management. The project limits should be wide open to allow free rein to exploring minds, plus some encouragement to discipline the direction of learning by self-management.

## Reviews

In the early years, it is advisable to review the progress of all graduates at intervals of not more than six months. Their recent progress, their accumulating track records, plus conversations regarding their development career preferences, should be used to guide selection of their next assignments.

Of particular importance will be the tentative judgements of longer term potential and the choice of assignments which begin to test the limits of ability and to stretch individuals who appear able to progress rapidly.

At this stage, the process is concentrating on early assessment to ensure appropriate placements and to optimise personal growth. By continual reappraisal, any initial misconceptions can be sorted out and early development can settle into planned progress.

Remuneration must be reviewed in parallel with career development, for individual contribution and worth will evolve quickly from the recruiting valuation. The spread of salaries will begin to widen rapidly from a very early stage.

## Individual Development Plans for managers with high potential

As the development of individuals judged to have high potential must be planned carefully and then monitored, the need for IDPs is particularly strong. As development may involve a variety of broadening assignments and projects, it is logical to have *five to ten year horizon Individual Development Plans*. These should set out the most likely series of career steps over the period – perhaps four or five steps over a ten-year period – so that the most probable career path is clearly evident. Additionally, some alternative options may be detailed, with some indication of the factors which will affect choice. It is useful to see what standards of performance and development are expected of the individual in his current and next assignments: what does he have to do before being considered ready to proceed in the next level? As each assignment should be planned with more than one purpose, ranging from acquiring experience to meeting certain commercial objectives, commitment to the success of each task is essential within the process.

A feedback of progress on development assignments should be

recorded on IDPs so that a comprehensive track record accumulates. *If career limiting factors are identified, they must be recorded and action planned to overcome them* if possible. They do not disappear if they are ignored (as some people hope), and are liable to occur more severely and cause career difficulties if not tackled. Some, inevitably, may prove career limiting, but sound identification and analysis should restrict damage and ensure that evident potential is directed to ensure a substantial career along lines which are not threatened by a single factor.

As noted above, the optimum career path for a high potential candidate should be outlined for a five to ten year period, with ideal postings noted, selected to provide the mix of experience sought. If one of those positions is filled by a long-term incumbent, and it is considered essential to provide experience in that specific slot, then priority may need to be given to the longer term development of the high potential candidate and a fresh assignment found for the blocking individual. If this should seem ruthless, one might also consider the positive aspects of a fresh assignment for a manager who has become stuck in his present position.

Ultimately, further progress will become more directly competitive as the numbers of jobs at each level decrease. Even when people reach board level it remains essential to seek indicators of further potential, and continuing growth should be encouraged and tested towards the highest position.

## Future specialists

The 'dual track' or triple track concept (general management – functional management – specialist non-management streams; in each of which there are equivalent career streams providing comparable status and pay opportunities) has gained favour over the years in quite a number of large companies. In part, it reflects proper understanding of the complexities of the organisational balance, but also recognises that some individuals can make outstanding contributions without having to manage operations. In fact many of the most fundamental elements in the development of a business may be determined by staff people, not by making the line decisions, but by identifying opportunities and developing strategies, and then influencing busy line executives.

The human resource area is an excellent example where this

should occur, where senior specialists have the expertise and the time to determine how to influence behaviour and systems and to make things happen. Much that is in this book that makes complete sense to line managers also presents them with problems of how to implement. It is for the business planning and human resource specialists to quietly guide and assist their colleagues to achieve the desired end results.

As high ability people go through Assessment Centres at around age 30, a few will show the qualities to develop into effective specialists – and little inclination (or ability) to manage. The career development of such people needs to provide massive broadening of their understanding of the workings of the total business, but should not attempt to force them to develop managerial skills beyond their abilities.

Increasing specialisation is one of the major themes to emerge from future organisation, so that non-managerial specialists are likely to become a more significant element in the organisation structures which develop through the 1990s. They are likely to occur in most sub-functions, wherever the corporate culture provides for due recognition, status and opportunity to contribute for specialists. Research and development is one area where this recognition is already established to great advantage, and provides proper scope and utilisation for some highly innovative people who view managerial responsibility as a nuisance which reduces their real effectiveness.

Specialists will find strong roles in the project management culture, where their duties and objectives will be clearly evident and require minimal supervision; in much the way that a medical specialist might provide services in a hospital today, where a 'project team' assembles briefly round a patient, bringing together all the relevant specialist skills to determine an agreed course of action, and then disperses.

## High potential lists

Many organisations develop formal lists of individuals currently believed to have high potential. In some companies, entry to lists is difficult and removal rare, while other companies have 'fluid' lists which are continually changing with reassessments. The most important factor in listing is the question of ownership. It is virtually essential that they should be owned by the CEO and his board if they are to be of importance.

Monitoring fast developing younger managers needs to be done with some care. When such an individual moves to a fresh and demanding assignment, he tends to 'disappear' from any list of obvious high potential people as, faced with a new situation, and possibly a different function or move into a generalist role (but hopefully not both at the same time), he or she will be at a low point on a learning curve and making a minimal contribution for some months. Subsequently, those same individuals will get on top of the new challenge and progress to make a high level contribution. By that stage they are fully visible again as high potential candidates, *but* should they ever have disappeared? It should require a deliberate decision to remove a name from such a list, and careful monitoring of those going through a trough should be an essential part of each review. Removal from the list of 'hot prospects' should not be done casually.

Selection of the individuals to be included on the list was covered in chapter V.5 on 'Judgement of potential'. The list may look like example 29 which is fairly simple, but it should be backed up by a set of properly detailed IDPs and by recent Assessment/Development Centre summaries, where available.

As high potential people get on top of a job, they tend to become restless, feeling a readiness for new or bigger responsibilities. If these are not evidently coming quickly enough internally, they may begin to look outside – rather rapidly. These are very mobile people, and the task is to keep them fully stretched and growing as a priority which overrides the business need to keep them in one position for an extended period. The main purpose in listing high potential people is to keep a spotlight on their progress so that signs of dissatisfaction are picked up quickly and addressed.

Should listed people be aware that they are 'listed'? I see no reason why not, but equally no reason to draw attention to lists. It is far more important to stress the fact of individual development being planned to optimise growth within the limits of capability and ambition, and to talk openly with *all* individuals about their own development. After all, there are many other managers of great value to the company whose potential is no more than marginally less than the selected top slice, and whose long-term development and morale are similarly important.

| Age Group | Division | Name | Age | Position | Grade |
|---|---|---|---|---|---|
| *25–29* | New Products | Strike G. K. | 28 | Senior Designer | |
| *30–34* | General | Black Q. | 30 | Finance Manager | |
| | International | McMahon C. I. | 32 | Sales Director – Zimbabwe | |
| | Retail Operations | Smit R. C. | 33 | Distribution Manager | |
| | Manufacturing | Cameron F. S. | 34 | Production Controller | |
| | New Products | Stark L. D. | 34 | Head of Market Analysis | |
| *35–39* | Headquarters | Spencer H. N. | 35 | Patent Attorney | |
| | Retail Operations | Tomlinson P. | 35 | Director of Management Information Services | |
| | General | Patel E. | 36 | Service Operations Director | |
| | Components | Fletcher B. | 37 | Exports Director | |
| | International | Evans T. B. K. | 37 | General Manager, New Zealand | |
| | Manufacturing | Davies J. M. | 37 | Production Director | |
| | New Products | Wallis F. J. | 39 | Planning Director | |
| *40–44* | General | White I. | 41 | Personnel Director | |
| | Headquarters | Leslie G. M. | 41 | Treasurer | |
| | Components | Rice V. | 42 | Marketing Director | |
| | International | Timmins A. L. | 44 | Managing Director, Australia | |
| | International | Shah W. | 44 | Managing Director, Middle East | |
| *45–49* | New Products | Kennedy O. | 46 | Managing Director | |
| | Retail Operations | Meyer E. P. | 47 | Managing Director | |
| *50–54* | International | McAllister D. R. | 52 | President US Operations | |
| *55–59* | Headquarters | Ward N. H. | 56 | Group Chief Engineer | |

**Example 29** High potential: corporate resource list
*Note:* Potential for rapid advance: two organisation levels within 5 years, or apparent potential to achieve promotion to main board.

## Ownership

Development responsibility normally resides with the individual himself, with his immediate manager, and with *his* manager, but for individuals judged to have high potential, the responsibility needs to be shared more widely. All managers are part of the corporate management resource, but within that group the high potential listed people are such a critical resource for the company in the longer term that a degree of 'central ownership' develops.

Depending on the size and mix of the corporation, a CEO and his board need to take personal responsibility for identifying which individuals have the extent and form of potential to justify top level interest, and for 'managing' those resources – to oversee and monitor the development of those individuals. The board which assumes ownership and responsibility must be able to provide the development opportunities to stretch those in its care.

Lists of the 'best prospects' will change from year to year as, in addition to the 'certainties', there is always a range of borderline cases with undoubted ability but with various queries about ultimate potential. These may come and go from the list. Equally, there is a need to ensure that good people are not overlooked. To ensure proper dedication to the task of identification of potential, it is not unusual for the individual bonuses of top managers to be directly affected, perhaps with 'plusses' for achieving listings for subordinates! On the other hand, virtually all managers have some potential, and there is a need to encourage optimum growth by the listed *and* unlisted people, as well as to refine the quality of the highest flying stream.

Example 30 shows pictorially the relationship of the corporate high potential stream to top management as seen by a chief executive. The categories of people noted on the chart summarise the individuals whose development and deployment should properly be under the eyes of the top board, as the single most critical resource potentially affecting the future of the enterprise.

## SUMMARY

The high potential stream should be seen as the primary source of candidates for future middle to top management positions and is, therefore, of vital importance to the company.

Within the management resourcing and development process most managers have some potential, so that it is essential to identify the extent and direction of each individual's potential and to identify the exceptionally able; then to stretch, test and monitor the growth

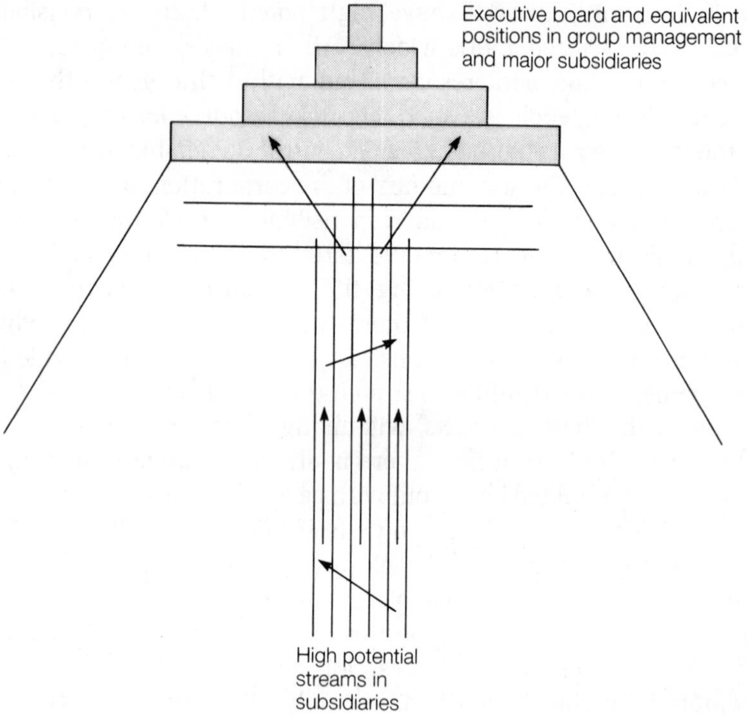


**Example 30** The 'centrally owned' management resource

of those individuals systematically using individual development programmes which progressively increase your knowledge of their abilities, strengths and limitations, and to ensure optimum rates of personal growth towards more senior positions. This process continues, with on-going evaluation and development of potential, right up to preparation for the chairman/CEO position.

Because this cadre is so crucial to the future competitiveness of any enterprise, it is appropriate that the chief executive and his board should take personal responsibility for managing the development of this vital corporate resource.

# V.10

## *Self-development*

### INTRODUCTION

Every manager should be acutely interested and active in progressing his own development. The days when an individual accepted that his development and career would be 'taken care of' by the company, that he would do the jobs to which he was assigned and go where he was sent, have long gone. Today, each manager not only expects to be involved in the direction of his career development, but is likely to express strong views on his preferences and to be taking initiatives to support the achievement of his own career objectives. Ideally, development becomes a partnership, with the company pursuing its needs in open discussion with its staff.

The manager assessing his own future prospects is likely to look for a number of general pointers to the company's attitude, for signs of scope to develop, and for indications of potential hazards. He may look for:

- signs of effective development planning
- signs of interest in his development
- apparent scope for advancement (as opposed to blocked paths)
- the availability of particularly attractive jobs
- managers who develop subordinates well.

By taking a look at these five pointers, we may obtain a greater understanding of the support for self-development which needs to show.

## Signs of effective development planning

An individual thinking about his own future looks round the organisation and observes staff movement. He is likely to look for signs that movements have been thought through and prepared for. When managers are moved, does the movement appear to have been planned to satisfy individual development preferences as well as company needs, or was it haphazard? Is the changeover as people retire or leave smooth and planned, or does it show signs of last minute panic? Do managers appear to leave in frustration because they do not progress?

He will also look for the factors which have influenced the selection of those promoted, for the behaviour of those promoted will indicate 'required behaviour' and will therefore influence the behaviour of others. If merit is evidently the key factor, all is well, but if some form of favouritism or nepotism is dominant, people may try to adapt to the company style – or will leave. From personal analysis and discussion, the individual will judge whether the top management and human resources staff are competent people to participate in the development of his career.

## Signs of interest in his development

The obvious sign of company awareness and interest is a career move or promotion, but actual movement is likely to be infrequent. While the frequency of moves may average something like 18 months for the young high flier, more usually there will be intervals of two to three years, and frequently longer, between appointments.

More significant and frequent are the performance and career discussions with the individual's manager, which are much appreciated provided they are meaningful. The employee is talking about his career, a delicate subject on which he is highly sensitive. He looks for genuine interest from his manager, appreciation of his value and potential, and real intention to encourage and assist his career progression. Words without commitment soon become obvious.

## Apparent scope for advancement

A company or function with a large number of staff in one age group may present a serious problem to a young manager looking ahead. The feeling that there is a queue waiting for any vacancy is oppressive, and the younger person with talent but short service may be justified in moving on, and may be retained only if he can be convinced of early prospects of advancement.

In a growth company where new jobs are appearing steadily and being filled by individuals recognised as being good internal appointees, other employees are likely to feel confident that their own efforts will pay off. But should appointments be more haphazard, with many going to outsiders, there is a clear message about company development philosophy, and good people will not stay long.

## Availability of attractive jobs

Most individuals have views about the jobs they would particularly like to obtain. These may be acknowledged 'plums' which invariably seem to lead on to even bigger things, or they could be certain line jobs which provide ideal 'bridges' from staff positions. Observation on the way these positions appear to be filled provides the basis for a cold assessment of the probability of the individual being able to obtain a preferred position. His conclusions, and a judgement of personal willingness to accept something less, will combine to influence any stay or leave decision.

## Managers who develop subordinates well

In every organisation there are some managers who seem to have a 'golden touch' with the development of their subordinates. People in their areas are encouraged and guided to develop rapidly, and subsequently feature strongly in the lists of promoted individuals. In contrast, there are other managers who appear to place a dead hand on the careers of their subordinates. Inevitably, there is competition among the best younger managers to join one of the forcing houses, and great concern to avoid getting trapped in a dead end.

SELF-AWARENESS

Observations on the development environment enable a manager to decide whether the company will be supportive in helping him to develop his career along the lines he has in mind, but, while this support is invaluable, the main drive and effort must come from himself.

## Assessment seminars

Self-development is logically preceded by self-awareness. Some organisations now run short seminars or Development Centres for groups of bright younger managers, which are designed to increase self-knowledge or self-awareness and to help clarify the soundness and achievability of personal career objectives and development plans.

These sessions will draw out information on a range of aspects. They should provide insights into personality and how other people see the individual. For example, a degree of introversion and generally poor people relationships, which may not have been understood previously, might be highlighted, although potentially career restricting. The process would also explore how the individuals learn and their style of learning, and may explore and challenge the personal philosophies of the participants. As a result, a number of young workaholics suddenly become aware that they dislike what has begun to happen to their lives, and realise that they have deep-rooted preferences for a different life style. Perhaps this might have remained dormant if it had not been drawn out, but its emergence five years later in a career might be even more traumatic.

From these seminars, or from private thinking, or from separate discussions, the perspective on personal aims will clarify, so that associated career objectives can be resolved and addressed.

## Career development options

It is unlikely that the forward view will provide a clear single career line. Invariably there will be options, and to some extent the options which are ultimately taken will be heavily influenced by the timing of opportunities becoming available. The chance to take a promotion is difficult to turn down if the preferred alternative is less immediate and less certain.

The task facing each individual is to identify a range of options which seem realistic from the starting point, and then possibly to add some less realistic possibilities with notes of the additional actions which would be required to make them achievable. For example, the individual trained as an accountant is likely to identify a range of straightforward options associated with progression from his initial functional training, but if he wants to progress to general management, there will be a range of additional criteria to meet. However, if the accountant decides to become an architect, he may have to return to the beginning of professional training in order to make that possible.

Each individual needs to assess the options available from 'where I am now', weighed against preferences, ambitions, mobility, and generally against what is sought from life, and then to determine the strength of preference for a particular track. I recall one individual who worked his way steadily and rapidly into senior management until, at age 40, he resigned suddenly and bought a hill farm in Wales. This had always been his real ambition, but first he needed a different career which enabled him to accumulate sufficient capital! Each individual, then, must balance the available options against all other factors, and identify his or her overall preferences, priorities and ultimate ambitions and once these are clear, decide how they are to be achieved.

However, not all managers have such a clear view of their preferred future. For some people, the implementation part of their self-development is focussed largely on continuous effort to improve performance and get right on top of the present job, so as to reach a 'ready to move' state before targetting the move itself. It is probably true to say that such people do not have a long-term plan, unless it is simply opportunist. Their attitudes are close to old style development, for the individual is leaving everything to the company or to chance, being content to accept almost any higher level post.

## THE DEVELOPMENT PLAN

Preparation of IDPs (see chapter V.7) should form a key part of the development process, provided that the plans properly incorporate the preferences of the individual as well as an objective assessment of his capabilities, and realism about opportunities within the organisation. Assuming that there is an excellent relationship between the manager and his boss, there should be ongoing career development discussion, permitting informal lobbying for consideration for particular opportunities, and agreed actions to develop skills and experience in preparation for the favoured options.

Inevitably, there is competition for most vacancies (*all* vacancies are development opportunities), and disappointment for some contenders. The timing of completion of a previous agreement may not be ideal, for example, so that a favoured post becomes occupied or 'blocked' for the next two to three years. This may be serious if the list of 'favoured' posts is rather short. Most high ability people involved in their own development tend to have an eye on external, as well as internal, opportunities, particularly at moments when an incident appears to go against them. It is to be expected that a number of them will be lost to ideally timed opportunities outside, although this risk is minimised by close communication between manager and subordinate, and frank review of both lost opportunities and fresh ones to come.

Career development is a partnership owned jointly by the manager and *his* manager, but neither has total freedom of action and their objectives are not identical. The manager has fairly specific ambitions and will be seeking satisfying and testing assignments which allow him to progress in the right direction. He will expect to gain full value from, and to contribute positively to, each assignment; and will not expect to move too quickly. The senior manager knows that he must plan to meet the management needs of his organisation, based on business objectives and environment. In parallel, he will want to deploy the full inventory of managers as efficiently as possible, while optimising development opportunities for all individuals. There will be some imperfect matches in this Review process, but these can be minimised by forward planning, and the linking of local Reviews into the corporate network.

A further advantage of the integration of local Reviews into the corporate whole is that if the senior manager finds that he has an excess of managerial resources, he may be able to open up available opportunities for some of his people in units outside his own sphere, and then discuss with his people the acceptability of available moves. Or he may be a net importer of corporate talent. In either case, he is able to involve his people in discussions to enable them to contribute properly to their own career decisions.

## SUMMARY

Recognition that the individual manager has considerable interest in, and probably strong views on, the development and direction of his own career is necessary in all company initiated career development activity.

Self-development can only be fully effective if the individual really knows himself well, so that his ambitions or objectives are in tune with his capabilities and personality. Self-awareness seminars can be useful aids for young managers who are still forming their personal objectives, or where their declared ambitions seem ill advised.

There is a need for clear communication between the individual and the company to ensure that IDPs achieve a balance which meets both company needs and opportunities, and the abilities and objectives of the individual; and to recognise that development planning involves a partnership.

Open communication based on this company philosophy, and evidence that planned development does get implemented, are critical elements in attracting high ability people to the organisation and then retaining them. Development practices are highly visible, and the thinking manager will read the signs on how effective development planning really is; how well plans are implemented; how much interest is evident in his own development; what scope there is for his progress, particularly the accessibility of the more attractive jobs; and whether his own manager is effective as a developer.

# V.II

## *Training needs*

### IN GENERAL

*Development* is about total growth of the knowledge, experience and abilities of an individual, the development of the 'whole person' as he progresses towards his ultimate potential. Development is long-term and future orientated; provides new perspectives and encourages strategic vision. In contrast, *training* tends to be narrower and shorter term, concerned with helping people do their jobs better, or contributing to preparation for future positions. Training is one part of the development process, to which it contributes by providing supplementary opportunities to acquire knowledge, skills and attitudes largely off-the-job, to help achieve desired performance or levels of knowledge.

A broad business justification for training might be to ensure that all employees are provided with the necessary knowledge and skills to enable them to operate efficiently and for business objectives to be achieved. Additionally, and as an investment, training should provide able employees with knowledge and skills which they will require in future assignments.

Beyond that, there is a divergence of attitudes to training. At one extreme is commitment to the total development of the individual as a 'whole person', with open access to training and knowledge-expanding sessions, including self-development interests (some of which may not be relevant to present or future jobs anticipated by the employer). At the other extreme is the view that training should be focussed narrowly on business performance improvement with an early bottom line impact, which might be achieved (for example) by putting a 'training cum business consultant' into a project team to improve project performance, but with no real concern for people development. A good middle-of-the-road objective is that all training actions should be in response to legitimate, business-related training needs. As one consultant put it, "If you think training is expensive – try ignorance!"

THE ROLE OF TRAINING IN PERSONAL DEVELOPMENT

## On the job or formal training?

The greatest part of a manager's personal development will take place on the job, learning from the boss and learning from doing, as he is progressively exposed to an increasing variety and complexity of assignments and new levels of responsibility. However, formal training is part of the management development process and, carefully planned to complement each step of a manager's development, can make a significant contribution to improving current job performance and preparing the manager for further stages in his career.

## Identifying training needs

All training must have clear purpose and value. It should be designed to meet defined needs, identified for individuals, or to meet company needs. The design should be both time- and cost-effective and should take into account individual learning abilities.

Not only must all training respond to the needs of individuals and the business, but it is essential that you:

- ensure that training adds value and has a direct influence on business performance
- re-establish training needs at regular intervals
- design, or review and update, the content and form of all training programmes to maintain high standards of quality, and to meet training needs in the most cost-effective way
- endeavour to measure the effectiveness of training in relation to the required impact on performance.

## TYPES OF TRAINING NEEDS

Training needs arise from the requirements of the individual within the business, or from the business itself. They arise from the individual:

- to help him improve his performance in his present post
- to assist in his preparation for a different or higher level position

or from the company:

- to respond to changing environmental factors which alter the objectives of the company and its managerial jobs, and the knowledge and skills required by its managers
- to respond to changing technologies or environmental changes which affect the ways in which managers will do their jobs.

At least once each year, normally following on from performance appraisal, a comprehensive updating and analysis of training needs should take place. Example 31 shows the process in flow chart form.

### Individual training needs

A range of activities provide sources of data on the training needs of individuals. Most of this information is assembled on IDPs, where it is integrated into career plans so that the requirement is properly defined, the urgency established, and provisional timing set. Most of the more urgent requirements will be scheduled for action in the immediate 12 months, while some longer term training related to future assignments may be scheduled for subsequent years. This great range of precisely identified needs will have to be summarised before a corporate training plan can be assembled.

Contributing to IDPs, particularly in respect of actions which may improve performance in the present job, is the *performance appraisal* process. This should provide a clear analysis of the individual's ability to do his job at the performance standards required, should identify shortcomings in performance and what can be done to overcome them, and include agreement on specific training actions. Further, the appraisal discussions should cover training needs, as seen by the individual as well as by his manager.

Any performance problem needs careful analysis before any corrective action can be initiated. The nature of the problem has to be

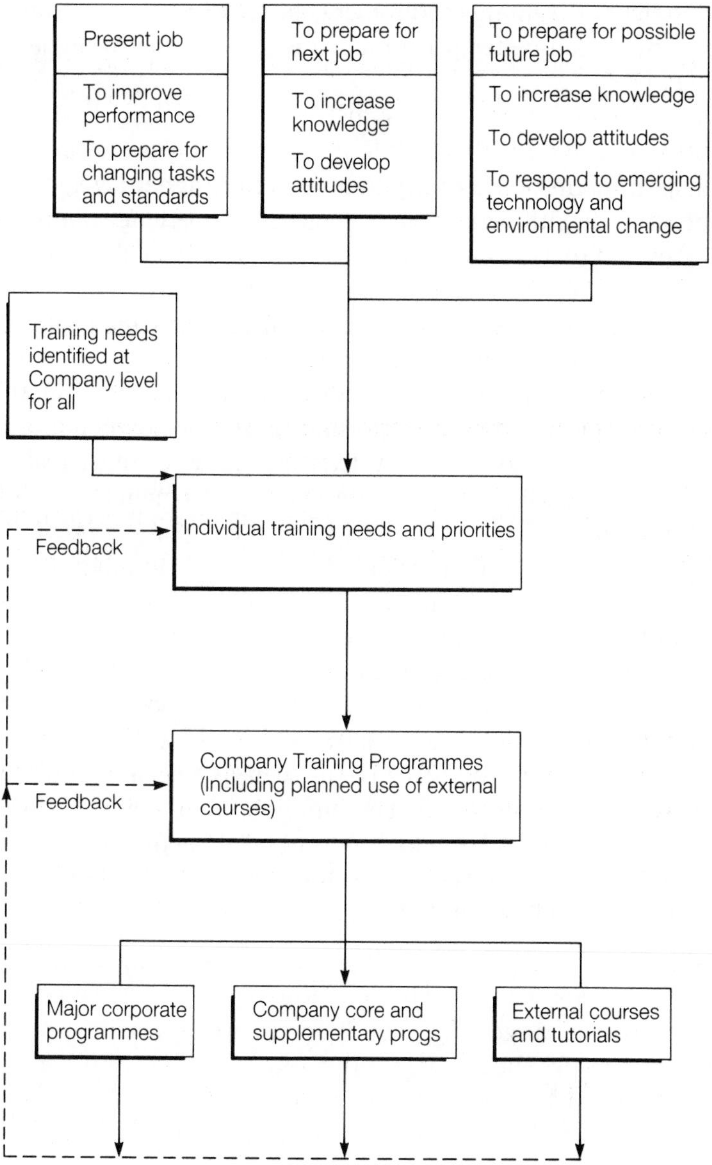


**Example 31** Training needs determine training programmes

understood before there is any probing into competency or experience deficiencies which may be the source of the problem. Only when the means of overcoming the limitations are clear can the development or training requirements be specified properly, and the process by which better performance is to be achieved made clear and agreed.

The other major contributor to IDP's will be *Assessment Centre* conclusions and any other aids to the *judgement of potential*. As part of the assessment of the ability to do other or higher level jobs, it is essential to identify gaps in knowledge, experience, and competencies and to evaluate how much it is possible to fill these in (for our purpose here), specifically by any form of training. Actions which can be taken should be incorporated into IDPs, even if the appropriate timing is two to three years ahead.

As a supplement to the individual training needs which are identified to meet company performance and deployment requirements, an analysis of company training needs to meet *individual growth objectives* is likely to generate some requirements for training, which may or may not fit in with what a company is prepared to provide. For example, there is an increase in the number of young people who want to obtain an MBA, and a parallel increase of external full- and part-time courses, some with company sponsorship. For this type of course, a major commitment is required from the employee, but his knowledge and value to the company may be increased significantly. Most employers are willing to provide some support, even where the MBA is not seen as relevant to the individual's present work, as the combination of company knowledge and enhanced overall knowledge has to be attractive.

There must always be a query as to whether the company process of establishing individual training needs is adequate.

> As a part of its annual survey of needs, one management set out to check whether they were missing key needs. They began by asking a wide range of individuals for their views on their personal training needs. These were written out on several hundred cards, and grouped by apparent categories. Further individuals were asked to place the cards in order of priority, first by category and then within categories, and a picture of perceived needs was assembled. In this particular study, no significant area was found which had been overlooked, but there were some important messages about the way priorities were perceived.

## Corporate needs

An *organisation capability audit*, based on business plan objectives and the changes expected in the environment, is quite likely to identify blocks of knowledge or skills which have not been relevant in the past, but which are about to become almost universal needs. A typical study might show a need for much higher levels of understanding of the acquisition and use of improved competitor information; or a recognition that internationalism of markets needs to be understood by managers in all functions; and perhaps an awareness that the workings of corporate culture should be more widely comprehended.

Factors which are expected to alter the operating environment and lead to a demand for new or different knowledge or skills require serious attention. The ways in which the necessary skills are to be acquired may involve a combination of external recruitment and internal training, possibly in a relatively short time scale. One issue may be recognition that the company needs a rapid advance in its use of information technology, likely to alter the jobs of many middle managers, where the training contribution will be critically important.

These real needs should not be confused with 'top management demands' triggered by incidents. For example, a series of poor presentations should not justify all managers being sent on a course on how to make a good presentation. Some managers may need it, but it is worth exploring the circumstances of the 'poor presentations'. Were they really poor, for example, or was the unreceptive attitude of the audience the real problem?

# TRAINING NEEDS ANALYSIS

## The importance of analysis

The mass of detail on the training needs of individuals, plus the blocks of training required to meet corporate needs, have to be analysed and summarised to produce an overall statement of the company's training needs and priorities. This will provide the source for planning and booking individual training commitments for the immediate period (for at least a year ahead). It will also provide the justification for modifications to established company or corporate training programmes, the specifications for new programmes, and the numbers and levels to be covered.

Where this process is not yet fully established, the principles remain true: there are no other meaningful sources of training needs data. In a poor situation, it may be possible to draw impressions of needs by interviewing line managers, but without an analytical base these will be of poor validity.

## Form of analysis

The analysis of training needs should be set out in a formal way so that it can be seen to be comprehensive, and to enable training to be designed and scheduled to meet the needs. A format for a typical analysis of training needs is shown in example 32.

Sorting out a large number of individual training needs into a logical pattern does take time and effort, as the detail of the needs must not be lost. The objective is to group together all needs which are related, for example all finance-related training requirements, so that the best means of addressing them can be determined.

Some companies transfer these data to computers, with classification of each entry for subsequent analysis and print out. Others use cards for each requirement and shuffle them into heaps, or simply list under selected headings.

*Functions and skills*

Example 32 uses the list format. Down the left-hand side is a breakdown of functions or skills (or competencies). I have seen a company-wide analysis on sheets where the listing covered some 200 headings, so choose the extent of your breakdown with care.

The first breakdown is likely to be by major functions, but in a large company, the volume of individual needs will require further detail. Each function may be sub-divided into obvious sub-headings, plus a general category. Then there may be a series of multi-function headings, such as human resource/employee relations in manufacturing or optimising product cost in design. Requirements for generalist training will frequently have a functional slant, such as financial management or marketing skills for general managers. Clearly these headings can be numerous and possibly overlapping.

| ***Summary for:*** ........................................................... Department/Division<br>............. Date | | |
|---|---|---|
| Categories | Detail specific areas and levels against individual names | Timing/ urgency |
| 1 ***People management***<br>Skills | | |
| 2 ***Functional management***<br>Indicate:<br>• Own function/other<br>• Level of knowledge required basic–advanced<br>• Practical operating/ management appreciation<br>• Specialist areas/general | | |
| 3 ***General management*** | | |
| 4 ***Language training*** | | |

**Example 32** Analysis of management training needs: format

*The level of training*

The analysis must also indicate the 'level' of training required, covered in example 32 under the heading 'Detail specific areas and levels against individual names', using the categories:

*General* This indicates a requirement for 'general' knowledge of the subject, sufficient to enable a manager to supervise or direct the activity, without being or becoming a functional specialist.

*Familiarisation* This indicates a requirement to cover the subject in sufficient depth to enable the manager to work with a functional specialist in the subject, for example, with systems and programming specialists upgrading an information system in a functional department, or to give a technical man a basic comprehension of financial controls.

*Detail: basic* This covers the basic training in the subject for staff who will be engaged in that field, or who are broadening into it.

*Detail: advanced* This level is concerned with operational knowledge of the subject, to enable an established specialist to advance his detailed knowledge of his subject. Most training would cover specific and generally narrow segments.

In the first two categories, it is possible to arrange training for people at a variety of hierarchical levels, with different needs, as distinct from the level of involvement in the subject. Against each entry in the analysis, some indication of urgency needs to be added.

*Identifying relevant needs*

It is important to stress that the training needs which are identified and incorporated into the analysis should be relevant to the business, and fit the cultural climate. It is easy to flood the analysis with non-essential 'needs' and then to run large volumes of training which have no impact on the business operation. This is sometimes known as the 'leaky bucket' approach to training, as new skills and knowledge are poured in but promptly drain away in non-use.

For the training needs analysis to be meaningful, the sources of information, the IDPs and individual appraisals of performance and assessments of potential, should be as realistic and accurate as possible. This calls for competence on the part of each manager in identifying and then specifying relevant training needs, at least in respect of the positions reporting to him; and subsequently on the part of the personnel or training staff involved in extracting data as they prepare the training needs analysis. The same care is also essential from those involved in any form of organisation or job restructuring, where training or retraining may be a key part of implementation.

As a further illustration of the complexity of this analysis, one need look no further than a typical profile or set of competencies for a middle manager, which is unlikely to be met in full and will require training to help meet some of the demands. As a specific example, if we look at the job and present competencies of an engineering manager, we might find a need for additional skills in a whole range of areas, including:

Some additional basic technical knowledge, or updating.

A creative element, to improve the ability to apply the technical knowledge to meet a stated requirement, or a new situation.

Cost awareness – a knowledge of alternative materials and their qualities and costs.

An understanding of how things are made, so that his designs can be manufactured within equipment and cost limits.

An understanding of selling, and of customer requirements which can temper his design inclinations. Also an ability to 'sell' his ideas.

Reasonable personal relationships with his manager; with his equals; with subordinates. This probably includes an ability to communicate well.

Most middle to senior management jobs have a wide range of competency requirements which incumbents should match for effective performance of the job. Examination of the needs of this sample engineering manager indicates the scale of the requirement for more know-how related directly to the job; more general knowledge about other functions; and invariably the strong need to improve some aspects of 'people' skills.

It is sufficient here to draw attention to analysis of the competencies required, and the role this plays in determining training needs (and, ultimately, training programmes). Analysis of existing competencies can provide indications of whether individual managers will tend to be naturally successful in learning new skills, by making simple comparisons between the skills already acquired and new skills proposed – a valuable guide where retraining and redeployment are involved.

## TRAINING PRIORITIES

A typical response to completion of an analysis of current (one year) training needs is that the company will need two to three years to get through it all! Sorting out priorities should not prove too difficult, but may involve going back to source material and judging the urgency of each element. Some of the larger requirements will stand out as essential and urgent, while others will clearly be less so.

Any tendency to postpone or put aside training in aspects of man management skills should be resisted. Many managers seem curiously reluctant to participate in training to improve their skills in counselling and interviewing, although these may be essential to their effectiveness. Some of the largest and best managed companies expect *half their total management training effort to be spent improving man management skills*.

The completed analysis provides the detail to be turned into training actions for the next cycle of 12 months.

## SUMMARY

Training is one part of the development process. While the primary source of learning and development is through the planned provision of job experience, this is supplemented by training. Some learning is best arranged off-the-job, and some training is to provide new knowledge or skills in preparation for future jobs. Training is designed to meet these needs, but first the needs must be determined.

All training actions should be in response to legitimate, business-related needs. Views of what should constitute a need vary widely, ranging from restricting training to essentials with an immediate impact on profitability, through to open encouragement of development and learning in the belief that this boosts motivation and business generally.

Training needs arise from individuals – to help the individual improve present performance or to prepare for future positions – and from the business – to provide new ranges of skills or expertise to enable the company to respond to changing environment and technologies.

An analysis and summary of training needs is required from time to time, drawn from a variety of sources, ranging from IDP's, performance appraisal and judgements of potential, through organisation capability studies, business plans, and current business performance problems. This summary provides the basis for determining overall training requirements, training priorities, allocating resources, and developing actions to provide the training.

# V.12

## *Training actions*

### THE BASIS OF TRAINING

Training is concerned with creating a rapid learning situation for identified groups of individuals with similar needs to increase their knowledge, skills and experience of predetermined activities, functions or behaviours. As managers learn continuously from daily events, training should encourage more directed and intensive learning in specific areas, to bring knowledge up to a desired level or performance up to a required standard, and should also enhance the managers' learning abilities.

Training is work- or activity-related. 'Academic training' or 'education' has its emphasis on systematic intellectual teaching, the provision of a base of theory. There is no boundary between education and training, only a difference of emphasis.

All training actions should be in response to legitimate, business-related training needs. Once those needs are identified, summarised, and priorities determined, a programme of *training actions* can be developed.

### MEETING THE NEEDS

#### How people learn

As the purpose of training is to impart knowledge or skills to those being trained, for training to be effective, some understanding of how people learn, or can be motivated to learn, is necessary. Training and learning are two different things. To quote the old proverb, 'you can take a horse to water, but you cannot make him drink'. In the same way, you can put someone through a training course, but you cannot make them learn.

If you want people to learn, it may be appropriate to assess their suitability for learning. For example, entry to an academic course is likely to have an 'entry gate' of successful completion of a preparatory or lower level course, which indicates an ability to comprehend the subject matter at the level required; an intellectual standard. Some training courses have (or should have) comparable entry gates in the form of some assessment of individual ability to cope with the training programme, as some individuals do get placed on courses which are at too advanced a level, and others may have intellectual limitations or some form of learning difficulty which may place them at a disadvantage.

The approach to teaching is of vital importance. It has been suggested that formal education systems tend to 'immunise' adult students from learning; that much of what we learn as adults is picked up in less formal settings. This provides an initial pointer to the sort of learning environment and structure of training required to optimise learning by adults.

A situation where the trainer sees himself as the 'giver' and the trainees as 'receivers' in a childhood school sense is evidently not going to be effective, particularly with high ability people. The training manager may need to tutor and counsel managers on how to tutor and counsel in turn, so that they provide leadership and support their subordinates, provide an environment in which learning is natural and encouraged, and, as far as possible, is owned, designed and paced by all participants. In this way, management training is moving out of the training centre with its lecture rooms, and into the business operation.

The adult learner does not like to feel 'dependent', and seems to want to take both responsibility for his efforts and full credit for achievements. He is likely to have strong views on his own training needs and how these may be met, influenced by past learning experiences.

Ideally, he will want to be involved in determining the duration and content of learning and to be an active participant rather than a passive recipient. He is likely to seek some measure of the effect or effectiveness of the training experience, and will be influenced in his judgement by his degree of enjoyment of the process.

*Action learning*

The most effective form of learning from training at senior levels is likely to come from some form of action learning. This can take much of the activity outside the training centre, although some theoretical input or grounding may be needed, which will generally be accepted if it is well presented with active, participatory discussion. The main learning is generated from questioning and problem solving, using case studies which are live and therefore very real and detailed. Action learning requires participants to work in small groups, and to clarify learning by questioning their individual learning objectives as a preliminary to team working on these live projects. Learning is primarily 'by doing' and 'from each other', and the team should be expected to carry projects through to implementation rather than present a conclusion and walk away. 'From each other' has several facets, from sharing experiences constructively, through interactions with team members involving both criticism and advice, to reviewing with each other the lessons learned from the actions agreed.

Involvement in a real life business problem which requires a solution and action alters the perspective enormously, taking training out of playtime into reality, and the learning effect is multiplied. Realisation that there is rarely enough information in complex, real time decision-taking may be one of the key lessons. These real problems move 'training' into 'development', for one of the best development situations is an assignment in a lively project team. The distinctive 'flavour' of this training comes where managers participating in the programme are teamed with specially selected 'training' staff operating in the mode of business consultants to address real problems, and where the 'consultants' support and steer the learning from within the project.

Learning in these situations is from demanding and practical experience, from which the 'manager students' will reflect on their observations and construct their own patterns of concepts or generalisations. The end result is a learning experience where the impact may visibly pass through to the bottom line.

*A learning culture*

Ultimately, individuals will learn if they choose to. However much effort is put into the design of training situations, if there is resistance to learning, the training will not be effective.

This may stem from management attitudes and a consensus that training is a waste of time. That sort of cultural resistance is not unusual and is very difficult to dislodge, but it can be done.

In a large construction group, I identified a range of current operational problems which were clearly hitting the bottom line, and assembled a management training package to show in practical terms how some of these could be tackled. To fit the 'macho' image of the senior managers, the course was designed to run for three 14-hour days, beginning on Sunday evening. The members of the trial group duly arrived for their 'holiday' – a phrase they dropped, two hours into Monday morning. The involvement in new approaches to real problems caught their interest and we had to fight off demand for places on the programme until the top 200 managers (including all directors) had been through. And it really did have an impact on the bottom line.

In more enlightened organisations, the recognition of the value of learning is high. I emphasise *value* of learning, not necessarily 'training', for training is no more than one opportunity to learn, with experience providing a much better source!

A learning culture encourages learning by everyone in the organisation, by providing many opportunities for learning, but, more importantly, encourages a way of thinking where everyone *wants* to learn and takes positive initiatives to that end which go well beyond any normal job-related requirements. If some new development occurs in the business, everyone wants to know about it, about the implications, and about the opportunities it may create elsewhere in the business. Expert help is called in to run some evening own-time seminars, and everyone participates.

This is the same attitude that you get with groups of individuals who are 'naturally dissatisfied' with the present state and are convinced improvement is possible to all things. It fits into a culture of openness and total encouragement for development; of selecting people who want to grow, and then doing more than just giving them their heads by creating a 'hothouse' to maximise their growth and development.

Of course, you cannot just go out and do this in any 'ordinary' company, for it would terrify many of the managers, but, as a vision to work towards, it is something for many human resource staff to savour and for some to achieve.

## Structure of training programmes

Once training needs have been identified and priorities established, (as covered in the last chapter), the means of addressing the requirements can be planned. The bulk of training in any organisation of size should be internal and local, supplemented by corporate and external activities, depending on the size of the organisation and the degree of specialisation and one-off requirements in the needs.

*The core of internal training*

The core of internal training will take the form of a nucleus of essential preparation for advancement level by level, plus a range of functional, technical and man-management courses associated with the needs of the overall business and the broadening of its managers. It will also instil and ensure an understanding of basic corporate values. Core programmes are likely to have an individuality related to industry and culture and the corporate approach to development and training.

The purpose of the core training programmes is to ensure that individuals are properly prepared for each major step forward as their careers progress and, where appropriate, acquire a common understanding of corporate culture and systems. Definition of the basic knowledge and skills or competencies which are essential to provide smooth transition to each new level provide the basis for the core training modules, from entry level through middle management. There may be variations for different streams, such as the core knowledge for all graduate entrants or all finance staff, or all people with supervisory responsibilities. Example 33 shows a typical corporate structure.

*The intake level*

At intake level, there is likely to be some general induction covering the company structure, philosophy and general administration, followed by industry and product familiarisation, basic financial management and human relations skills, and company operating systems.

The pattern of training following intake is likely to be streamed by functions, concentrating on the development of specialised knowledge. For example, the graduate intake may divide into a technical stream where the requirements of progressing to, say, chartered

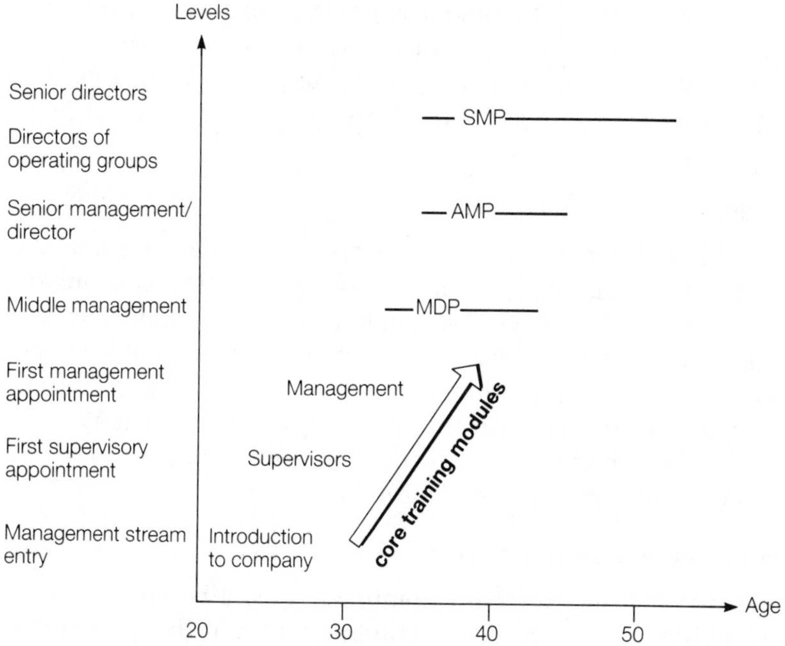


*Key:*
SMP – Senior management programme
AMP – Advanced management programme
MDP – Management development programme

**Example 33** Management training structure

engineer status are catered for; or an administration stream, with sub-groups progressing towards post graduate qualifications in finance or information systems, etc. In parallel, other entry streams may be working towards a range of professional qualifications, in accounting, or as actuaries, or in personnel or marketing. The main objective at this stage will be the 'pumping in' of relevant professional knowledge to match the growth in experience and responsibilities, to meet the requirements for professional qualifications, and to prepare for planned career development.

Company requirements will require training in a further range of 'grounding' skills, covering company systems, developing man management skills, covering the basics of how to write a report, make a presentation and read fast. There may also be finance for non-finance people, marketing appreciation for all, and relevant technical briefings. Company culture is likely to come through strongly in these programmes, with great emphasis on any new thinking, attitudes or behaviour felt to be critical. For example, most programmes involving major cultural change have been backed up and reinforced by heavy and repetitive 'training' to hammer home the message.

*The first supervisory appointment*

As individual careers develop, the first supervisory appointment should be preceded by a core of deliberate preparation, covering the continuing development of relevant functional skills and knowledge of financial systems, but with emphasis on the development of man management and leadership skills. As management is essentially about getting things done through people, and as management becomes more participative, the development of these skills will be of fundamental importance to future managers.

*The first managerial appointment*

Later, the first managerial appointment should be preceded by a similar, but more advanced, programme; with a further programme before the individual begins to manage other managers. In these programmes, the primary element is the man management cum leadership focus, which determines the potential effectiveness of the individual as a manager/leader, however able a technician he may be. There should be parallel programmes for individuals progressing up the specialist route, which should still include a significant element on interpersonal relationships.

At this senior level, many organisations will look outside their own boundaries, perhaps to group headquarters if they are part of a very large organisation, or to the major business schools and management training establishments. Example 34 suggests how this transfer might be handled, where the training expertise required is more specialised and less easily utilised to the full within a company. Typical of the first of the top level programmes would be an 'Advanced Management Programme', targetted on senior managers and directors to provide participants with increased breadth and depth of understanding of the way they can contribute to the improvement of business performance.

A typical in-house programme at this level might start with rapid refresher coverage of functional expertise, including marketing, finance, operations and management information and control.

| Operating company organisation level | % of operating company involvement | Operating company activities | % of corporate involvement | Corporate activities |
|---|---|---|---|---|
| Entry level to middle manage-ment | 95% | Conduct needs analysis<br>Design programmes<br>• Orientation to business<br>• Industry related skills<br>• Basic supervisory skills<br>Conduct all courses | 5% | Audit programme quality<br>Assist in programme design |
| Middle manage-ment | 80% | Conduct needs analysis<br>Design programmes<br>• Skills broadening<br>• Management skills<br>Conduct most programmes | 20% | Audit programme quality<br>Advise on curriculum<br>High potential<br>Package programmes<br>Finance<br>Leadership |
| Upper to senior manage-ment | 10% | Conduct special one-time seminars, e.g. Economics Outlook<br>Conduct Company specific programmes, e.g. Team Building<br>Recommend participants for corporate programmes | 90% | Conduct needs analysis<br>Design programmes<br>• General management<br>• Leadership<br>• Finance<br>• Marketing<br>• Operating<br>Conduct programmes |

**Example 34** Allocation of corporate management training activities

Human resource management and organisational issues should also be covered. The programme can then broaden to look at environmental change and its implications, economic and political influences on strategic decision-making, and advanced marketing issues, and then concentrate on one or two current issues with a requirement to contribute to corporate decision-making.

Learning on these programmes comes from the acquisition of conceptual and factual knowledge, the development of managerial skills, and from critical communication of attitudes and behaviour. Self-appraisal and development of self-confidence are natural outcomes of the interactions between the executives on such a course.

*Building up the programme structure*

The detailed structure of each module through this range of training programmes needs to be built up from the identified needs, knowledge of the targetted participants, and how they are expected to learn. The structure may emerge as a consensus, following discussion and argument between the training course owners (the senior managers whose subordinates will be participants) and the training staff. If the subject matter or content is unproven or may be controversial, a 'preview' with selected participants is advisable so that the module can be 'de-bugged' before being used live.

The form of modules is variable. Provided that they are designed to meet the needs of participants, the variation in the ways the needs are achieved can be enormous, influenced particularly by corporate culture and both management and training staff preferences.

*Cascade*

The introduction of any new corporate system, or of a culture change programme, is frequently backed up by training programmes which are more in the nature of communication exercises. Training may be considered as communication with a specific purpose, and the use of training resources and techniques to present and sell new practices does create a learning situation and is legitimate.

For example, the launch of an updated appraisal programme should be presented with strong training support. So too should some significant change in the company's information systems of wide interest and concern; or an increased emphasis on marketing which requires universal understanding and support; or some legislative change which will have an influence right across the business and possibly require some change of behaviour or business practice.

To be effective, these special programmes must be seen to have been started at the top, and to cascade down level by level so that all managers are seen to participate, and so that everyone has a common understanding and language. If the interests of the various organisational levels differ, then the primary message may be adapted, but must not be distorted or changed as the complexity of content or language is modified.

## Training design and operation

For training to be most effective, great care will have been taken to ensure that the training needs of all the participants on a course are roughly at the same level, and have been matched to the designed course content. However, the personal expectations of the trainees are likely to be more varied than is immediately obvious, and some time at the beginning of a course should be devoted to exploring, and perhaps recording, those expectations.

Also at an early stage, there may be value in looking at how individuals learn, and discussing individual learning styles and preferences which may influence how the sessions should be run. If this preparatory work is done to clarify expectations and means, the course objectives can be more closely focussed and relevant. This implies that there must be some flexibility in the designed content and running of every course.

Courses for managers need to be designed to optimise use of time. To help achieve this, all necessary factual information and basic data should be covered by the provision of carefully selected and concise pre-reading. Then any 'information transfer' which must take place within designated course time should be presented crisply, with opportunity for discussion to ensure full understanding. The controlling hand must have a light touch, but these basic sessions do need firm control in order to cover the 'syllabus' fully in the allocated time.

If some operational practice of course elements is required, this should be linked with straightforward case material and role playing to develop some realism, plus discussion to consolidate understanding. If role playing is used, the subsequent discussion and analysis also need the most delicate handling. The participants must be encouraged to make their comments and discuss the conclusions first, as comments from the observing members (and particularly from the 'teaching staff') will 'contaminate' and distort their initial feelings. Also, they can admit any obvious errors rather than be told and lose face. The tutor must play a low key role, posing questions rather than commenting.

The most stimulating part of the course, likely to provide maximum learning, should be expanded to the maximum possible proportion of time, and should use current problems for projects if possible. Historical case studies have only a fraction of the impact of a live project. If the end stage of a live project is a presentation of recommendations to a decision-making body, with some potential for being required to take those recommendations through into practice, the commitment and 'electricity' generated can be enormous. Where two or more teams are on the same project and are competing for acceptance of their proposals and assignment to implement, the level of drive reached over a short period can be very exciting.

In these situations, the role of the 'trainer' is completely altered, to become business expert, consultant and mentor to the project team. The level of expertise required in this role is substantially greater than is found in most training managers and closer to that of an experienced general manager, and needs to be resourced very carefully for full value from this approach to learning. As an incidental, people learn a lot about team working.

At the conclusion of each programme, some form of 'rounding up' of the learning is valuable, to clarify what is felt to have been learned within the group, and also to give some immediate feedback on the effectiveness of the course design. This is a time for blunt language and clear messages.

## NOMINATIONS FOR TRAINING

The selection of individuals to attend any course at every level must be evaluated carefully. Attendance must be linked to their agreed training needs, and the individual must be capable of understanding the training and benefiting from it. But, even more important, it is fundamental that attendance should follow a personal commitment to participate enthusiastically and to complete the intensive and demanding self-development opportunity which any training course provides.

Nomination and selection of delegates for top level corporate programmes should be made with reference to current corporate succession and development plans. Where possible, the nomination of a delegate to *any* programme should be timed to coincide with an anticipated job change or promotion, or some reorganisation that will affect job duties and responsibilities. It should be seen as part of the essential preparation for a future career move.

It is absolutely essential that people attending a training course should understand and support the objective. Attendance is normally sponsored by their immediate boss, who has a responsibility to brief the 'attender' fully, so that expectations from attendance at a programme are clear. Attendance should *never* be a 'company requirement'! There has to be choice and commitment by the participant.

The sponsor (and *his* boss) have a further responsibility; to ensure that their nominees do attend courses as booked, and are not distracted or withdrawn. Programmes are expensive to organise and run. Apart from the fact that the full costs should be charged when withdrawal occurs at a late stage, the opportunity to use the place for another individual may be lost.

On return from a training programme, the sponsor should debrief the participant to ensure the purpose of attendance has been achieved, encouraging the participant to do most of the talking. I find it useful to request a written report, giving a full assessment of the course and the learning obtained, and to follow this up after, say, three months, with the question, "What have you done in the last three months as a direct result of attending the course?" If the answer is "nothing", you must enquire why.

## EFFECTIVENESS

Training effectiveness is not easy to measure, and rather subjective judgements are frequently necessary, especially in regard to management training. The objectives of training, based on identified needs, may be clear enough, but the measure of how well the participants have absorbed the knowledge and skills, and whether they are inclined to use what they have acquired, is difficult. One approach is to try to assess changes in behaviour some time after the training has taken place, but getting reliable and quantified before and after data is unlikely, particularly when isolated individuals have been involved from across a large organisation and a variety of other factors may have influenced behaviour change.

## Evaluating effectiveness

Deliberate effort to evaluate training might lead to evaluation of:

- *Trainees' initial reactions* However carefully any course or seminar is designed and run, individual reactions vary widely, but the discipline of writing a short immediate comment on each session will enable any generally agreed responses to influence subsequent programmes.
- *Learning* Where the subject matter is clear, such as for specific inputs of functional knowledge, it is possible to get some measure of before and after proficiency; but for most management courses the knowledge areas and levels are not definable with sufficient precision to use in this way, and one looks at the use of knowledge and at behaviour.
- *Behaviour* Changes in job-related behaviour may be evident, as in the construction industry case mentioned above, and in that on critical path scheduling below. So too may other introductions or developments of particular competencies. While these are evident in individuals, use of acquired skills may be inhibited unless the surrounding managers possess and are using these skills.
- *Organisation behaviour* Where large groups of people attend the same or similar programmes, the reinforcement provided by many people trying out the same new ideas can lead to acceptance and consolidation. Measurement may still be difficult, but it is universally evident that certain changes have occurred. On a smaller scale, any team which has worked through a competitive live project will have been stimulated sufficiently to carry on with the project, and using the skills they have acquired. If, when split up or returned to their original environments, they find their learning cannot be successfully communicated and absorbed, they will tend to revert to previous attitudes.

Evaluation can be attempted as people leave the training centre, but measures of effectiveness really need to be based on permanent changes in behaviour back on the job and in the company. The effect of the corporate culture on the use of acquired skills, and the influence of a wide variety of other factors, make it progressively more difficult to be specific about the impact of training. Ultimately, one looks at progressive improvement in corporate performance, and can attempt some judgement of the influences which have contributed to change, which will include training.

Some of the most effective management training, in terms of evident change of behaviour, follows cascaded presentations covering the entire management population, so that everyone becomes familiar with a set of ideas, concepts or techniques over a short time, and has a common language to discuss experimental introduction which further heightens the learning effort. I have seen enormous savings being generated following such a programme; for example, following a programme which introduced the entire management team to critical path scheduling on large building contracts where avoidable delays had been invoking time-related penalty clauses.

To monitor effectiveness of individual training modules, it is worth restating and testing objectives each time the module is to be run, and then reviewing how well it went (as seen by training staff, line managers involved, and participants) after the event. These reviews must be challenging. Before the event, examine the possibility that the requirement is changing or that the knowledge of the participating group is atypical. After the event, an immediate review might be followed by a more reflective one, a month or three months afterwards. Just as the environment and business are changing continuously, so will be the training needs of the participants, so that updating is essential and should be on-going. It is a feature of many of the most successful organisations that they appear almost overly self-critical, and naturally extend this approach to their training. Perhaps this approach is a key element in their success, and it is not a bad feature to apply to training.

## The time element

Apart from the effectiveness of the training itself, we should also *analyse time*. Very many training courses are longer than necessary. Some are designed that way to justify the price being charged! With in-house training there is no justification for padding, and, because the training is designed to meet the specified needs of a known population, the content and format can be tailored to concentrate on essential material, to stretch the participants and to minimise the time required. Time is a critical cost element, as training costs should really include the total remuneration costs of participants for the period away from their jobs. Almost any factor which will reduce training duration (but not reduce training effectiveness) will provide cost improvement.

## The contribution factor

In an ideal situation, training effectiveness would be measured by its contribution to the achievement of business objectives. All training is likely to contribute something, but unless the training is directed to improving performance in a defined unit and is clearly measurable, it will be very difficult to separate the influence of training from that of effective line management.

### SUMMARY

Training actions should be in response to legitimate, business-related training needs, and should be designed to meet those needs as efficiently as possible.

Learning does not automatically follow from training, as some forms of teaching will generate resistance in adults. It is necessary to recognise that programmes should be tailored as closely as practical to participants, who should be encouraged to 'own' the programme.

'Action learning' involves taking training out of the training centre and into the current work situation using, for example, important current projects as the learning basis, with careful guidance by 'business consultants' rather than traditional trainers.

Training involves creating a learning environment within which a selected group with closely similar training needs is led through carefully designed learning opportunities. Companies with a 'learning culture' stimulate controlled learning widely within the work situation.

Company training programmes should have a core of essential learning which provides relevant preparation for progress to each further level in the organisation, and is supplemented by detailed knowledge of the relevant function. There needs to be substantial emphasis on man management skills at each level as participative management becomes the new norm.

Where a major training programme or a training-backed culture change exercise is in progress, it is logical to cascade this down from the top to cover all managers level by level in order to achieve maximum impact.

The efficiency of training actions is very difficult to assess, but is best addressed by examining the immediate responses of participants to the achievement of course goals. Further review of changed behaviour some months later can give strong feedback, but may be influenced by other factors.

Participation in any training programme requires a high degree of both support and personal commitment, so nominations to training courses must be carefully selected, and briefing carried out by managers before and after participation.

# V.13

## *Management continuity: succession plans*

### PART OF THE REVIEW PROCESS

Management continuity focusses strongly on the top levels of the enterprise, as succession is particularly important to the top management group itself, but this slice represents no more than the tip of the iceberg, for continuity and effective resourcing are important at every level of the organisation. It is to do with the passing of responsibilities from one generation to the next; with ensuring that every management position is filled with a competent individual at all times; with having at least an 'heir and a spare' suitably prepared when a planned requirement is scheduled; and with having cover in emergencies.

Management continuity or succession planning is a major concern in the Review process, discussed in chapter IV. This Review process is the 'master programme' within management resourcing and development activities, and is concerned both with short-term management deployment and with the longer term three to five and five to ten year projections, integrating organisation development and management deployment with business development in the changing environment. In addition to being concerned with ensuring effective resourcing and continuity of management at every level, it also provides an occasion to assess the effectiveness of management development policies and strategies.

Succession planning, then, is essentially part of the ongoing Review process. In this process, the corporate vision of the future, the business objectives, the scenario of changing environment, corporate systems and culture are 'translated' into required organisation structures and management specifications at a series of points in time, and into supporting human resource strategies. The Review brings together these requirements with the inventory of individual managers – their diverse abilities and degrees of effectiveness, rates of growth, career preferences, and so on – to match the supply of people with the requirements or demand. The periodic succession plan report records this process (as a snapshot of current thinking at one point in time), and provides a basis for a subsequent audit of progress.

Within the overall Review process, the particular concern of succession plans is to ensure continuity of management at a high level of competence throughout the organisation and in depth, to achieve the future business objectives in the anticipated environment. The Review/succession plans indicate required structure and manning options over the period of the plan. These *options remain open until appointment decision points are reached*, so that the forecasts of management requirements and the track records and suitability of nominated successors and other contenders can continue to be

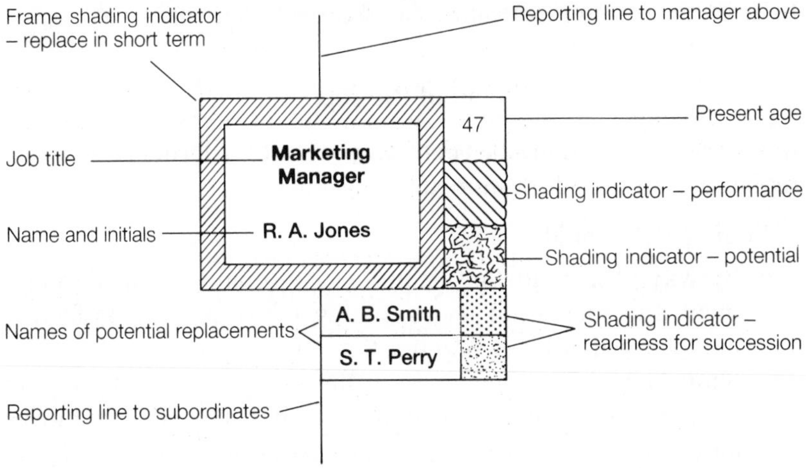


**Example 35** Detailed 'plot' covering one post from a succession planning chart

reviewed up to the time when final selection decisions are taken.

Present organisation and appointments provide the starting point for discussion and review of the plan, probably set out in stratified organisation chart form. A summary of the information available on each position and person can be shown on the charts. Example 35 shows an example of one 'plot' from a succession planning chart, showing coding of some information by colour indicators. When discussions take place, it will be appropriate to have IDPs and more detailed personnel data readily available. Subsequent stages of the plan should also be set out in chart form where possible, as the pictorial representation highlights the changing organisation shape.

## THE MANAGEMENT CONTINUITY REPORT

The management continuity or succession report which most organisations require from time to time, may represent the final summary of deliberations which have taken place over several months, or may be a 'snapshot' at a single point in time of the current stage in a continuous process. Its evolution should be based on the detailed Review process covered in chapter IV, so that the top level plan represents the top slice of extensive activity down through the organisation. In the plan, there may be some current problems, but the main emphasis will be on the longer term and the adequacy of the managers being developed through the system to meet the requirements anticipated three to ten years out.

### Form of the report

In a larger corporation, the board may set out the form of the report required from subsidiary companies as follows:

> Your report should:
>
> 1 By way of introduction, state the key management development and succession issues, noting relevant business factors and planned or likely organisation changes.
> 2 Show succession plans for your immediate reporting line and the next level, supplemented by broad notes on planned moves for current job holders, and the preparation of individual successors. *How* are people to be made ready?
> 3 List your high potential people who do not yet appear on the top succession charts, particularly those in the 25–35 age group, with individual notes on your star achievers.
> 4 Detail the actions you have taken to improve the quality of your graduate (and other future management) intake, and to speed the progress of the most able.
>
> In order to make our discussions more productive, I am asking our group management development advisers to discuss the position

with you to identify and agree the key issues as the agenda for discussion with the board.

It is clearly evident from this that succession plans cannot be presented baldly – that there has to be a scene-setting statement by way of introduction.

This introduction needs to set out the ways in which the organisation and management positions are expected to change during the period of the plan, so that the plan is concerned with resourcing the anticipated requirements rather than a past structure. It has to recognise that some positions will retain titles unchanged, but anticipate drastic changes in required competencies which may unseat incumbents. The introduction should incorporate a statement of the anticipated future organisation, and only after that should the report get down to questions of the deployment of individuals.

## Introduction to the continuity plan

The most serious fault in most succession planning is that it gets oversimplified. Managers begin to find problems with the complexity and uncertainty of assessing how they expect individuals to develop through the coming months and years, and the difficulties of matching individuals against possible vacancies. They baulk at adding further uncertainty in the form of changing organisation and competency requirements, and prefer to assume status quo on future organisation and jobs. One large company, about to introduce some radical organisation change, still carried out its annual succession planning with a written 'assumption' of 'no organisation change for ten years', believing that the succession planning task would have become impossible otherwise! At best, this approach will give an indication of current strengths and emergency cover, and identify individuals thought capable of advancement. This provides no more than a sort of inventory, and is of no help in determining what action is necessary to prepare people for future positions. Nor does it give any indication of the company's ability to provide sufficient and suitable people to resource a future organisation.

Continuity planning is virtually meaningless unless it is carried out against the best available projections of the organisation's future shape and management requirements at a sequence of points in time. The business is *not* going to be the same in future. Many aspects of the business environment are already changing, and further evolution is inevitable. As these are reflected in the business plan, the future management requirements are visible, and many of these changes will alter the skills you require in your managers.

*The succession plan needs to be introduced by a statement of these changes*, to set the scene and lead into a clear picture of requirements at specific future points for which succession (or resourcing) must be planned. For example, the combined impact of advanced information management and changing attitudes to work and leadership will lead to flatter organisation structures and alter most management jobs, independent of all other change. How will existing managers adapt to the changing demands placed upon them in their present jobs?

The introduction should cover an assessment of the impact on organisation and human resourcing of all the business and environmental factors, and then go on to explain the projections of the organisation required for the next two to ten years which incorporate forecasts of the numbers, categories and levels of managers required over that period. (As elsewhere in this book, I use the single word *manager* to include all management, up to and including the chairman of the board, regardless of title.) While the succession plan will be based on the business plan with its associated scenario and assumptions, some other options may be thought serious enough to cover with contingency plans. Possible merger, acquisition or disposal considerations might also be covered, for they may have significant management implications which should be evaluated. Even a straightforward demerger can alter the management requirements significantly.

Against a particularly fluid future, a continuity plan based on the most favoured scenario should be backed by a comprehensive inventory of existing managers, with some comment on the extent of individual flexibility within. Further comment on excessive uncertainty is included below.

Finally, an overview should summarise the strengths and limitations of current managers and their readiness to assume anticipated forward positions against this background. This should include comment on the identified high potential stream which may not yet have begun to feature on the major succession sheets, but which represents the major source of longer term successors.

The review should not concentrate solely on line and functional management, for there will be an increase in the requirements for high ability specialists through the 1990s, and these people will form an essential part of the future organisation. The supply of some of these 'non-managers' may prove very difficult to meet. You need to accept that some specialists in narrow functional areas will not have careers in one company simply because their numbers within one organisation are too small to provide adequate career ladders. Some will leave, and their replacements will be recruited. Even so, encouraging their personal development will ensure optimum contribution while they are with the company.

As the whole continuity process operates at every level, there is a need for an adequate two-way flow of information, so that managers at the lower levels can take into account the availability of people from other areas, as flagged by their seniors, as they carry out studies for their own levels.

## Minimising uncertainties

Situations do arise where the uncertainties in the forward business scene appear to be too extensive to enable an optimum scenario to be developed. Analyses of these situations tend to show that the most serious uncertainties involve timing. There may be a recognition that a range of identified business changes are coming, but that the precise form of change is still evolving and the timing of 'impact' remains uncertain (within a specifiable period of, perhaps, several years).

The objective should be to pin down the anticipated changes against separate aspects of the business or against separate business units, then to develop a forward view of the 'most likely' organisation and note the variable time scales. An assessment can be made of how this future organisation might be staffed against several timetables. For example, it may be possible to prepare individuals and achieve effective staffing at a later date, but there might be difficulty if the timing were to be brought forward; or alternatively there may be people ready shortly who can not be kept 'on ice' for delayed introduction. The business plan, of course, will require achievable solutions for every time variant.

## Succession plan impossible!

If it is concluded that the degree of uncertainty in the available options makes any attempt at succession planning impossible, an 'emergency approach' is required. From a business point of view, you have to assemble the best possible assessments of the abilities of managers to fill the range of possible future organisations, and identify any managerial limitations to these possible courses of action so that contingency plans may be prepared.

Where a number of uncertainties exist it may be possible to match the range of management requirements as they occur in different divisions or subsidiary companies with candidate 'readiness' from a central management inventory. Of course, the preparation of candidates would need to be more general than for a single post, but this in itself is healthy, and in periods of exceptional change may become the pattern for the future in some companies.

A variation on uncertainty, as seen by one CEO, was that "We simply cannot see all the things we are going to have to do." Almost all business change, even in relatively static, slow changing industries, appears to produce new or 'different' problems and needs from those identifiable from prior experience, and unanticipated people requirements. The visibility of these new or different needs invariably occurs at a late stage as a new situation begins to bite, and the information needed to manage it and the manner of managing become evident. Then the required competencies must be obtained by matching those already available internally, by an unplanned transfer, or by urgent external recruitment. Hopefully, the inventory database enables you to match the need internally, and to rely on there having been sufficient broadening in the overall management development process to have developed the necessary competencies to a sufficient degree.

I suspect that, in those industries coping with the most rapid developments in their business environments during the 1990s, we shall see a considerable development in the use of management inventories as the focus of management development and succession planning. The concern will be to optimise the growth and development of all managers to the fullest extent of their potential, against a wider range of possible business scenarios and less than acceptable probabilities of choice. This approach has the disadvantage of needing unusually wide-ranging reviews of management deploy-

| Succession plan | | | | | | | | |
|---|---|---|---|---|---|---|---|---|
| | Current job holder | | | Planned successor | | Ready within 10 yrs | | |
| Job title / Job grade | Date in / Year out | D.o.B. / Age | Name | Name | Year / Age then | Name | Age Now | Year Ready |
| | | | | | | | | |
| | | | | | | | | |
| | | | | | | | | |
| | | | | | | | | |
| | | | | | | | | |
| | | | | | | | | |

**Example 36** Succession plan: format 1

Enter job titles and grades of current jobs, plus any roles which are currently absorbed within others but which would *normally* exist separately. Also enter titles for any 'new' jobs which are planned to come into existence during the planned period, with proposed appointments.

Current job holders (enter details as follows):

| | |
|---|---|
| Name | Show *surname and initials*. If the holder also simultaneously holds a more senior job, put the name in brackets. |
| D.o.B./Age | Enter date of birth above the bar and *age at the year end*, below the bar, e.g. $\frac{7/38}{51}$ |
| Date in | The date on which the job holder took up his present responsibilities, or at least the large bulk of them. |
| Year out | The year in which the current job holder is planned to give up the role. If by retirement, add 'ret'. |
| Planned successor | Enter *surname and initials* of planned next job holder and *year* of planned succession.<br><br>If a job is planned to disappear from the structure without a further appointment after the current incumbent, enter the fact in the name section and give the date, e.g., 'Job eliminated 199X'.<br><br>If a new job is to be created, enter the planned first job holder into the 'Planned successor' column and the date.<br><br>Where a change of appointment is anticipated during the period of some three years, from now to the end of 199X, a planned successor should be named. No *planned* successor need be named if the present incumbent is expected to remain in post beyond 199X. |
| Ready within 10 years | The name(s) of *all candidates* who are expected to develop to be fully capable of doing the job, plus the *earliest* year by which each would be ready. That earliest year could well be before the next planned change of job holder. List the names of candidates in order of their readiness and, where appropriate, *include the planned successor.* Where no successor is expected until after 199X *underline* the name of the favoured longer-term successor where he/she is identified.<br><br>One person may well be a potential successor to several jobs. If there are more possible successors likely to be ready within 10 years than can be accommodated in a single space, all those with potential to reach the position within 10 years are to be listed. |

**Example 37** Completion notes for succession plan form

ment, and at more frequent intervals, as events clarify the path of environmental change.

However, recent analysis of the application of some inventories developed to respond to this type of situation have shown disappointing results. The analyses were designed to audit the provision of suitable candidates for unplanned new jobs. It was anticipated that a high degree of individual flexibility would have been achieved so that acceptable candidates would be available to meet all needs. The hard facts showed that virtually all individuals were felt to have further potential; the *form* of that potential had not broadened or changed significantly from earlier judgements. Each individual was assessed as being suitable or ready for a very limited selection of positions, generally in a single functional area or closely related types of general management post. It appeared that a combination of personal preference, personal strengths and personal style strongly influenced the fresh assessments, in spite of the broad spectrum of development and training which had been attempted.

I do not, at this stage, feel able to draw absolute conclusions from these results, but there does appear to be some very real limitation on the effectiveness of growing able and flexible people to progress to 'any kind of job'. It is certainly necessary to seek a high degree of adaptability (and willingness to adapt) in the personalities concerned.

## Timetable

The management development function is likely to include a review cycle, along the following lines:

| | |
|---|---|
| Month 1 | Board defines issues to be given special attention. |
| Months 1–7 | Subsidiary companies prepare draft report and briefs for review. |
| Months 5–7 | Initial discussions between subsidiary companies and corporate management development staff to establish 'key issues' for agenda. |
| Month 8 | Preliminary reviews by subsidiary company board members. |
| Months 9–10 | Final reports completed and collated for sub- |

**Confidential**

*Plans for board and management committee* | *Organisation: Excelsior Electronics* | DATE: November 1990

| Position<br>Incumbent<br>In position since: (Month/Year) | (Age) | Replacement plan 1991 | 1992 | 1993 | 1994 | 1995 | 1996 | 1997 | 1998 | 1999 | 2000 | *Comments* |
|---|---|---|---|---|---|---|---|---|---|---|---|---|
| Chairman & Chief Executive Officer<br>Tony JONES<br>4/85 | (61) | | | | BOSTON (52)<br>– – – – –<br>JONES to retire | | | | | | | Organised with a Chairman & Chief Executive Officer, and a President & Chief Operating Officer, the ideal structure would have one with a marketing/sales background; the other with a financial/human resources background. Boston was previously Senior VP-Marketing. |
| President & Chief Operating Officer<br>Joe BOSTON 5/90 | (49) | | | | APPLEBY (56)<br>– – – – – –<br>BOSTON to Chairman | | | | | | | Appleby is the only internal candidate and is highly qualified for the position. |
| Vice-President – Finance<br>Hank SMIT<br>3/83 | (64) | APPLEBY (44)<br>– – – – –<br>SMIT to retire | | | JENKINS (32)<br>– – – – –<br>APPLEBY to President/COO | | | | | | | When Smit retires in March 1991, Appleby will become VP-Finance in preparation for his move to C.O.O. |
| Vice-President – Logistics<br>Fred APPLEBY<br>1/88 | (43) | JENKINS (35)<br>– – – – – – –<br>APPLEBY to Finance | | | HANSON ?<br>– – – –<br>JENKINS to Finance | | | | | | | When Appleby moves to VP-Finance Jenkins will succeed him for three years, probably followed by Bill Hanson. |
| Vice-President – Marketing<br>Ian MACDONALD<br>5/90 | (43) | | | WILLIAMS (43)<br>– – – – – – – –<br>Transfer to Corporate HQ | | | | | | | | MacDonald is one of this company's highest potential executives, and his next move is planned into corporate headquarters. |
| Vice-President – Human Resources<br>Anne SLOAN 2/87 | (52) | | | | | | | | | | | |
| Vice-President – Manufacturing<br>Charles HARRISON<br>10/89 | (56) | | | SCHWARTZ (49)<br>– – – – – – – – –<br>HARRISON to retire early | | | | | | | | Harrison should be replaced no later than mid-1992 when the current reorganisation is completed. He excels in day-to-day management but not at board level. |

**Example 38** Succession plan: format 2

| | |
|---|---|
| | mission of succession plans to the central board. |
| Months 11 | Board review of succession plans. |
| Months 12–1 | Prepare and discuss action plans and priorities for the next cycle. |

Most reviews at board level will require the succession plans to be set out concisely and in a standard format. Example 36 showed such a format and example 37 provides associated 'notes for guidance' on the detailed content. As these forms vary from company to company, I have included two further styles in examples 38 and 39.

## CEO succession

One very special element in continuity planning is succession to the CEO. Every CEO knows that he needs a successor, and that finding and appointing that successor will be one of the most important things which he will have to do, but few CEOs are in a hurry to let go. The incumbent CEO and his likely successors have big egos, and the potential for bruising conflict is significant.

There are a number of routes to succession. Ideally, one wants a civilised process with planned and agreed succession. This may be most easily achievable where (in the USA) a chairman/CEO stands down in favour of a suitably groomed president/COO; or (in the UK) where an Executive chairman stands down for his CEO. Where such a one-over-one structure exists, the successor is identified and is being groomed and, if all goes smoothly, succession is straightforward, the new top man having time to select and induct *his* successor.

The process ceases to be so easy where there is no one-over-one structure and the range of serious contenders is more substantial. A top man with two or three deputies, or a 'deputy' who will not be the successor, leaves a more open, competitive situation. Smooth succession requires the incumbent CEO to name his successor sufficiently in advance, otherwise a 'competition' will develop where the competitors are publicly competing and the 'losers' are likely to leave the company. It is inevitable that, in any sizeable organisation, the contenders will be big on intellect, vision, leadership qualities and charisma, and there may be a temptation for the

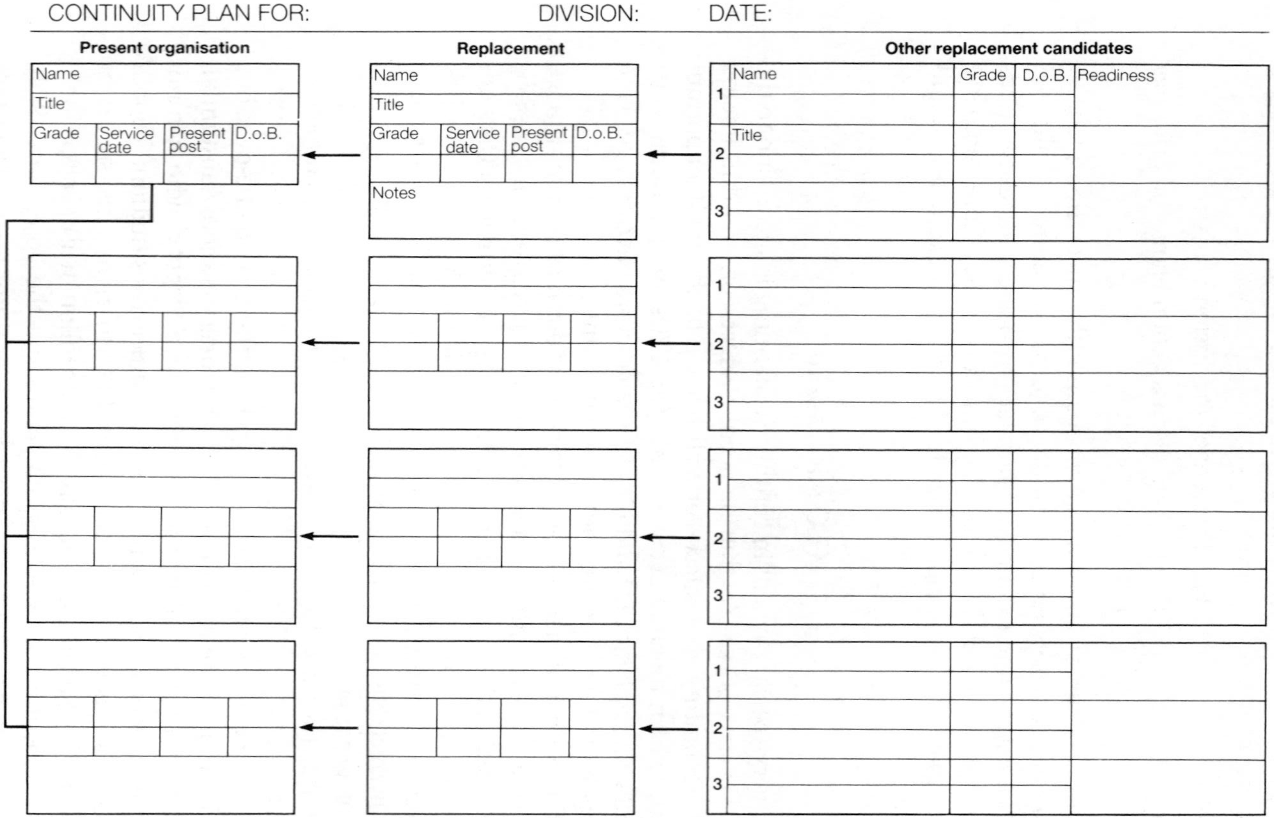


**Example 39** Succession plan: format 3

incumbent to leave his contenders to fight it out. But one expects a more responsible approach. It would be proper to expect him to explore the personal aspirations of contenders and their vision of the corporate future; to discuss his views with the non-executive members of his board; and move to a recommendation on which he could expect to achieve consensus.

From time to time, it will be recognised that the individual required to take the corporation through the next decade does not exist in the organisation and that external sources must be used. Again, a concensus of key people should support this view and be privy to the actions taken, to define the requirement and consider the contenders. If someone is to join from outside, there will probably be an expectation of rapid change, and a need to ensure that the incoming appointee really understands what the board expects and has the ability to succeed, harnessing the support of his colleagues in the process.

The next generation of CEOs will, inevitably, differ from their predecessors – as with all other levels of manager. In particular, they will be more at ease with risk, and are likely to have managed high risk projects before taking full profit responsibility for a unit. They will have a global view and probably a second language. They are likely to have worked overseas and understand other cultures. They are likely to be younger, and will probably be in the company already. And they will have excellent political contacts and sensitivity.

## Preparation of individuals who are possible successors

The agreed succession plan needs to be integrated with plans for individuals, the IDPs, to ensure that people are prepared for the positions planned for them.

For implementation to be effective, there needs to be ongoing questioning of the future management profiles, as these provide the specifications for which individuals are being prepared. If they turn out to be wrong, 'prepared' candidates may not be suitable for the positions planned for them, and identification of suitable alternative internal candidates at a late stage is unlikely.

The succession plan identifies the best candidates for anticipated future vacancies, ideally an 'heir and a spare', enabling individuals to be assessed against specified requirements so that any shortcomings are identified and remedied. While it may be possible to modify organisation and job specifications to fit an individual, the usual objective is to prepare the candidate to meet the requirements.

Realistic IDPs are essential. If a successor candidate has some career limiting quality, it does not help to turn a blind eye. If a limitation is critical, it must be addressed and the implications accepted. The development plan must set out the clear course of development actions required to prepare the candidate for the intended appointment; it must be implemented; and the implementation responses monitored to ensure that the planned preparation is being effective.

Throughout the 'preparation' stage, all options on appointments remain open. Inevitably some planned successors will falter, or be head hunted away, while fresh candidates may 'come from behind', developing faster and better than anticipated. The plan remains a plan up to the point of the decision to implement, and is properly open for reconsideration as the detailed position evolves.

It may or may not be appropriate to take someone fully into confidence about their career development plan. It should be certain that a provisionally planned appointment conforms to the known personal preferences, ambitions and mobility considerations of a candidate, but there may be alternative options or other candidates, so that the ultimate proposal to a candidate, or the timing of a move, needs to remain open.

IDPs should cover all development required against the likely options, and should incorporate (or have attached) confidential notes on those options; suitably compared with other contenders; and criteria on which judgements may be made. The purpose is to ensure a disciplined and monitored approach to subsequent management decisions.

In planning management continuity, the nature of existing teams and the fit of a possible addition will be important. If a candidate, who is 'ideal' in terms of experience and track record, has a personal style which is alien to the existing management team, there may be a high probability of failure, or risk of destabilising the existing culture.

## Ready to move

In the short-term part of the succession plan, there is a need to plot the career advance of younger high potential managers who may move from post to post at intervals of around two years – even shorter on occasion.

As these individuals get on top of their jobs, they gradually become 'ready to move'. When they reach the stage where they can learn little more from continuing in their present jobs, and particularly if they are also ambitious and keen to take the next step up their career ladders, the pressure to achieve those moves is very strong; interest in their present jobs begins to flag.

The most able people are also potentially the most mobile, and at each career 'crossroads' the young high flier will be looking at any available external option as well as pressing for an internal move. This is a time of maximum vulnerability to external persuasion, so that the period of uncertainty about his next assignment must be minimised and the attractiveness of forthcoming internal opportunities stressed.

The Review process, and succession planning, must highlight the approaching 'ready to move' state of all high ability people, and give high priority to identifying the next best step for each one. If necessary (and, given sufficient lead time, it should be possible), clear the way for an advantageous career move to take place on the required schedule.

As discussed earlier, the highest ability people who are on a career path towards top management positions make up a critically important corporate resource. Their career development must be under the direct eye of the CEO, who must ensure that all necessary action is taken to ensure their ongoing growth – which should continually test the limits of their capacities and seek to stretch them to further growth. And this must be planned through the Review process and as part of succession planning.

## The continuity section of a succession plan report

Examples 40 to 43 represent a sequence of actual planning charts, although suitably disguised. These are in black and white, although the company (and many users) makes use of colours. Symbols and shadings are used to represent colours in the examples shown.

The example series is set in a subsidiary of a major group, but might equally be in a smaller independent unit. The sales turnover is in excess of £100 million. The product, which needs continuous technical research in addition to product development, is sold through a network of technical salesmen in the United Kingdom and through agents in overseas markets.

At the beginning of the sequence, the 'old-stagers' are still running the company. However, the impact of the coming, younger regime is strongly felt in the planning, perhaps too strongly at one or two points, but reflecting an aggressive chairman's interest at head-office.

For simplicity, the charts reproduced cover only the two levels below the managing director, although subsidiary charts exist to cover all supporting management and supervisory posts. Charts are prepared and held by all managers covering their own subordinates.

The first chart shown, example 40, represents a statement of the present position. Each post is shown in relative order of value to the company, using the grade-level scale shown down the side. Against each post is shown the present job holder, his age in the current year, and an indication of his performance and potential, which is backed by supporting papers, including IDPs. In addition, the names of potential successors are shown under the boxes, in all cases for the top line and, where especially relevant, for other posts.

On the original company charts, substantial use is made of colour to highlight performance and potential ratings, etc., as indicated in example 35. For example, posts held by staff aged over 55 are surrounded by a red border to attract special attention. And the readiness of staff to take on a particular post for which they are named as possible candidates is shown by coloured dots and symbols to provide a quick reference which differentiates between the immediate candidate and the longer term prospect.

Before analysing this chart, take a quick look at the content of the sequence – examples 40 to 43. Each shows the same upper levels of the company organisation plan, set out to show the distinct jobs and their relative levels at distinct points in time. No further appraisal data are included, but the (often relevant) age is retained. In addition, potential replacements are shown wherever possible. In the last of the series, the lack of identified suitable candidates is highlighted by the appearance of blanks and queries.

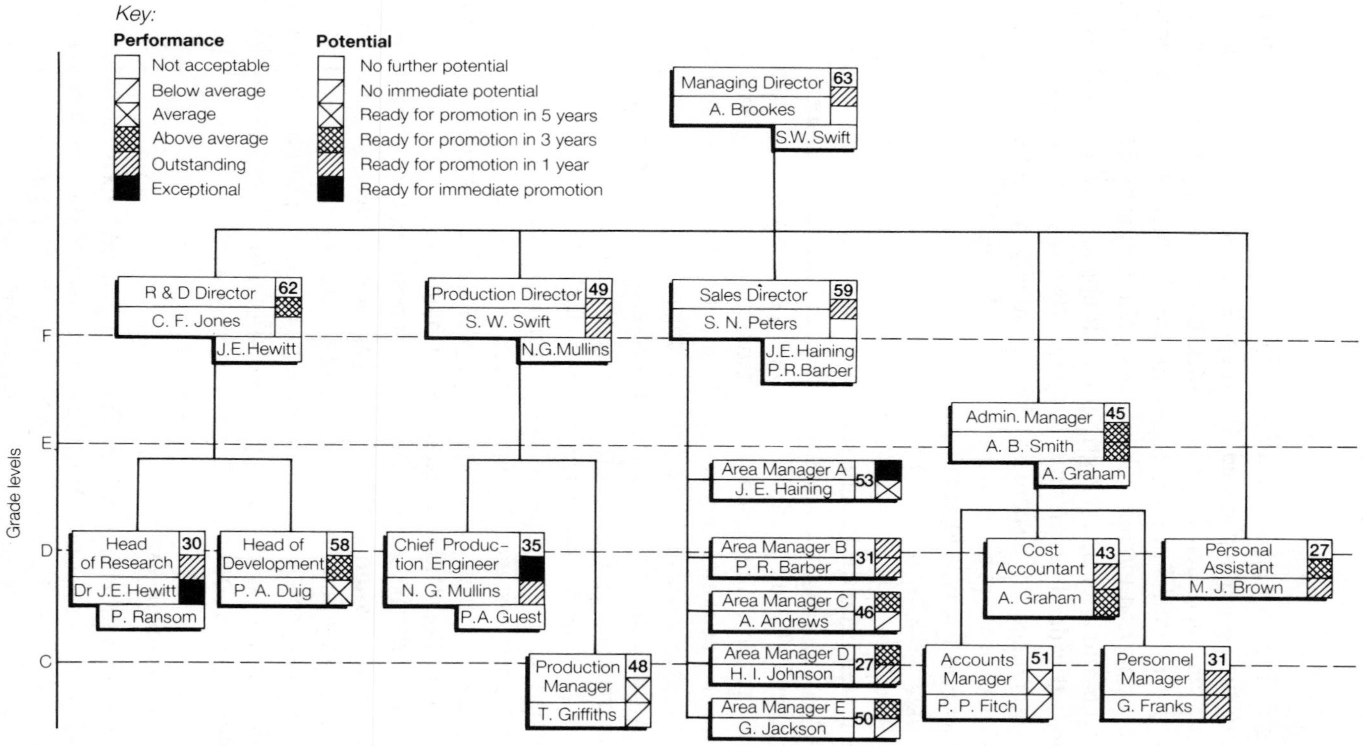


**Example 40** Original succession planning chart

*Analysis of example 40*

Several of the senior posts are filled by older men whose retirement during the period is planned. However, in most cases, a number of bright, younger men have been identified as ready to step up, so that the overall situation is not acute. In fact, some deliberate preparation had already taken place. The major problem is in the research and development group which appears rather poorly supported, the deadweight of older men (below the levels covered) having tended to discourage better quality younger men from seeking careers on the development side. We shall look closer at this problem on the development plans.

A bigger problem, which was discussed in the plan introduction but which is not brought out on the current chart, is that of anticipated growth. Progression to greater turnover and company capacity, increased competitiveness and more sophistication in management, will gradually change the competencies demanded and raise the value of some jobs. This means that the growth in a manager's personal capacity may be wholly absorbed by parallel growth in the size and complexity of his present job.

It is this pressure which sets the problem, shown most clearly by comparisons of job positions against the grade-level scale at the side of each chart. Basic specifications for the main positions were sketched out in the organisation and manpower planning exercises at each growth stage and support the need for future grade changes. They also set provisional 'person specifications' which help candidate selection and individual career planning.

Completing the review of the present position, take a preliminary look for succession problems. All top posts appear to be covered adequately by potential replacements, although the administration director's cover looks thin in relation to future growth. However, at the age of 45 in this company environment, Mr Smith is unlikely to leave or die, so the short-term risk is acceptable.

*The one-year plan: example 41*

The changes scheduled for the first year give an indication of further developments to come. A gradual handover of the top post is to be arranged by Swift moving up to deputy managing director and handing over his old post. We expect Dr Hewitt to 'champ at the bit' at this stage as he waits his turn to move up as well, and

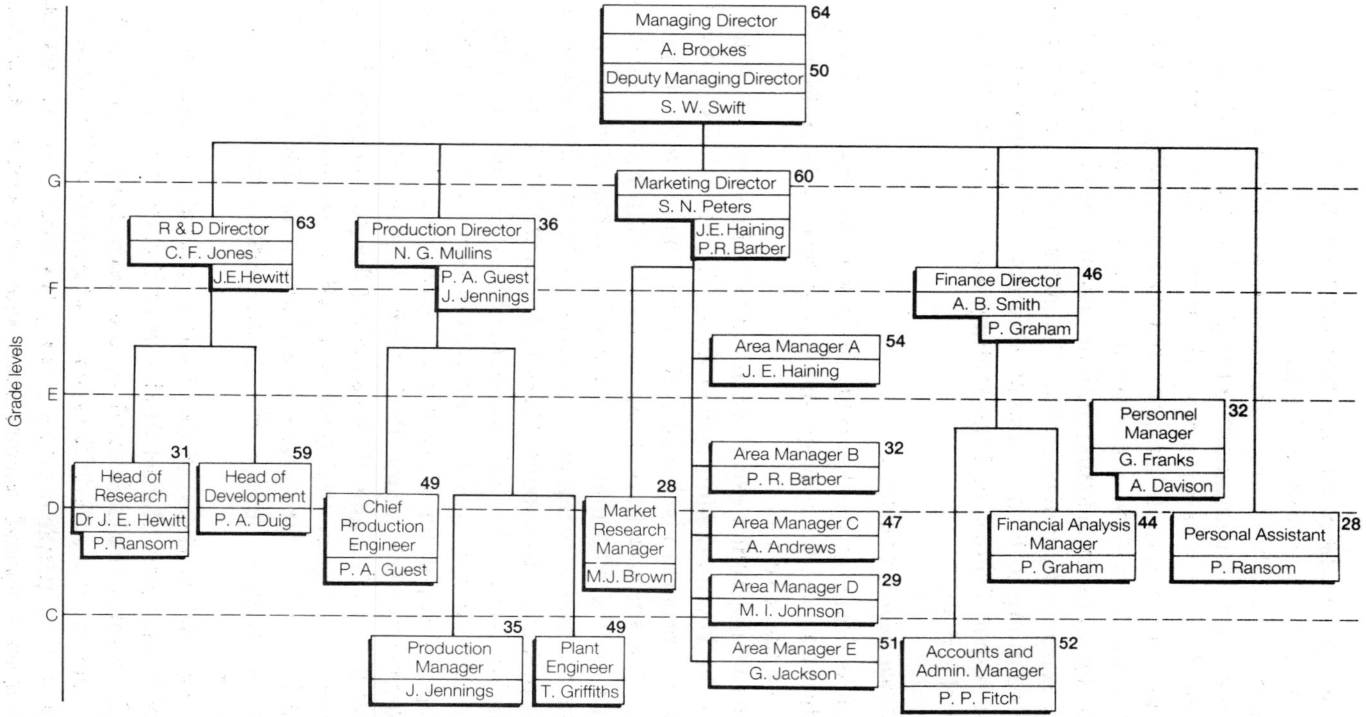


**Example 4.1** The one-year plan

anticipate the possibility that a concessionary title of 'deputy' may help. However, it need not be charted.

In the marketing function, evolution from straightforward selling into a marketing organisation can begin. The present PA to the managing director is an economist who is being 'broadened' before his assignment to initiate market research and intelligence work. His place as PA will be taken by the young research scientist, Ransom, again for broadening until he becomes head of research.

Other scheduled changes include the alteration in job emphasis from accounting to finance, the passing down of routine administrative responsibilities, and the splitting away of an independent personnel activity.

*The two-year plan: example 42*

Mr Swift is firmly in the top seat, Dr Hewitt has been appointed R&D director, and the average age in top posts is down from the present 56 to 43 years.

The remaining senior executive in sight of retirement age, Peters, holding the key marketing responsibility, has no clear successor. The choice appears to be between the older Haining, only six years younger than the present occupant, and the younger Barker, a man of high potential who may not have sufficient experience to cope with the big and growing post. Looking five to six years ahead, it may be preferable to appoint Haining as 'caretaker' for five years until Barker is ready, but this would not be an ideal arrangement.

So, in the two-year plan, the new post of sales manager is created as a preparation post for whichever one is to succeed Peters. During the intermediate two years, Barker will be given every encouragement to grow fast and, if he can stand the pace of growth, will step above Haining at that time. The critical decision cannot be delayed longer than two years, and if serious doubts about both men still remain, an outside appointment will be made to ensure succession.

The potential weakness of the R&D organisation is also clearly revealed by this plan. Should Dr Hewitt or Ransom leave, there are no replacements available, and no successor exists to cover Mr Duig's sideways move. A deliberate recruitment effort is required to bring in suitable people over the coming two years, and an interim organisation of 'special' appointments may be necessary to attract good people without involving personality clashes.

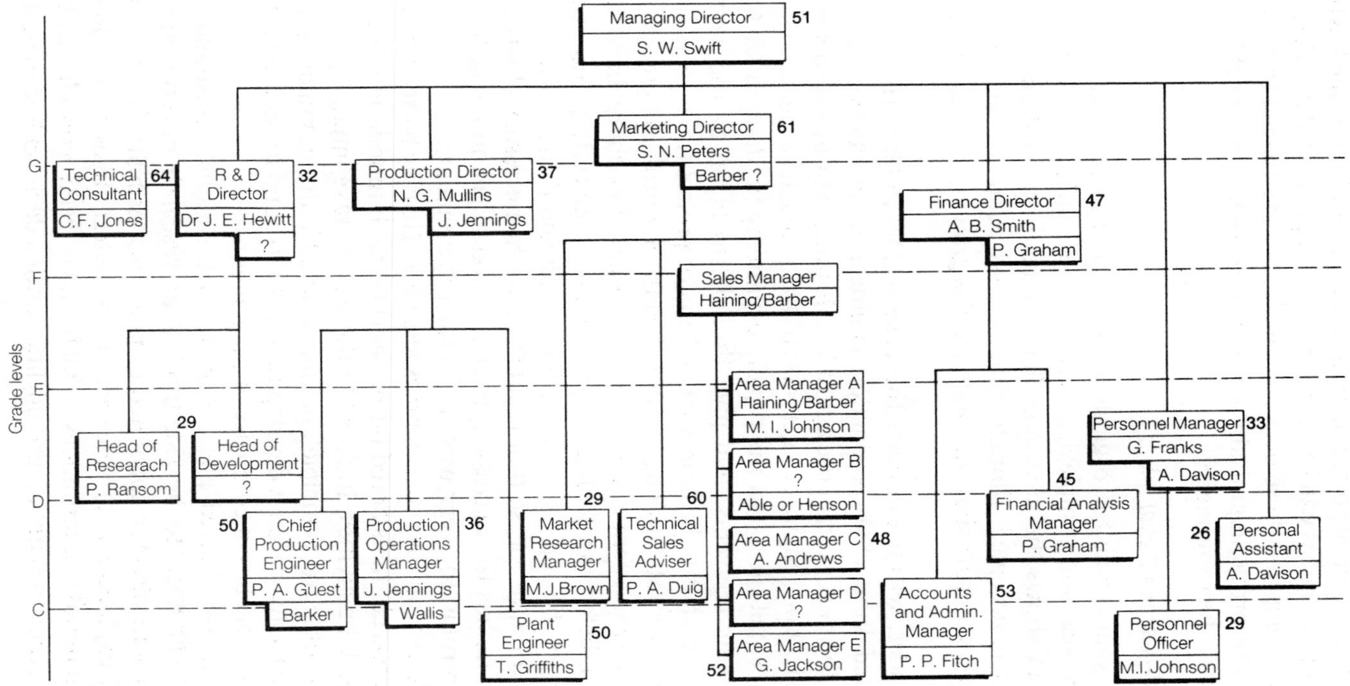


**Example 42** The two-year plan

Some shortage of potential area managers is also revealed, which the company hopes will be overcome by a reappraisal of its salesmen. As often happens, these outside employees have tended to be overlooked on formal appraisal exercises, and several are insufficiently known to their managers.

*The five-year plan: example 43*

In five years' time the organisation will be substantially different, and the size and complexity of the top jobs substantially greater. The plan shows the men most likely to be in the positions at that time. It is accepted, though, that this selection will be regularly reviewed to ensure that each individual is growing at an appropriate rate.

Consider, as an example, the case of Mr Mullins. He is to be promoted from chief production engineer to production director within the next year, at the age of 36. He must 'run-in' his successor as production engineer, get down to a much wider range of problems, get on top of the rapidly expanding production facilities and labour problems, and give thought to planning the second factory which is to be launched as a major project three years after he takes over. Mr Mullins is a qualified mechanical and production engineer who spent some time as a production chargehand and foreman before switching to production engineering and rising rapidly to the top. A well balanced individual, he wants to be production director, so that in addition to the necessary ability and energy, he has the necessary determination to get on top of his job and control it. In every way he fits the requirements.

Dr Hewitt, on the other hand, is less ideal. Heavily biased towards basic research, he is bored (at present) by such mundane things as commercial activities. Inclined in the past to take impulsive action for some obscure 'principle', he may find difficulty in building up a highly effective product development activity, and in taking part in the upper reaches of company management.

Should the charted plan begin to look seriously unsound, Dr Hewitt will need to be side-tracked as research director and a development director appointed to take responsibility for the commercial exploitation of research. These alternatives to the main plan, generally alternatives which have been considered but rejected, must remain on the sidelines until a decision is irrevocably taken.

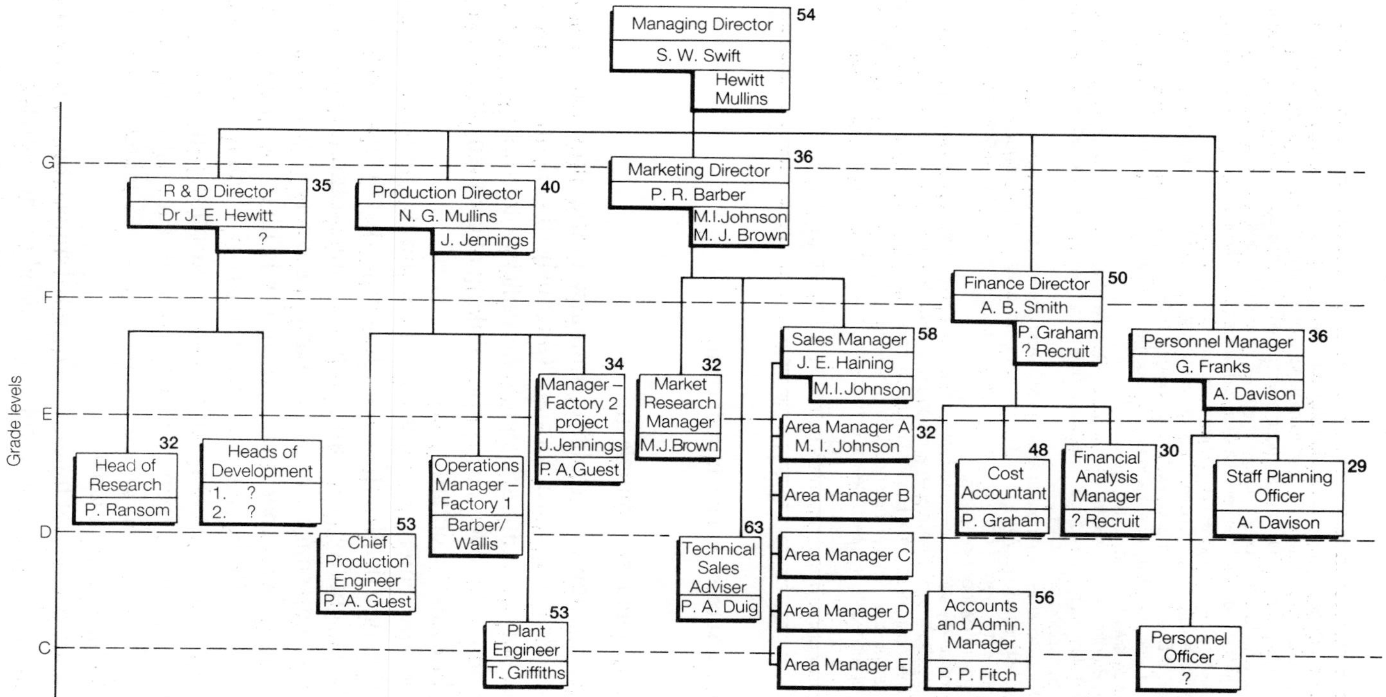


**Example 43** The five-year plan

No major changes of the organisation structure are planned during the five-year period. Growth in business volume will lead to most jobs growing and some restatement of responsibilities will occur. The business environment will become more competitive and the emphasis on further product development will increase the scale of development activity and require closer links between sales and development. The importance of our human resources will be recognised by an upgraded personnel function.

The immediate task is to carry through the planned succession to the Managing Director and R & D Director, and to cover the vacancies created below. While the changes are planned, considerable upheaval in the management structure will need to be managed sensitively over the one- to two-year period.

Alan Brookes will retire early next year and Sam Swift will move up to be deputy MD for Brookes' last six months. Nigel Mullins has been fully prepared to succeed Swift and there is strong support below him.

Cliff Jones retires two months after the MD, and Jim Hewitt is already taking on parts of Jones' responsibilities. While Hewitt is underpinned on research, development management is weaker and we are recruiting for senior people with the potential ability to head major development teams.

The other key succession is to replace Stanton Peters when he retires in three years' time. We shall need to develop marketing skills in any potential successor from the sales side. The most senior man (Haining) probably lacks the ability. Paul Barber is young, but he will be advanced with Haining and the two developed in parallel. The possible need for an external successor is to be reviewed in one year's time and, if necessary, a special marketing post will be created to induct a new man.

All other planned appointments are discussed on the divisional sheets.

**Example 44** Succession plan introduction

*Discussion summary: example 44*

Example 44 shows a simplified summary of the discussion above, using a fairly standard format. Obviously the detail is greatly reduced, but the summary should be sufficient for the group chairman to obtain an overview of the thinking at company level before sitting down to the detailed review.

Should any 'emergency' loss occur during the first year (due to resignation or a death), the strength of immediately available cover is clearly evident from the data on the starting positions chart. Some companies make a feature of specifying the emergency action to be taken against every position. If turnover is high, planning emergency cover will be an important part of a plan, but where unplanned losses are comparatively rare, insufficient thought may be given to covering them. In that situation, the real thinking will be done when an emergency occurs and the so-called 'emergency plan' will have been a waste.

Once a full plan is put together, a detailed supporting commentary is required to demonstrate the 'achievability' of individual preparation required and to highlight any vulnerability in the plan.

Also, options may be discussed and contingencies presented in the event of business variances.

Concluding the discussion of this example series, which happens to show no inter-company movement in the style of a small independent unit, I suggest that the planning approach is fairly typical, as far as any approach can be typical when no two situations and cultures are alike and the range of variation is enormous.

## SUMMARY

Management continuity or succession planning is an ongoing task at every level of management, concerned with the effective resourcing and continuity of management on into the future. It is an integral part of management resourcing and development strategy, and top level succession planning is the most critical management level in the Review process which is at the heart of that strategy. Continuity plans tend to be recorded in detail and reviewed in depth once each year, but this is a continuous, everyday activity.

Any report of the succession situation represents a 'snapshot' which is immediately out of date, but it enables the assumptions and scenarios towards which future appointments are being prepared, and the progress, suitability and planned preparation of designated candidates, to be challenged and monitored.

A full introduction to the plan should be prepared. It is important that succession planning should be based on the best judgements of the way the business, its environment, its culture and management organisation and management competency requirements will develop over the period of the plan, so that future managers are prepared for that future. We do not want to develop cavalry colonels for a nuclear age!

Continuity involves naming the preferred candidate for each future position, plus other serious contenders. This provides the basis for their ongoing development and testing against the demands of the future positions, and does not involve making any final commitment prior to the point where a successor must be named.

Finally, an examination of the quality of the high potential stream coming through, and their ability to meet the envisaged longer term requirements of the corporation, together with a review of the whole process of management development, is properly part of any management succession review.

# V.14

# *Remuneration issues*

Remuneration issues cannot be separated from management resourcing and development. From the point where recruiting begins, the adequacy and form of the remuneration package influences the quality of applicants and the ability to recruit. Pay is certainly not the only issue, but it does influence resourcing and retention. Once the recruit joins, he can be directed to priorities by salary and bonus practices which 'reward' achievements and favoured behaviour and will be *perceived* as reflecting corporate culture.

Of course, 'reward' has aspects other than remuneration. I prefer the word 'recognition' – one form of recognition of achievement or contribution being financial. Even more significant than remuneration is recognition in the form of career progress or promotion (where remuneration may provide a supplementary consideration). This form of recognition may be influenced by conforming cultural behaviour as well as the primary achievement.

## POLICY

### Remuneration policy

Remuneration policy should be viewed as an extension of the management resourcing and development strategies which are designed to support achievement of business objectives in the anticipated environment. It is essential that *remuneration policies should support and encourage achievements of the key accountabilities, selected priorities, and the behaviour required*, and any conflicting influences should be identified and removed. In view of the degree of change occurring in the business environment, remuneration policy and practice need continual review and updating.

For example, pay policy should ensure that corporate pay levels at least match market values for the combination of person specification and performance standards required. If this is not done, it will put achievement of staffing quality at risk – and therefore achievement of business objectives at risk.

A long-established salary policy might make insufficient allowance for the recent trend to greater differentials between market values associated with high performance compared with the 'good average' performers, providing insufficient financial incentive to stay with the company and to achieve exceptional performance. If achievement of corporate objectives is dependent on attracting and retaining high ability people, giving them wide-ranging scope in their jobs will not motivate them adequately if they feel underpaid. In such a case, the remuneration policy should be updated as it is not providing sensitive and adequate support.

Some other influences and the response required in remuneration policy might include the following:

- A tough market environment and aggressive sales objectives will require high person specifications for marketing and sales management. This must be reflected in competitive levels of pay for people meeting the specifications, and be backed by incentives to direct effort to priorities and to motivate achievement.
- Changes in management competencies and/or changes in the behaviour required to respond to anticipated environmental change may require changes in salary and bonus standards, so that these are associated with future and not past requirements. For example, continuing high achievement of sales of low margin products may have become unacceptable and may be penalised if the requirement is to boost sales of a new, high margin product range.

Remuneration policy and practice should be reviewed and restated in parallel with changing views on operating scenarios, updated company objectives and strategies, and the associated management resourcing and development programmes, to see how remuneration practice may be adapted to provide support.

The overall remuneration strategy may be 'to use remuneration to help attract, retain and motivate staff who are well suited to the jobs in the company and are capable of adapting to the jobs of the future'. It might go on to state an intention that remuneration standards should compare favourably with those of competing employers, or to pay particularly well for achievement of high standards of performance. These general objectives might be supplemented by considerations such as:

- developing wider performance-related differentials to encourage achievement of high performance standards
- providing and publicising 'exceptional contribution' bonuses in addition to the existing bonus based on achievements against objectives
- ensuring pay progress in line with potential for listed high potential people, rather than on their current performance on the current assignment, to ensure their careers can be broadened and driven ahead without any demotivating restriction by remuneration policy
- ensuring, where customer contact is a significant part of a job, that achievement of excellent customer relationships is used as the sole factor for awarding 'merit' increases for one year, in order to reinforce the behaviour required from these staff
- ensuring that the pay potential for top professionals in staff positions is on an equivalent basis to line appointments in order to discourage key staff people from seeking to move to line positions for which they are less suited.

Obviously many other considerations may be relevant, and influence either overall policy or short-term practice.

## Future policy

As future organisations move away from hierarchical structures and become more knowledge-based, as structures become less power/authority dominated and more influenced by knowledge and the ability to contribute from all levels, then the emphasis within salary structures and policies will shift.

The most significant change is likely to arise in the approach to grading practice, where there will be a move from *job* grading (based on the responsibilities and authority vested in the job) towards some form of *personal* grading (based on ability to contribute to the business). The basis for this in the fluid structures will consist of two or three prime elements – knowledge; application ability; and possibly a 'position related' factor.

Knowledge will be judged initially on qualifications, as with the graduate intake at present, but including professional qualifications. It will be supplemented progressively by measures of wider and deeper professional knowledge; experience-based knowledge; and knowledge of other functions, including 'generalist' knowledge.

Applications ability will be judged on how well the individual can use that knowledge effectively in the business, and the ability of the individual to contribute generally in his specialist area, in multi-discipline projects, or on business strategy.

The third factor covers management/leadership skills, which will be critically important, but the overall approach to establishing personal 'ranks' will ensure that the high level specialist will command equal rank with 'leaders' on the basis of their potential contribution to critical elements of the business.

### STRUCTURE

Remuneration practice generally involves a number of elements. Typically, a policy will require:

- job information and person specifications
- job grading structures
- market surveys
- salary structures
- appraisal systems
- salary progression systems
- bonus systems.

The role which each of these plays, both on remuneration matters and on other aspects of importance to company operation and efficiency, is reviewed below.

## Job information and person specifications

For any remuneration structure to be meaningful, it is essential to have clear information about jobs, associated objectives, and the person specifications. These last are effectively translations of the jobs into detailed statements of the skills, abilities and personalities of the individuals thought most likely to be effective, given the demands, the environment and the culture in which they are to operate. Considered and accurate person specifications are very important, as they can vary enormously for jobs which appear to be very similar on the surface. Differences in environmental factors and in the relative toughness of the performance standards required, not always evident from the job description, can justify wide variations in person specifications. In turn, this can have a marked impact on remuneration levels, so overspecifying will inflate remuneration costs.

## Job grading structure

There is a variety of approaches to job evaluation, and the method selected may be influenced by the demands of the business. Grading structures indicate not only job value relationships, but also provide the basis for constructing career ladders within functions, or more widely.

It is relatively straightforward to develop a grading structure across one function as the factors on which value decisions are based are compatible and, because there is some career mobility within the function, market values tend to fall into closely related patterns. However, value relationships between jobs in different functions which are established by a grading process are artificial and may be quite different from relationships based on market values.

One approach is to develop an across-the-board grading structure to show 'felt-fair' internal relationships, and then to accept that a series of different salary structures may be necessary, appropriate to the market values of the various functions or job groups. This can provide an indication of 'equivalent levels' for inter-functional career moves, while maintaining reality in relation to the market place.

An alternative approach with a 'universal' grading structure is to override the market place where it is out of line with the internal view of relative values. For example, a decision to provide equivalent career status and remuneration to managerial and non-managerial engineering people can be implemented by grading decisions, even if it is not supported by the market. However, this strategy can only be applied to raising grade levels to values above market values and not to depressing them.

## Market surveys and salary structures

The level of salary structures are generally determined from detailed market surveys, which need to be done with great care. While there is a broad correlation between the size of a managing director's remuneration and the size of his company, this gives only the loosest indication of market worth, and much deeper analysis is required into job content, objectives and performance expectations, operating environment, and logical person specifications.

Once data have been collected, a significant influence on setting the level of the structure will be the performance expected of the job holders, as, where performance standards are set at a tougher-than-general level, the associated remuneration must be related and set at levels which reflect the values of individuals capable of matching these standards. If pay standards are pitched below the values of people capable of producing the required performance, there will be difficulties in recruiting and retaining people of the required standard, and company performance may suffer.

## Appraisal systems

This subject is covered in chapter V.4. Application to remuneration is generally secondary to the primary purpose of appraisal, which is to guide performance improvement. But there must be some input regarding relative performance to justify salary decisions, not least because the company will want to motivate people to perform well, and to reward those who do, in pay as well as in other ways.

## Salary progression systems

Salary tends to be more negotiable at the point of joining an organisation than at any other stage. Subsequently, salary administration policies and procedures provide a means of control over the overall movement in remuneration levels, and salary reviews establish revised individual salaries and relationships.

'Merit' is the general heading placed on salary adjustments within a salary range, but these vary, from incremental adjustments with little or no flexibility, through to variable adjustments in 'open plan' salary ranges which allow maximum discretion for line managers to determine individualised adjustments. In these latter structures, one expects to see the salaries of ordinary performers in the lower half of the range, and those of more substantial contributors moving into the higher section.

If there is to be a determined effort to reward achievement, retention of any incremental progression system is likely to conflict, in that the barely adequate performer may have his salary progressed at much the same pace as that of the substantial achiever. Only where management is prepared to tell the barely adequate performer that a salary a quarter of the way through the range is a generous statement of his personal worth, does there begin to be encouragement to do better; a knowledge that results will be reflected in reward.

In general, achievements against pre-agreed objectives will provide the best guide to performance for remuneration purposes, and is adequately factual; but it will always be necessary to look carefully at the career progression of fast rising people, where achievement may be better measured in terms of getting on top of the new task and ignoring any initial shortfall in achieving business targets. Here, the progressive rise in personal value and the longer term significance of the individual to the corporation should override any short-term apparent dip in value while newly in an assignment.

## Bonus systems

Whether a bonus should be seen as an integral part of the person's payments or as an 'icing-on-the-cake' supplement is open to discussion. Preferences vary, as do the defined purposes of bonus schemes.

If a bonus is integrated into a structure with salaries pitched below market values, there is a risk that a bad year may result in unacceptably low total earnings. If this approach is to be attractive to good people, it will need to be a rare occurrence which is more than off-set by high potential earnings in good years.

More usually, a bonus is a supplement over market value salaries, payable for real achievement. Amounts may be generous for substantially better than planned results, with acceptance that non-achievement means no bonus. Apart from key business measures, 'results' can include a range of factors which are not always quantifiable, such as progress on cultural change or achievements in management development.

The purpose of any bonus scheme is to focus attention on objectives which are considered the priorities. Most are one-year objectives with financial measures, but key accountabilities to improve management development, customer relations, quality, or to launch a new product in three years' time, may all be used as additional criteria. Longer term financial objectives are better associated with stock options, where the end result in cash terms is linked to a rise in the share price – assumed to result from improved corporate performance and increasing profitability.

## Pensions

Pension policy can also be considered a part of management resourcing and development/remuneration strategy as it can be used to encourage or facilitate the early retirement or departure of managers who are running to seed. It is important that this facility strikes the right balance, avoiding excessive generosity which might encourage the more able managers to seek early release and a further career elsewhere.

### SUMMARY

As noted above, remuneration policy should be viewed as an extension of the management resourcing and development strategies which are designed to support achievement. Used wisely, remuneration provides a potent tool to influence managers to concentrate on key accountabilities, particular priorities, or to modify behaviour. Business requirements which can be supported by this means should be identified and remuneration policy (including stock options and pensions) adapted accordingly.

# PART VI

# Effectiveness

# VI.I

## *Assessing effectiveness*

Most of the activities described in this book require commitments of management time and effort, resources which are invariably in demand and heavily committed. Managers at every level who have made the commitment will want to know what return they are getting on their investment.

Many of the aspects of management resourcing and development are long-term in nature, so that to look for a clear return after a few months would be pointless. Freshly initiated development activities may take up to about five years to show clear effects, although some indications may be evident within two or three years. Ten years will be required for investment in new graduates to show through into established management.

Effectiveness is a measure of how well the *total* activity has achieved its *overall* purpose, as defined by each company. This purpose will generally be concerned with ensuring that the organisation is properly resourced to achieve its business objectives in the changing environment; to gain a competitive edge; and to prepare for management continuity in the longer term. There will be various pointers which enable a subjective judgement to be made, but most indicators involve multiple factors. For example, no assumption of the effectiveness of management development would be justified solely from the fact that business objectives had been achieved.

Various human resource strategies will have been implemented to support the achievement of business objectives, or at least to ensure that achievement of the plan was not adversely affected or limited by human resource or cultural factors, and you need to know how effective each has been. That provides a fairly wide target so that effectiveness is impossible to quantify with any precision. To get a thorough assessment of effectiveness, it seems necessary to look at the contributions which had been required from each of the elements, and then to look at the actual achievements.

OVERVIEW

## Competitive advantage

Does the company have any advantages over its competitors, and is the present position in line with what was planned? There are many variants on this question, depending on the starting point and objectives, all of which come down to "Did you achieve what you set out to do?".

Whether reinforcing past achievement or striving for improvement against a long-term vision, you will know whether you are 'on track' or failing. Any more detailed assessment should come from a fresh analysis of the organisation's capabilities and achievements, as set out in chapter II.2. If things are not working out, you need to know why – and the analysis should point up some answers.

If you have established a real edge, your strategy must be to retain and enhance that advantage. Competitive advantage comes from people, and particularly from managers, but it develops from a combination of clear and challenging vision, objectives and purpose; able people (the right people to implement the strategies); and a supportive corporate culture which provides managers with a free rein to think, innovate, move quickly, and continually act to gain competitive edge.

On the other hand, if you are striving for that elusive edge and not achieving it, you may need to be looking for something beyond normal effectiveness. The requirement may be for a degree of insight which enables some major dislocation to be achieved which changes the rules and disadvantages key competitors. A major contributor to achieving such advantage is likely to be highly effective management *resourcing*, with retention of the advantage dependent on management *development*.

## Culture

The most significant influence on achieving a really effective business operation, and the effectiveness you need from your management development, is an appropriate corporate culture.

If, within your broad vision of the corporate future, you can identify business opportunity, and match it with organisation and with managers who provide leadership, intellect, breadth of vision and appropriate flair, who are excited rather than frightened by high abilities in their supporting staff, and who have the freedom to speak out to those above, then virtually anything is achievable. For a high ability team in a supportive corporate culture, nothing will ever remain a limitation!

Culture must be supportive, which means that the ways things are thought about and done must be wholly suited to the business you are in and the needs of the customers. But culture is complex and difficult to change.

Because corporate culture grows out of a concensus of what the people in the corporation believe and the way they behave, as people mature and as the mix of people changes, so corporate culture changes – obviously influenced strongly by the senior management, which may be dominated by a small clique.

Businesses are also changing, so that the perfect cultural fit may become less so as the 'corporate personality' and the customer environment and requirements evolve independently. Early recognition of this situation is essential to avoid an adverse effect on business efficiency and performance. Management development effectiveness might be judged partly by the timing of recognition of a need for some cultural change (at an early stage or nor until crisis point), and then by the quality of diagnosis and the action planned to achieve the desired change. The ultimate measure must be related to the effectiveness with which cultural factors are judged to be supporting or inhibiting the achievement of business objectives.

Not all companies are 'culturally aware', so that their published management development policy may be rather different from actual practice. Written policies provide clear statements of the 'way we wish to act', but the reality is the collection of all the ways in which individual managers actually behave. Their actions are influenced by their interpretation of the written policies, and by their personal beliefs – and also (particularly in strongly hierarchical companies) by the example of top management's behaviour. The end result may be visibly different from the public statements, but that visible behaviour will be recognised as representing the real policy.

In contrast, in more participative companies, the policy statements tend to be based on an agreed view of actual practice, the standards which everyone strives to beat. 'Challenge' is everywhere, arising from that curious dissatisfaction with the status quo which always seems to be present wherever really able people are doing anything really well. Everyone seeks to do things better, all suggestions are taken seriously, and no-one says, "No, we don't do things that way around here!". Behaviour and style are clearly visible and the culture is unmistakable, tending to give such companies a clear competitive advantage over those less able to utilise their human resources to the full. It is people who create that advantage, but it is the culture which attracts the high ability, free thinking, achieving people.

## Improving capability

The foundation for the next round of business growth must be the organisation and its resources as they are being managed now. This is the starting point, but there may be a number of actions which can be taken quickly to provide a swift and dramatic boost to capability. Chapter II.2 covered analysis of the opportunities for raising the base level for building the next stage of business development. You need to know whether planned actions were implemented quickly and whether they were effective.

Perhaps the company still needs a grander vision and a less cautious business plan; needs to look more positively for opportunities in the changing business environment, and be more adventurous in its human resource strategies. As perceptions shift, you can consider whether even greater capability is possible. If the conclusion is that greater things could have been achieved over the last year, and you can see how you should have redeployed your resources, there is an opportunity to grasp. Perhaps there always will be, for very few organisations use their total resources to the maximum.

## A planning approach

How effective was your business planning in the immediate past year? If you have been preparing five- or ten-year plans for some time, how much change do you have to make to your last year's projections beyond year one?

How good are the projections of various aspects of the business environment? If poor judgements are being made of competitor activity, the achievability of your planned business growth may be seriously threatened and the balance of the entire plan upset. It will follow that your human resource strategies will be wrongly directed, and these have formed the basis of your management development priorities. It is obvious enough that *any* serious deviation in the business scenario should trigger a reappraisal of the whole plan and the assumptions on which it is based. It should be natural for the human resource imperatives to be updated as a part of this process. Planning is never easy, but every error provides a learning opportunity so that the company can avoid making the same mistake twice.

## The managers you need

The business development plan scenario is followed by the planning of forward organisation. As with culture, the quality you seek in the planned organisation is that it should facilitate business development and in no way restrict or inhibit necessary freedom of action. One measure of effectiveness, then, is that it should not have been found necessary to change the planned organisation because essential things were not getting done.

A further measure would be the number of non-anticipated positions introduced because there were new demands which had not been foreseen (although these sometimes arise from new legislation).

Changing organisation, and changes in corporate systems and culture, may have a dramatic impact on the shape of many management positions and the competencies required in them. As effective management development is dependent on accurate projection of future requirements, one measure of effectiveness should relate to the degree of accuracy in future person specifications, which can be judged in part by whether people have been adequately prepared for the positions to which it is planned to appoint them.

If internal appointments are not being made because internal candidates are 'not right for the job', are the person specifications and capabilities defined within the plan correct, or is the plan out of step with the real world?

## The Review process

The most important check of all is on the effectiveness of the ongoing Review process, which brings continually updated information on organisation and management requirements together with the latest data on the full inventory of individual managers, to determine deployment and individual development decisions.

First, is this happening at all? A full Review should take place at least once each year (more frequently in fast changing environments). Some companies feel they can muddle through without one, and others lack thoroughness, so an *audit* of what is actually done should be carried out. It is impossible to optimise personal development for corporate or individual advantage if the process is not comprehensive, and it is equally impossible to optimise use of corporate management resources.

The Review process is a demanding one, but when managers become lazy and begin to find excuses for putting off Reviews, this can be very serious. Deployment actions stick and the implementation of IDPs is allowed to slip. The whole effectiveness of management development begins to diminish.

This process must be fully accepted as an integral part of the total business management process, for it brings into fine focus all the deployment and development opportunities currently critical to the business, so that they can be handled effectively; and it highlights business requirements from all management resourcing and development activities. One further contribution of the Review process is to provide the basic succession plan data, which is discussed further below.

## Resourcing

The most important immediate measure of effectiveness of management development for some managements is to be seen in the adequacy and quality of internal short lists for all senior vacancies. This is a useful measure once the full system has been operating for several years, but it can be frustrating for the management development specialist through the early stages of a difficult recovery situation requiring a five-year build up, when the CEO continues to complain of inadequacies which result from the damaging period of inactivity.

Management development should not be expected to provide short lists of perfect candidates for every management vacancy, but statistics which examine the numbers of adequate candidates for all vacancies will show whether actions over the past several years have been effective in developing candidates. Most expected vacancies (other than for highly specialist posts) should have an identified 'heir and a spare', and there should be useful candidates for many of the unexpected vacancies which occur – and enough flexibility to release them.

A surprising number of organisations set objectives of having 'better managers than the competition', and then find that they are struggling with definitions about competition and with the standards which can measure 'better' or 'best'. To me, 'the competition' means the companies with which one competes for good candidates – which will vary for different categories of job and not always be related to the industry or area. Regarding quality, it seems you should be thinking of 'good' against the person specifications which you set. The company next door, which happens to be in the same industry, may address different market segments, have different human resource requirements, may set different person specifications, have an alien culture, and be generally irrelevant in any comparisons.

Acquisitions and disposals, or radical organisation changes, can result in substantial changes in management requirements which cause difficulties with over and under supply, but it remains necessary to balance supply with probable future demand, from graduate entry upwards, and to monitor progress and adequacy.

## Appraisal

The purpose of appraisal should be clearly defined so that the effectiveness of the appraisal process in achieving that purpose will be evident. The value of appraisal diminishes sharply where the purpose is not clear or has conflicting objectives.

An appraisal scheme which is not backed up by proper employee involvement and counselling will be ineffective. Ask a cross-section of people about whether they are appraised and counselled (in line with company policy) and you may find a wide variation in responses. Probing questions may confirm that counselling is universal, but that the manner and quality (and effectiveness) do vary widely, in spite of considerable efforts to achieve high standards.

## Potential

Identifying individuals able to make exceptional contributions, or to advance quickly to higher levels of responsibility, is immensely important to the present and future well-being of the enterprise. This identification and the subsequent development of these managers form vital components in the management development process.

It is very difficult to determine whether very able people are overlooked, as they tend to leave, still unrecognised. Similarly, exceptional people may be lost in the recruitment process because their potential goes unrecognised, and there can be no measure of these losses.

The best safeguard may be a periodic audit of the process of identifying able people. This should examine how the company registers all signs of potential and then investigates its likely form and scale. Wide use of psychometric test batteries and discussion groups to supplement interviews for the graduate intake provides the maximum possible data and off-sets the lack of track records; while the use of Assessment Centres for people in their late twenties or early thirties can provide valuable additional data relevant to higher level requirements, to supplement track records. These are not the only aids which can be used. The key is to ensure that sufficient objective data are always assembled to ensure that assessments of the degree and form of likely potential for all management staff are competently made.

## Development

Development does not just happen: it needs to be planned and implemented with care on an individual basis, after first determining its intended direction and pace.

The first test of effectiveness concerns the existence (or not) of some form of IDPs. If these exist, they confirm that some thought has gone into the intended development of each person, and that there is a basis for monitoring whether the plans are implemented. While the form of IDPs is not particularly important, the quality of thinking and planning is likely to be evident from the content, on which a more subjective judgement must be made.

The ultimate measure of the effectiveness of development is found in the 'readiness' of people to fill positions for which they are scheduled. I recall one succession plan which regularly identified good candidates three to five years ahead of intended appointments, but rarely confirmed the appointments. Having made their selections the top management did little or nothing to prepare the candidates to take over the higher level posts, so that most of them were simply 'not ready' when the time came. Development requires very positive action, first to identify development needs, then to establish how they are to be met, and finally to ensure that the necessary action is taken.

Other questions about development might include:

- Is there a partnership between managers and subordinates on development?
- Does development continue throughout the employee's entire service?
- Is management development relevant to the business and to the individual, and to the time?

## Training

The effectiveness of training activity tends to be under closer scrutiny than most other elements of management development, due to the visibility of its cost and the volume of management time which it absorbs.

The first issue is about the need and justification for training, but the response should be straightforward as all training needs should have been established in advance as being necessary to the business.

The follow on question is about the effectiveness of the training done. In a few situations, it may be possible to see some effect flowing through to the bottom line, but for the bulk of training, you need to look for changes in individual behaviour, more effective performance or, if the course was part of core training, evidence that all managers at a level are knowledgeable to the target standard and can operate company systems effectively. If the training was more an investment in the future, you may seek confirmation that the individual is better prepared for his planned next appointment.

## Succession planning

The Review process and succession planning are very closely related, but succession planning usually requires an annual report which records the current state of play – and provides an ideal opportunity to audit the overall effectiveness of management development.

If the succession (or continuity) plan has been carried out simply against the current organisation, there is a high probability that it will not be effective. Considerable effort should have gone into resolving the future organisation shape, the future form of managerial jobs, and the range of competencies likely to be required. Any succession plan must be concerned with the manning of that future structure.

The text of the report should provide adequate assurance that not only can most of the appropriate positions be resourced by the development of internal people, but there is some reserve to cope with unforeseen needs and some flexibility to deal with variations in business development.

## Remuneration

As with all management development-related activities, remuneration systems need to support other efforts to achieve planned business development. As we assess effectiveness, we look for any negative signs. For example, is there any indication that remuneration policies inhibit or discourage effort on key programmes?

If the company is pressing for strongly entrepreneurial behaviour by its managers, an incremental basis for pay progress should be giving way to a more appropriate open structure to enable large adjustments (or no adjustment). The same situation would be even more strongly supported by a bonus scheme, permitting substantial results-related variation in payments.

It would be reasonable to ask for an extract from the human resource strategies covering remuneration, to examine first its general suitability against business objectives and other human resource strategies, and then its implementation to determine effectiveness.

## SUMMARY

The effectiveness of the management development process should be assessed by comparing its achievements with its intentions, against the background of the evolving business with its requirements for management resources. If any part of the business plan was poorly constructed or is not achieved, the whole plan may be adversely affected. This audit should look at the overall effectiveness of management resourcing to support the plan, any revision to it and response to subsequent events.

The other half of the review concerns the effectiveness of the individual segments of the management development process and the contributions they were expected to make to the business. Ultimately, management development can only exist as one facet of the management process, and it must be totally integrated into the business. In driving a business ahead, any one function can misjudge the task and throw the plan off balance, but these judgements will have been made by *people* in the function so that some part of the 'blame' comes back to the effectiveness of management resourcing – to the assumptions made about the competencies required and to the preparation and provision of the managers concerned.

But just as you can trace back all business difficulty to people decisions, so also you can trace all the great successes to the people who created the opportunities and made things happen. If leaders have vision and the culture is right, able people will gather and, in any business environment, they will challenge the limits of what is achievable and make their mark at the competitive edge – and still believe that there is even more to achieve.

# *References and further reading*

The list which follows has been selected primarily as suggested further reading on the chapter subject. In some cases, the publication has influenced material in the chapter concerned, in which case the author has been quoted in the text.

## II.1 Planning: a vision of the future

H. I. Ansoff, *From Strategic Planning to Strategic Management* (Wiley, New York, 1975)

J. Argenti, *Practical Corporate Planning* (George Allen and Unwin, London, 1980)

M. E. Porter, *Competitive Strategy* (Free Press, New York, 1980)

## II.2 Corporate capability now

R. H. Waterman, *The Renewal Factor* (Bantam Press, London, 1988)

## II.3 Environmental change

K. Barham, J. Fraser and L. Heath, *Management for the Future* (Ashridge Management College, 1988)

P. Drucker, *Managing in Turbulent Times* (Heinemann, London, 1980)

ERT, 'Education and European competence', *European Round Table of Industrialists Report* (1989)

G. Hamel and C. K. Prahalad, 'Strategic Intent', *Harvard Business Review* (May–June 1989), pp. 63–76

T. Peters, *Thriving on Chaos* (Macmillan, London, 1987)

H. Serieyx, 'The company in the year 2000', *Personnel Management* (June 1987), pp. 30–32

A. Toffler, *The Adaptive Corporation* (McGraw-Hill, New York, 1985; Pan Books, London, 1985)

## II.4 Human resource strategies in the achievable business plan

C. Fombrun, N. M. Tichy and M. A. Devanna, *Strategic Human Resource Management* (Wiley, New York, 1984)

## III.1 Organisation planning and development

W. Bennis, *Organisation Development: its Nature, Origins and Prospects* (Addison Wesley, Reading, Mass., 1969)

P. F. Drucker, 'The coming of the new organisation', *Harvard Business Review* (Jan–Feb 1988)

P. F. Drucker, *The New Realities* (Heinemann Professional Publishing, Oxford, 1989)

W. G. Dyer, *Contemporary Issues in Management and Organisation Development* (Addison Wesley, Reading, Mass., 1983)

A. Kakabadse and others, *Working in Organisations* (Gower, Aldershot, 1987)

N. Margulies and A. Raia, 'The significance of core values on the practice of organisation development', *Journal of Organisational Change Management*, vol. 1, No. 1 (1988), pp. 6–17

N. Margulies and A. Raia, *Organisation Development: Values, Process, and Technology* (McGraw-Hill, New York, 1972)

T. H. Patten Jun. and P. B. Vaill, 'Organisation development', in *Training and Development Handbook* ed. R. L. Craig (McGraw-Hill, New York, 1976), pp. 20.3–20.21

G. M. Robinson, 'Management development and organisation development', in *Handbook of Management Development*, 2nd edn, ed. A. Mumford (Gower, Aldershot, 1986), pp. 315–334

## III.2 Culture

W. W. Burke and G. H. Litwin, *A Casual Model of Organisation Performance* (N. G. Associates, Chorleywood, 1989)

P. Dobson, 'Changing cultures', *Employment Gazette* (Dec 1988), based on paper presented at IPM National Conference, October 1988

F. R. Kluckhohn and F. L. Strodtbeck, *Variations on Value Orientations* (Harper and Rowe, New York, 1961)

N. Margulies and A. Raia; 'The significance of core values on the theory and practice of organisation development', *Journal of Organisational Change Management*, vol. 1, no. 1 (1988), pp. 6–17

N. Marguiles and A. Raia, *Organisation Development: Values, Process, and Technology* (McGraw-Hill, New York, 1972)

T. Peters and R. H. Waterman, *In Search of Excellence* (Harper and Rowe, New York, 1982)

E. H. Schein, *Organisational Culture and Leadership* (Jossey-Bass, San Francisco, 1985)

P. Stemp, *Are you Managing?* (The Industrial Society, London, 1988)

## III.3 Competencies

J. Burgoyne, Talk on 'The strengths and weaknesses of competency approaches to management development', IPM National Conference, October 1988

S. Bevan, Talk on 'What makes a manager?', Institute of Manpower Studies, Brighton, 1989

IPM, Consultative paper on the proposed National Framework for Management Development (IPM, November 1988)

R. Jacobs (ed.), 'Assessing management competencies', Report by Ashridge Management College (1989)

R. M. Kanter, *When Giants Learn to Dance* (Simon and Schuster, London, 1989)

L. B. Korn, 'How the next CEO will be different', *Fortune (22 May 1989)*, pp. 111–113

## III.4 Leadership

B. Bass, *Leadership and Performance Beyond Expectations* (Free Press, New York, 1985)

W. Bennis, 'Transformative leadership', *Harvard University Newsletter* (April 1983)

L. L. Neider and C. A. Schriesheim, 'Making leadership effective: A three-stage model', *Journal of Management Development*. vol. 7, no. 5 (1988)

V. H. Vroom and A. G. Jago, *The New Leadership: Managing Participation in Organisations* (Prentice-Hall, Englewood Cliffs, N.J., 1988)

## III.5 Teams

**R. Meridith Belbin**, *Management Teams: Why they Succeed or Fail* (Heinemann, London, 1985)

B. Critchley and D. Casey, 'Teambuilding', in *Handbook of Management Development*, 2nd edn, ed. A. Mumford (Gower, Aldershot, 1986)

C. Hastings, P. Bixby and R. Chandhry-Lawton, *Superteams* (Fontana/Collins, London, 1986)

## III.6 Future requirements

K. Barham, J. Fraser and L. Heath, *Management for the Future* (Ashridge Management College, 1988)

G. McBeath, *Manpower Planning and Control* (Business Books, London, 1978)

## V.3 Resourcing and recruitment

D. Mackenzie Davey and P. McDonnell, *How to Interview* (BIM, 1975)

E. Sidney (ed.), *Managing Recruitment* (Gower, Aldershot, 1988)

M. Smith and I. T. Robinson (eds), *Advances in Selection and Assessment* (Gulf Publishing, Houston, Texas, 1989)

## V.4 Appraisal of performance and counselling

M. S. Kellogg, *What to do about Performance Appraisal* (AMA, 1965)
M. S. Kellogg, *When Man and Manager Talk – A Casebook* (Gulf Publishing, Houston, Texas, 1969)
A. Mumford, *Making Experience Pay* (McGraw-Hill, Maidenhead, 1980)
V. and A. Stewart, *Practical Performance Appraisal* (Gower, Aldershot, 1981)

## V.5 Judgement of potential

J. L. Moses and W. C. Byham (eds), *Applying the Assessment Centre Method* (Pergamon Press, New York, 1977)
V. and A. Stewart, *Tomorrow's Men Today* (IPM/Institute of Manpower Studies, 1976)
J. Toplis, V. Dulewicz and C. Fletcher, *Psychological Testing – a Practical Guide* (IPM, 1987)

## V.7 Development: Individual Development Plans

E. H. Schein, 'A critical look at current career development theory and research', in *Career Development in Organisations*, ed. D. T. Hall (Jossey-Bass, San Francisco, 1986)
V. and A. Stewart, *Managing the Manager's Growth* (Gower, Aldershot, 1979)

## V.9 Development of high potential

W. A. G. Braddick and D. McAllister, Report on management development practices in the European Round Table of Industrialists Group of Companies (1988)
D. L. Handy, 'Managing the high flier', *Training Officer* (July 1987)

## V.10 Self-development

IPM, *Continuous Development*, IPM code (1987)
T. Jaap, *The Steps to Self Development* (HRA Publications, Paisley, 1979)

## V.12 Training actions

J. Lawrence, 'Action learning – a questioning approach', in *Handbook of Management Development*, 2nd edn, ed. A. Mumford (Gower, Aldershot, 1986)
M. Pedler (ed.), *Action Learning in Practice* (Gower, Aldershot, 1983)
R. W. Revans, *ABC of Action Learning* (Chartwell Bratt, Bromley, 1983)

## V.13 Management continuity: succession plans

L. Gratten, *Heirs Apparent* (Basil Blackwell, Oxford, 1990)
W.F. Mahler and W.F. Wrightnour, *Executive Continuity* (Dow Jones–Inwin, Illinois, 1973)
R.F. Vancil, *Passing the Baton: Managing the Process of CEO Succession* (Harvard Business School Press, Cambridge, Mass., 1987)

## V.14 Remuneration issues

G. McBeath, *Salary Administration*, 4th edn (Gower, Aldershot, 1989)

# Index